COUNT DOWN

The Past, Present and Uncertain Future of the Big Four Accounting Firms

Second Edition

COUNT DOWN

The Past, Present and Uncertain Future of the Big Four Accounting Firms

Second Edition

BY

JIM PETERSON

United Kingdom — North America — Japan
India — Malaysia — China

Emerald Publishing Limited
Howard House, Wagon Lane, Bingley BD16 1WA, UK

First edition 2015

Second edition 2017

British Library Cataloguing in Publication Data
A catalogue record for this book is available from the British Library

ISBN: 978-1-78714-701-0 (Print)
ISBN: 978-1-78714-700-3 (Online)
ISBN: 978-1-78743-011-2 (Epub)

ISOQAR
REGISTERED

Certificate Number 1985
ISO 14001

ISOQAR certified
Management System,
awarded to Emerald
for adherence to
Environmental
standard
ISO 14001:2004.

FSC
www.fsc.org
MIX
Paper from
responsible sources
FSC® C013604

INVESTOR IN PEOPLE

CONTENTS

v

Contents

PREFACE TO THE SECOND EDITION

When Emerald Publishing released the first edition of *Count Down* in December 2015, aiming chiefly at its core audiences in the academic and scholarly communities, it was also my desire to extend its reach more widely.

Recent months have not been happy for the Big Four accounting networks — despite their extended market dominance and the growth of their combined global revenue, reaching $128 billion in the latest year — making timely this revised and extended second edition:

- Deloitte's Brazil firm in December 2016 incurred an $8 million penalty, the largest ever imposed by the PCAOB, and practice bars and other sanctions against twelve partners and employees, over confessed alteration of documents, false testimony, and lack of cooperation with the PCAOB's inspections and investigations. Lesser sanctions were also imposed on its firms in Mexico and the Netherlands for other PCAOB violations.

- EY in September 2016 was the target of two SEC enforcement actions, involving censures, fee disgorgements and fines of $ 4.4 million and $ 4.9 million, and practices bars against its personnel, over charges of loss of independence based on "close personal relationships" between engagement partners and client personnel — in one case a romantic relationship and in the other, significant expenses paid for travel, entertainment, sporting events tickets, and family vacations for the client CFO and his family.

- KPMG in April 2017 fired five partners and an employee, including its Vice Chair of Audit and its head of Audit Quality and Professional Practice, over its receipt and handling of advance inspection information leaked by an employee of the PCAOB. Meanwhile in the United Kingdom, pressures remain on the Financial Reporting Council and the Financial Conduct Authority over their treatment of KPMG's role as auditor of failed bank HBOS.

- PwC's delivery of the wrong "best picture" envelope, and the resulting tumultuous ending to the February 2017 broadcast of the Academy Awards, evoked outbursts of public ridicule — which were pale in significance compared to the potentially fatal financial impact of two multi-billion dollar lawsuits, relating to its audits of Colonial Bank and MF Global, where jury trials in process in August 2016 and March 2017, respectively, were discontinued in favor of settlements for confidential amounts.

The corrosive effects of these and other events on credibility and the public trust have left the Big Audit model increasingly fragile, yet still standing — so far. While fresh issues will no doubt displace this sampling, the central issues retain their relevance and urgency, and drive the importance of their scrutiny.

Those with directly affected interests include not only the auditors, but all participants in Big Audit whose professional or business positions, activities, investments and financial security are exposed to the flaws in the structure by which the Big Four provide audit opinions on the financial statements of the world's large public companies:

- Executive and financial leaders and the directors and audit committees of the corporate issuers.

- The community of financial information users: investors large and small, lenders, bankers, customers, and other sources of credit and capital.

- Professional standard-setters along with government agencies of oversight and law enforcement.

- And especially the accounting professionals themselves — the partners and employees of the Big Four networks that dominate the sector, and their no-less-affected colleagues in the smaller firms.

Extending my appreciation for their support to the Emerald team led by Charlotte Maiorana, series editor Gary Previts of Case Western University, and my agent Carol Mann — I believe in both the importance of assurance to the successful functioning of the capital markets and the necessity of full engagement by all parties in examining the challenges in today's model, and welcome this opportunity to contribute to the dialog.

Paris
May 2017

FOREWORD

At a meeting in the spring of 2001, I was taken aside by a senior partner of one of the large international accounting networks. It was, with hindsight, the quiet before the storm. Six months later, Houston-based energy giant Enron Corp. collapsed, followed rapidly by the criminal indictment and demise of the 88-year-old accounting firm of Arthur Andersen.

Here was a man at the peak of his career, with an executive position in his firm — not Andersen. He had stature and recognition both in his own country and internationally, and financial security and prosperity.

"My two children are both happy in college," he said. "And I have achieved my goal in career guidance. Neither one is going into public accounting."

How profoundly sad, at the personal level, despite his evident satisfaction, delivered with no trace of irony. This apparently successful professional, at the top of his form, did not see the value to society of the firm to which he devoted his entire working life as worthy to pass to the next generation.

How disquieting. One of the accounting profession's illustrious and respected members thought so little of its career potential that he would take satisfaction in dissuading his children from following in his steps.

A year later, I had as much reason as anyone to be dismayed at Andersen's flame-out. From 1982, I had been a senior member of Andersen's in-house legal group. For 16 years, I had been a partner in the uniquely successful Andersen worldwide organization, sharing fully and enjoying its prosperity and its handsome profitability.

I had recently reached the firm's early retirement age. I left with a generously promised package of retirement benefits, promptly blown to bits in Andersen's post-Enron collapse and inflicting a multi-million dollar hole in my retirement expectations.

There was real pain to go around. Andersen's active US partners lost their capital. Retired partners lost their unfunded benefits. A handful of senior management, labeled "toxic" for their proximity to the disaster, disappeared under the career-ending taint of responsibility for the disintegration of an institution often cited as the profession's "gold standard."

But there were few enough of us to mourn Andersen's demise. The non-US firms of the Andersen network relocated promptly into the cautious if welcoming arms of the other large networks. In the United States, Andersen's 25,000 employees mostly licked their wounds and went on — moving into the regional practices of the other large firms or combining into new niche practices with geographic or industry specializations.

Andersen's world-class roster of departing clients showed an absence of loyalty to the firm in its death throes — believing, correctly as events proved, that they could obtain elsewhere the same services of equal value, with ease and at times even at less cost. The reduction of the large global networks from five to four involved creaking and groaning adjustments, but was accomplished with a minimum of real disturbance.

This book is not a memoir. It is not the story about Andersen. Although relevant in the classroom, it is not a textbook, but a business-oriented narrative, addressing Big Audit as a critical component in the functioning of the world's capital markets. Nor, to my regret as a story-teller, does it feature a central personality — a hero to cheer or a villain to hiss.

It is about the questionable value and the uncertain viability of Big Audit — the business, regulatory and legal model by which audit services are delivered to the world's largest companies by the surviving global accounting networks: the Big Four — Deloitte, EY, KPMG and PwC.

Today the standard audit opinion is an outmoded product that nobody values, at a cost that nobody wants to pay. Its requirement by regulators inhibits evolution to assurance of real usefulness, and exposes the Big Four to litigation exposures that they cannot afford.

How Big Audit came to this fragile state, why the proposed quick and simple fixes are unachievable and how assurance of real value might be designed and delivered instead — these are the topics.

After the Introduction for context and history, the story proceeds in these parts:

- A review of the events leading to today's troubled and urgent state.

- An examination of the so-called "solutions" — none of which can withstand scrutiny as practical, effective or achievable.

- Scrutiny of the attitudes and behaviors of the major players in Big Audit, who by their very DNA and their mutually conflicting and antagonistic interests are constrained in their ability to bring coherence to a positive process of change.

- To finish, a last section — to which the impatient are referred if unwilling to wait or unable to defer — that outlines some of the necessary, and possible, elements of a re-engineered approach to financial reporting and assurance — a newly structured Big Audit model, sustainable to meet the needs of the 21st century.

Addressing along the way the discomforts caused by the present dysfunctionality, I will propose a complete re-structuring of Big Audit, either following its collapse as presently threatened or, much more desirably but highly unlikely, under forward-looking leadership prepared to accomplish the sweeping changes needed to avoid that collapse.

As a preview: Newly designed audit firms, perhaps evolving from and built on the present Big Four and others, would be free to supplant today's obsolete "pass-fail" opinion with assurance specifically tailored to the needs of issuers and users. New business models would include flexible forms of organization, permissibly associated with any other client services, drawing upon the support of corporate ownership or third-party capital. Firms would no longer be constrained by the obsolete limitations of "appearance of independence" or restraints on the scope of their ancillary services.

Regulators and law enforcement would retain authority to oversee both issuers and auditors and to enforce appropriate investor protections, while assurance reports would only be published subject to strict limitations of liability.

Because today's Big Audit model is unsuitable beyond salvation, it may be emotionally wrenching for many of its players to surrender beliefs they have clasped closely for decades. Difficult as it may be to imagine, however, only such a dramatically new model will allow for a sustainable Big Audit function, fit for purpose in the complex world of the modern capital markets.

I

INTRODUCTION — THE PAST — HISTORY AND CONTEXT

"WHERE *WERE* THE AUDITORS?"

The end of Big Audit started with events that are now familiar.

The Arthur Andersen accounting firm, founded in Chicago in 1913 and a pillar of its once-noble profession, died in the winter of 2002, under a deluge of accusations, investigations and recriminations.[1]

Painfully and in full public view, Andersen faced and lost a fight for its life — a fight that turned out to be unwinnable, under the crushing combined weight of law enforcement investigations, a media circus of multiple legislative hearings, and shareholder class action litigation claiming damages measured by Enron's $67 billion bankruptcy.

Andersen was mortally wounded from the very outset of the Enron debacle. At the time of Enron's collapse, Andersen was already laboring under a litigation inventory that included such crippling exposures as Waste Management, Sunbeam and Baptist Hospital. Had it not disintegrated under the influence of its criminal indictment in Houston, it had waiting the additional potentially devastating impacts of WorldCom, Qwest and others. Its financial resources, its solvency and its existence were in no way answerable to the inflictions it faced.

Andersen's inevitable demise was accelerated and sealed by its criminal indictment, announced on March 14, 2002. The United States Justice Department charged Andersen with obstruction of justice and destruction of evidence, for the exercise in document and files cleanup led by its then high-flying young partner, David Duncan, in Andersen's Houston office.

Trust in the Andersen franchise — both internal and external — was irretrievably lost. When Andersen's management failed to negotiate a plea bargain with US Justice that could have avoided the criminal indictment of the firm, the trickle of departing clients and partners became a flood. Practice units of the firm in the United States, unable to find a single merger partner willing to risk inheriting Andersen's litigation legacy, splintered into regional deals and start-up niche practices. The international network dissolved almost overnight as its separate national practices around the world were thrust into shotgun marriages with the other large networks' local firms.

Convicted after a trial in Houston on June 15, 2002, the Andersen firm in the United States announced that it would cease performing audits and surrender its professional licenses as of August 31. Not ever formally bankrupt, even at this writing, the firm effectively shut itself down.

Although the US Supreme Court rarely intrudes into the conduct of trials by the lower courts, it accepted Andersen's petition for review, and in 2005 gave its Pyrrhic judgment setting aside Andersen's conviction.[2] By that time, any hope of survival or revival was long since lost.[3]

Where did the world think Andersen had been?

One answer came at a House Energy and Commerce Committee hearing. On January 24, 2002, Congressman James Greenwood (R-Pa) unloaded on David Duncan, Andersen's engagement partner on the Enron audit. Although it was known that Duncan would exercise his constitutional right not to testify, the Congressman launched this sarcastic sound bite:

"Mr. Duncan, Enron robbed the bank. Arthur Andersen provided the getaway car, and they say you were at the wheel."

It was the same familiar outcry: "Where were the auditors?"

Heard with every outbreak of financial scandal. With every dramatic stock price collapse. With every disintegrated company that was once a fast-rising "new thing." With the evaporation of every darling investment taking in the funds of credulous investors in response to touting on the business channels.

A single example, inevitably not the last scandal *du jour,* was that of British food retailer Tesco, which in September 2014 announced a half-year profit shortfall that exceeded £250 million. Confessed irregularities in its accounting for supplier discounts and rebates accelerated the collapse of its stock price by 25% within a month.

Three years on, the Tesco story is still unfolding, with much agony to come. Shareholder class action litigations were promptly started in both the United States and the United Kingdom. The body count of jettisoned company executives reached eight plus the chairman himself. The Serious Fraud Office's investigation led to criminal charges in September 2016 against three senior Tesco executives. The company's stock price continued its fall through late 2014, to a low of 165 *p* that December.[4]

"Where were the auditors" of Tesco — namely PwC, which had served the company in the United Kingdom since 1983? It had been immediately speculated that the 32-year auditor/client relationship PwC had enjoyed with Tesco was at risk — a prophecy fulfilled in May 2015, when the company announced PwC's replacement with Deloitte.

Meanwhile, the financial cost to PwC cannot yet be calculated, although the only reason not to predict a major blow to the firm is that neither British regulators nor the courts of that county have a history of inflicting fines and damages on the scale imposed by the Americans.

So where had the auditors been? In the aftermath of financial scandal of any type — and despite the passionate arguments from the profession's apologists that "audit failures" are not strictly involved — the impact faced by the auditors includes spasms of righteous indignation, spite and recrimination, and years of wheel-grinding in the systems of law enforcement and litigation damage claims.

WHERE IS BIG AUDIT TODAY?

The global presence of the large enterprises audited by the Big Four is as massive as all of world trade. That population — roughly, for purposes here, the world's 1000 largest public companies — comprise the Dow Jones and S&P 500 indices in the United States, the United Kingdom's FTSE 100 and 350, the DAX 30 in Germany, the CAC 40 in France, the smaller groups of country-leading companies in the other G-20 countries, and the large but local state-sponsored financial and other institutions elsewhere.

The vast portion of the trading activity in the stocks of all public companies, by number and value, involves these large enterprises, whose presence dominates the world's markets.

The auditors' mission to serve the capital markets is spelled out in detailed legal requirements, and the footprints of Big Audit are everywhere. Audit reports are mandated for public companies, in language precisely prescribed by the national securities regulators, to permit their shares and debt to trade — the driving capital engine at the heart of the great machinery of the world's economies.

In the United States, every public company is under the legal obligation of the federal securities laws to file financial statements, examined and opined on by an auditor in good standing with the American regulators — the Securities and Exchange Commission and the Public Company Accounting Oversight Board.

How much is involved? There are some 2800 public companies listed on the venerable New York Stock Exchange (NYSE) alone — as a sample among the world's large securities exchanges. Together those companies have a total capitalization exceeding $19.3 trillion. The value to trusting investors of all of that $19.3 *trillion* is supported by the opinions of those companies' auditors.

The NYSE trades a daily average of 1.46 billion of these companies' shares, in transactions with a total daily average value exceeding $40 billion. *Every* trading day. Each and every transaction reflects the trust and confidence of the trading participants in the financial statements of the companies involved.

The Visibility of the Big Four

The business presence of the Big Four networks, as ubiquitous as the large companies they serve, is impossible to miss. (See the following *Sidebar*: *Counting the Beans — Facts and Figures on Big Audit*.) Completely dominating the delivery of audit services to the world's large companies, the Big Four together had global revenue for fiscal 2016 of nearly $128 billion. They employed close to 890,000 people worldwide. They are among the largest campus recruiters and providers of entry-level professional job opportunities at the world's leading colleges and universities.

Their partners' individual annual profits on average exceed one million dollars each. The firms' names and logos decorate prestige office towers in financial centers around the globe, with offices in more than 150 countries where they serve clients with material business presence in at least that many. As with the British Empire in the 19th century, the sun never sets on the world-circling presence of the Big Four.

With the pervasive presence of Big Audit, its successful functioning is a matter of direct personal interest to everyone who owns stocks — who expects a pension — who has a Keogh plan or a retirement account — who puts personal savings in a bank or anywhere but in the mattress — who works for a company audited by one of the Big Four or whose suppliers and credit-worthy customers are Big Four clients. In short, it matters to anyone holding this book, who has a nontrivial personal or family balance sheet.

It matters that the market for large-company audit services, represented by audited financial statements that are integral to the transactions at the heart of all of those relationships, is stable and functional.

But as the selective if colorful examples from Enron to Tesco make clear, the questions as to the value of Big Audit go to its very heart. Is there value in the audit report? If not, why is it still required? What justifies the cost of Big Audit, or its very presence?

The Expected Attitude of the Players

The great and the good across the political, regulatory and professional world periodically and consistently tell the world why Big Audit is important, making anodyne pronouncements extolling its importance:

- In her 2015 address at the AICPA National Conference, then-SEC Chairman Mary Jo White declared that auditors share the regulators' *"weighty responsibility to maintain high-quality, reliable financial reporting."*

- PCAOB member Steven Harris said to the International Corporate Governance Network on June 28, 2016, *"The independent auditor serves a vital role in our capital markets by providing an objective third party opinion on the integrity of financial statements that investors rely upon for investment decisions."*

- In a speech on December 9, 2013, PCAOB chairman James Doty:

  "As sophisticated as our markets and economy are, they are dependent on trust. We cannot take trust for granted. Independent audits provide that trust, and thus bridge the gap between entrepreneurs who need capital and lenders and investors who can provide capital."

- In 2011, the SEC's then-chief accountant, James Kroeker, testifying before a Senate committee:

  "Financial reporting plays a critical role in establishing and maintaining the confidence of the investing public. The objective of financial reporting is to provide information useful to providers of capital in their decision-making processes.

  Reliable financial reporting becomes even more important in a financial crisis, when concerns about a company's fundamentals are most acute .... An audit by an independent public accountant is key to investor confidence and the functioning of our capital markets, and independent audits have long been recognized as important to credible and reliable financial reporting."

The credibility of those acting as cheerleaders is at risk, of course, as these players would all be expected to talk the same upbeat messages. Their positions, their stature and their reputations are based on continuation of Big Audit's *status quo*. To expect otherwise would be like thinking that Santa's elves would risk their own unemployment by voting against Christmas.

To the Insiders, Big Audit Is So Yesterday

As a theme that will run through the entirety of this story, however, the most motivated and interested users of financial information — a key constituency among the roster of players in Big Audit — have cast their negative vote on the value of the standard auditor's report.

Namely, the bankers and others engaged in the large-scale management and deployment of investment capital now disregard the "pass-fail" audit opinion, using instead their own tools for the performance of due diligence, the assessment of earnings and asset quality of companies, and the evaluation of company management strategies and directions.

For these players, the traditional standard report is anachronistic and obsolete. Rapidly evolving opportunities in the "big data" algorithmic analysis of both the language and the figures of corporate reporting, and the wisdom and insights to be extracted from trends by industry and geography, have rendered irrelevant both the outdated statutory forms of annual and quarterly public-company filings and the sampling-based audits that are the legacy of models that time has passed by.

As will be expanded later, this dynamic environment should logically be a field ripe to be occupied by the technical training and professional experience of the Big Four firms (and, to be sure, their smaller and perhaps more agile but also less well-financed colleagues).

But until or unless the current audit report model is slated for complete replacement, the Big Four auditors can only offer these evolved assurance services for fees above those paid by clients for the statutory report alone. Frustratingly, however, it is precisely at this interface with the future that the inhibitions and proscriptions of the current Big Audit model clamp down:

- Regulators committed to an "audit-only" mind-set display increasing hostility to the Big Four's rapid expansion of their consulting and advisory competence and capabilities.

- The cost of already-required statutory reporting puts a heavy financial lid on the resources available to an audit committee or a chief financial officer to reach out for innovation.

- Conversely, pressures on the firms of time and budget are antithetical to expansion into new areas of assurance opportunity.

- And the obsolete obligations of "appearance of independence" and the understandable fear of being second-guessed in litigation close off the auditors from the opportunities to design, operate and access their clients' information systems where the valuable data reside and where the analytics can be performed.

To summarize, then — the regulators and politicians pay obligatory but sterile respect to Big Audit, to serve their own purposes, while the best-endowed users have no reason for any attitude but indifference.

To the Rest of the World — Accounting Is *So* Boring

What then of the larger population of investors? Beyond the self-protective posturing of the public servants, and the alternative strategies of the large market players, how is it that the broad population of information users shows such lack of interest?

Surprised and insulted at a Tesco or an Enron? When the shareholders of GM were wiped out by its government-led bailout, within months of the clean audit opinion from Deloitte? By the rolling series of bad news emerging from Fannie Mae, the quasi-governmental mortgage guarantor whose spectacular conflagration amid the financial crisis left in smoldering ashes the unqualified audit opinions issued by KPMG through 2004.

Admit it, straight out, as I have done with those who counseled against the boredom factor in setting out to tell this story: "Face it — accounting is not sexy."

Agreed. Pulses are not set racing. Big Four auditors do not sell racy novels, star in Hollywood blockbusters, or compete on celebrity television.[5] The profession offers no personality like that of Billy Bean propelling "Moneyball," or Lloyd Blankfein, the leader of Goldman Sachs, the "great vampire squid" of the financial crisis. The late comic Rodney Dangerfield had the best line about the profession: it's easy to spot the most dynamic auditor at the cocktail party — he's the one who looks at *your* shoes when he talks.[6]

For all the passions briefly aroused when "bad things" happen in the markets, and investors feel real pain in their accounts and their portfolios, their perspectives are filtered through their brokers, investment advisers and fund managers, so that the day-to-day public attitude toward the auditors remains one of distance and disregard.

Not so with the other professionals. Throughout the financial crisis that began in 2007–2008 with the fall of Bear Stearns and Lehman Brothers and the bailouts of institutions ranging from AIG to GM, other large institutions were demonized. Bankers were vilified. But there was no movement to "Occupy the Big Four."

In the Elizabethan era, Shakespeare's anarchic Dick the Butcher urged that "The first thing we do, let's kill all the lawyers." But for all the personal and institutional wealth that evaporated since the financial crisis began, nobody has ever aimed such murderous hostility at the auditors.

Instead, the accountants have received a pass. There has simply been no sustained arousal of insult, outrage, or even sustainable concern. To borrow baseball legend Yogi Berra's assessment of the public reluctance to buy tickets to see a losing team:

"If the fans don't want to come out, you can't stop them."

What accounts for the general public inattention to the work of the auditors, whose function is mandated by government and when so much seems to be at stake with their role in the free-market economies?

Familiarity

First, to look back, the role of the independent auditor was invented in the Victorian era in England and Scotland, in direct response to the desires of investors. Since then, over the entire course of economic history since the beginning of the Industrial Age, it has simply *always been there*.

Despite the massive changes in business and commerce over a century and a half, and the complexity of the transactions now reflected in corporate financial statements, the message delivered by the auditors is little changed since the 1850s, and the basic audit report is little evolved since the passage of the major American securities laws in the 1930s. The report language is regulated and standardized. Without seeing the logo or name of the issuing audit firm, a reader would be clueless to identify its source.

To modify the cliché, familiarity may not breed contempt, but it does breed passive indifference.

As familiar as water at the tap — electricity at the switch — television or music at the touch of a button. As dull and uncontroversial as any utility whose instant presence is expected and assumed.

Complexity Conceals

And yet ... Any can of worms looks simple with its lid on.

Beyond its boredom-inducing familiarity, a *second* reason for suppressed public concern is the daunting complexity of the financial markets in general. It is challenging enough to those on the inside, to comprehend the array of products, rules, standards and regulations. Perplexed outsiders confront the observation that "all professions are conspiracies against the laity."[7]

There was a time, as an analogy, back when fathers spent Saturdays under the hoods of the family cars and high-schoolers took Auto Shop, that common knowledge included the ability to gap a set of spark plugs or clear a flooded carburetor. Today, the percentage of car owners having the competence even to change a tire — much less any interest in ever having done so — hovers in the low single digits.

No less with the protocols of accounting and audit. Even though the principles are the same as those involved at the dawn of civilization when trade was invented, they have now evolved to eye-crossing complexity. A major cause of the financial crisis was the impossible intricacy of the financial products invented and sold by the investment banks — well beyond the understanding and risk evaluation even of the professionals. It was no wonder that even a knowledgeable investor could only stand by in wide-eyed incomprehension.

For both autos and auditors, we know much less in a more complicated modern world about the workings under the hood. Obliged to carry on with reduced familiarity about their inner machinery, we accept both benefits and hazards that are subject much less to individual understanding or control.

Big Audit Looks Like Any Other Utility

Third, Big Audit looks boring on the surface because its characteristics are those of a public utility:

- Market forces strictly limit the number of providers with the necessary scope, scale and economic incentive to deliver — whether a "natural monopoly" or, like the Big Four, a cartel with a few players. Examples are subway systems, cable providers and power grids.

- The product or service is standardized and undifferentiated among users — just as one telephone line or one bus ticket is pretty much like all the others, so is an audit report.

- The process and the product are highly regulated — whether by a public utility commission or a county water board or a transit authority — or for Big Audit, by the SEC, the PCAOB and their counterparts in other countries.

- The costs of switching to an alternative provider are dauntingly high, or choice may be simply impossible for want of another source.

- Innovation is not prioritized, for reasons running from history and culture to inertia and political protection of incumbent suppliers.

Customers of a utility display acceptance of their lot — expecting that water will appear at the turn of a faucet, that lights will go on with the flick of a switch, and that at the press of a remote, the cable system will deliver a sporting event or a news channel. And that buried deep in every year's corporate annual report, the same audit opinion will appear, and be ignored.

The reasons lie in the nature of a utility itself.

Change is constrained and inhibited when a utility enjoys official protection — as shown by the sluggish pace of change among the cartels under state ownership or sponsorship, in such fields as transportation, telephony and electricity.

The same with Big Audit. Laws and rules of the world's securities regulators require that public-company compliance and access to stock trading privileges include the annual filing of a standard-form auditor's report — the scope and language of which are strictly prescribed.

The mutually interlinked relationships among the players in Big Audit's market mean, in other words, that everyone's back gets scratched. Regulators set the rules of compliance so that only a handful of audit firms have the capability to fulfill them. Symmetrically, audit firms and their revenues are protected inside that system from the emergence of either new competitors or new forms of assurance.

The handcuffs are golden, and well-tempered by time and history.

Yet, government has another role in the typical utility model. It is the backstop of last resort when a delivery failure has occurred. Unlike breakdowns in a market of unconstrained competition, costs of a utility failure are effectively socialized, and spread across the population:

- By the widely shared inconvenience and distress — think of a power outage or a transport strike.

- By the financial burden put on a citizenry to adjust and cope with, for example, the nationalization of a failed railroad system.

Because utility customers expect that they will receive continuous, zero-defect service, they behave with both indifference and lack of influence. They are aroused only with a breakdown and even then, only to impotent complaints: "How long until the power is back on?" and "Where in hell is the cable guy?"

With no meaningful involvement in the repairs or the restoration of interrupted or substandard utility service, customers know only that eventually some anonymous *they* will plow the roads or repair the broken switch or reboot the transformer. And for the most part, *they* do just that. Sooner or later, after some level of public grousing and discomfort, the power is restored — the water flows — the trains run again.

What does not happen are consumer lawsuits against the utilities, or punitive cries that they should be put out of business for their substandard performance.

"Mind the Gap"

Just as consumers expect seamless integrated service from their other utilities, what much of the investor community knows — or think they know — is that the job of Big Audit is to protect the shareholders, to bless the stability and prosperity of a company, to assure the absence of corporate fraud or financial misfeasance and to stand guard over stock prices that should go nowhere but up.

But those views are clashingly inconsistent with the vision, mission, responsibility and capability of Big Audit — as is reemphasized anew, every time the cry is raised, "Where were the auditors?"

The difference between what users seek and what Big Audit has the ability to deliver is starkly known as the "Expectations Gap" — a yawning divide created in no small part at the profession's own initiative and responsibility, and which now threatens to engulf both the suppliers and the users of Big Audit.

Since securing the franchise to provide financial statement assurance for public companies, under the American securities laws of the 1930s, the accounting profession has borne self-inflicted responsibility for the creation and expansion of the Expectations Gap. Its actions included:

- Overselling the level of comfort its reports convey — going back to the inference of a "guaranty," conveyed by the unfortunate and now-replaced terminology of a "certificate," and the profession's futile inability to escape the lingering shadow of that language.

- Tolerating the misplaced label of "watchdog," as applied by jurists and academics whose presumption of guidance exceeds their real experience.

- Fostering the obsolete and intellectually fragile "appearance of independence" — a trope at odds with the "client-pays" model in place since Mr. Deloitte's era, which delivers neither protection for the auditors themselves nor enhanced comfort to users.

In addition, to be fair, responsibility for the users' side of the Expectations Gap includes in good part the challenge that Big Audit itself is complex.

Even at its best and working well, Big Audit involves a complicated set of tensile interlocking relationships among the players: standards that are as complex as the full range of business activities comprising the world's commercial economies, and expectations of users that are difficult to articulate, inconsistent with each other and harder still to reconcile.

Analysis and evaluation become even more difficult in the situations reflecting systemic stress. Resort to oversimplification is ever-present and tempting. Examples include such core topics as the proper balance between completeness of financial disclosure and reporting overload, or the competitive pressures of local-country regulatory autonomy and the desirability of consistent global standards, or the height of the bar by which to measure audit quality.

This challenge can at least be made easier to grasp by focus on the resemblance of Big Audit to other utilities — no different from that presented everywhere else in society's debates over policy choices about the allocation of conflicting priorities and scarce resources. Few of us know the engineering of a nuclear plant or the technology of a wind turbine, but we do have legitimate community interests in constant access to dependable electricity in our homes and offices. Only the experts can grasp the intricacies of phone and data service distribution, but we all expect our connected devices to work on demand, home or mobile, all the time.

The Limits of the "Utility" Metaphor

Here is the difference between traditional utilities and Big Audit: There is no "they" to provide a fix. Big Audit has become so structurally fragile that one more serious shock will leave it in catastrophic collapse. The liability regimes that permit death-blow litigation against the auditors could well deliver a result that is mortal.

Andersen's collapse showed that a large audit network *can* fail. It *could* have taught the public lesson that a systemic breakdown was and remains a dangerous possibility. But that lesson was not learned — at least not yet.

To round out the utility discussion, there are two additional problems with "socializing" the costs of a systemic breakdown of Big Audit:

First, among all the functions that government has tried with varying degrees of success to assume and provide, it has never been seriously asserted that nationalized "big government audit" could replace the current structure to the satisfaction of any of the players.

Other and better forms of assurance are available for design and delivery — a very lively part of the current discussion, to be visited in Part V. But it is unambiguously clear that whatever value may reside in today's commoditized audit report, it cannot be delivered by civil servants working under the same governments that have inflicted such nightmares as the Internal Revenue Service or the Transportation Security Administration, the National Health Service or National Rail.

Second, then, the socialized costs of the collapse of privately delivered Big Audit could come in the form of its extinction and complete disappearance, like the dinosaurs of old or the urban streetcar franchises of the 19th century.

If the Big Audit model fails today, there is simply no governmental authority with the vision, competence and authority to sustain and keep it alive. Which means that in its post-collapse absence, the model to replace today's Big Audit would have to be invented and constructed out of the available parts left in the pile of its wreckage.

Where Are the Critics?

There are commentators focused on the accounting profession who view Big Audit with unrelieved hostility — pointing to malign characteristics that range from client or agency capture to venality and downright corruption.

I decline to join their impassioned forces, chiefly because those critics take themselves out of active participation in any constructive dialog.

I am not an apologist. I believe that the profession has earned much of the criticism and general lack of sympathy bestowed on it, and that its leaders are fairly chargeable with a long history of lack of vision and a record of strategic and tactical ineptitude.

But I also believe that the profession's members are overwhelmingly people of good faith, with a resounding degree of technical competence, a basic commitment to their profession's central tenets and goals, and value to bring to the effective functioning of the capital markets.

To construct a bridge of comprehension and analysis across the Expectations Gap — rather than shout in futility from the opposing ledges — is a task of formidable dimensions. If this book does not reach the level of a blueprint for that task, it may perhaps at least be one form of a design proposal.

My goal here is to take the lid off the can of worms. To separate and look at the complex issues facing Big Audit, in blocks of comprehensible size. I realize that the examination of complex issues can only be simplified so far without degrading into simplemindedness, so there will be some use of terms and concepts that are technical or professional — no more than necessary, I hope.

FRAMING THE ISSUES

"None of us has a clue."
> — *Outgoing PCAOB Chairman William McDonough,*
> *to a reporter asking how regulators would respond to*
> *another failure among the Big Four*[8]

A basic reordering of the relationship between large global companies and their accounting firms is inevitable. Although evolution can be postponed, it cannot be stopped. But the need is neither well recognized nor openly discussed.

Auditors' reports on the financial statements of large companies have for decades been deemed important in the operation of the world's capital markets.

By tradition, consensus and eventually, law and regulation, "pass-fail" assurance on the financial information issued by publicly held companies has been provided to regulators, investors and other users by private accountancy partnerships organized into large international networks.

But recent events show this structure and the firms' business model to be unsustainable. Instead, the global organizations that remain from what was known for years as the Big Eight — often identified, inaccurately and without irony, as the Final Four[9] — are now down to an irreducible minimum.

Nothing good has happened since Andersen fell in 2002, which might relieve the threat that the Big Audit model may be unsustainable. Big Audit cannot survive another loss at the Big Four level. Vigorously as the ambitious leaders of the next smaller networks would assert their growth plans, challenges of global scope and depth of resources constrain their ability to deliver audit services at the top of the corporate size tables.

Yet the combined pressures of regulation and litigation are irresistible.

If another of the Big Four should go down — an acute and present peril — the investors, bankers and other users who for years have proclaimed the importance of Big Audit and the accountants' core product, along with politicians and regulators alike, will awake to find that the one-page document they have for so long either criticized or taken for granted is no longer available from any source.

A confluence of factors combine to threaten a profession that has served society with great value for over 165 years, and define the challenges under which the players in the world's capital markets will be obliged to adjust and cope.

Andersen/Enron — The Beginning of the End

"How did things ever get so far?"
— *Vito Corleone (Marlon Brando),*
"The Godfather" — 1972

The major lesson left unlearned by Andersen's collapse is that the litigation exposures and regulatory stress on the Big Four today are every bit as grave as Andersen's, and their financial capabilities and limited multinational cohesion are if anything more fragile.

To which, public indifference extends among their clients, the users of the issuers' financial statements, and the lawyers, regulators, law enforcement officers and politicians. Their simplistic reaction to the death of Andersen was, essentially, "Too bad — those auditors have just got to learn their lessons."

As one example: when he was interviewed in the fall of 2003, Sir David Tweedie, the then-chairman of the International Accounting Standards Board, was asked about the capacity of the surviving large firms to contribute the professional resources necessary to achieve the improvement and convergence of international accounting standards that are the mission of the IASB, in light of their surrounding structural pressures. His dismissive answer was that "they'll just have to do better."

In an environment of parochial interests and denial, as will be seen, a complex of interacting factors makes impossible the ability of the firms to "do better." This question is not answered, because it has gone unasked:

"If Andersen could not survive Enron, then who or what could save today's Big Four?"

The Diminished Value of Today's Assurance Product

The spate of financial scandals that started with Enron in 2001 in the United States continued through WorldCom and Tyco and Adelphia. It extended to such multinationals as Ahold, Adecco, Parmalat and Shell. Still to come was the financial crisis that began in 2007–2008 and tarred — or claimed — such iconic names as Bear Stearns, Lehman Brothers, AIG and Merrill Lynch, as well as banks and other financial institutions in the United Kingdom, Ireland, Iceland and across Europe.

The eruptions have continued steadily since — Satyam in India and BT in Italy, Tesco in the United Kingdom and Petrobras in Brazil, FIFA in Switzerland, Olympus and Toshiba in Japan, MF Global and Valeant and Wells Fargo in the United States — with the certainty that there will be more to come.

Recent history shows that the traditional standard auditor's report is obsolete and no longer relied upon. There is no differentiation in content among issuers of the standard product — showing commodity pricing and market behavior consistent with a utility product of diminished value.[10]

The Big Audit model does not reflect pricing premiums on audits of global companies — but, to the contrary, fee pressures and reductions, and relentless pressure on staff time and budgets. As with such commodities as brands of toothpaste, identical mid-sized cars, and gasoline at the pumps, the price-cutting effect applies no less to *verbatim* audit reports and their "pass-fail" opinions — identical and undifferentiated across both companies and their audit firms.[11]

Further, evolution in the capital markets has rendered the traditional auditor's report both obsolete and irrelevant.

Sophisticated investors have long since stopped relying on Big Audit's reports — dating back 30 years to the twin phenomena in the 1980s of junk securities and leveraged recapitalizations. In that era, no lawsuits against auditors were ever brought by the "smart guys" — the venture capitalists, the managers of private equity, or the financiers of leveraged recapitalizations — who glanced at an audit opinion under the cover of a corporate annual report, yawned, and went about their real diligence.

Less sophisticated investors also ignore audit reports confined to traditional financial reporting, as shown by the complete disconnection, during and since the bubble years of the 1990s, between share prices and audited financial results. Soaring prices were supported by neither assets nor earnings under generally accepted accounting principles — nor, in time, even by revenue. The analysts herded their clients, and each other, down roads paved with airy business plans, empty promises and inflated expectations. At the point of collapse, a clean audit report provided shareholder plaintiffs only with a ticket to the courthouse.

The Players in the Matrix — Their Interlocking Mutuality of Interests

Post-Enron, to the extent public awareness of the involvement of accountants in the creation and issuance of financial information was changed, the perception took the form of criticism and disrespect.

The diminished contribution of the profession — although it was deemed tolerably important to the effective operations of the capital markets, if both unnecessarily complex and terminally dull — only polluted further the stifled atmosphere in which the private provision of assurance now functions.

The central proposition is this: The imminent collapse of Big Audit would require the capital markets to adjust to the unavailability of financial statements examined under generally accepted auditing standards and bearing a "pass-fail" opinion. Players in those markets would be forced to identify alternative assurance products, sourced from a new configuration of suppliers, designed and implemented to be responsive to the needs of a world more complex than ever.

The structural components of the Big Audit model involve a complex interplay among the major players, each having both self-interested vision and limited influence and authority. They are:

- Listed public companies — the large corporate issuers of financial statements, examined and reported on by the auditors.

- The Big Four accounting firms themselves — the providers of the audit function and its standard commodity report.

- Investment bankers, analysts, rating agencies, investors, and other financial statement users — with their varying and inconsistent attitudes toward the auditors' opinions.

- The professional accounting and auditing standards-setting and oversight bodies — jockeying among themselves and in their respective jurisdictions for recognition and credibility.

- The regulators of the profession and of the world's securities and capital markets — thinly stretched, and motivated to drive actual audit performance toward a box-ticking exercise to satisfy their mechanistic inspection-oriented programs.

- Politicians and legislators — overwhelmed by market forces so complex as to be incomprehensible, and driven by the primary imperative of every office-holder, to be retained in the comfortable enjoyment of incumbency.

- Agencies of law enforcement — hampered by limitations of resources and jurisdictional boundaries, and caught up in the pressures of political accountability.

- The ever-present casts of lawyers acting for all of the above.

These differently motivated parties contribute separately to the current environment. But each of them operates under limitations of geographic and jurisdictional authority, organizational competence, and simple self-interest — limits built into their very DNA that constrain their capacity for change.

There have been frequent public statements to the effect that, after the fall of Andersen, no one actually desires the failure of another large accounting network. Which may well be so. Regulators have somewhat moderated their bellicose messages and tactics. There are even statements to the effect that "they" will not allow another of the Big Four to fail.

But as the acerbic Gertrude Stein said of an urban dystopia, "there is no 'there' there." There is no "*they*" — regulators, politicians, or others — having either the will or the authority to prevent the next failure. The concept of a rescue mission for a Big Four firm driven to the brink of failure, by an unbearable litigation award or an irresistible prosecution or enforcement proceeding, would be both politically unachievable and legislatively impossible.

In the matrix of Big Audit's interested parties, complex pressures on the issuance and assurance of financial information are combined and interrelated. As summarized here, and expanded and fleshed out later:

- Societal expectations about the value and function of auditors are mismatched with the reality of corporate behavior.

- Accounting and reporting standards — too complex for comparable implementation in their requirements for broad ranges of judgment and degrees of estimation — are exploited by financial statement issuers to the point of overt manipulation.

- Built-in limitations on the realistically achievable level of auditor performance are unrecognized.

- The last four large accounting networks — along with their smaller counterparts — suffer unbearable professional liability litigation exposure.

- The Big Four have consistently failed to achieve levels of practice quality to match the expectations of the users of large-company financial statements. Instead, they attract year-after-year criticism from regulators such as the PCAOB and, more importantly, an unbroken stream of litigation more than large enough to be life threatening. The Big Four and their partners lack the financial resources to withstand the potentially devastating impact of a "worst-case" litigation outcome, on the scale that rapidly spun Andersen to its destruction. Their available capital — thin if adequate to meet their routine demands — does not begin to match their exposures.

At the same time, the large firms' ability to innovate in the delivery of assurance products having real value to the capital markets is hobbled on multiple fronts:

- By scope-of-practice constraints imposed by the restrictions of the obsolete and intellectually unsound concept of "appearance of independence" — a system providing neither protection for the firms nor comfort for the community of users.

- By the "golden handcuffs" of a business model that requires delivery of audit opinions in the commodity language demanded by regulators — creating an environment in which innovation is stifled by the combination of client budget demands and anxiety at the prospect of regulatory second-guessing.

- By the impact of scale and the barriers to entry imposed by the demands of global clients for services in dozens of countries, making niche introduction of new competitors and new forms and techniques of assurance both unfeasible and uneconomic.

The players making up Big Audit have been talking past each other about its issues since well before the collapse of Enron. But the persistent recurrence of disruptions and scandals makes plain their ineffectiveness, and the lack of a suitable venue or forum to communicate, evaluate and mediate their disparate interests.

Because of the structural and political impossibility of a cooperative and holistic approach involving all of these important actors, there are a number of near-term scenarios under which the global accounting networks could be forced out of the audit business.

Most likely among these, overwhelming litigation would drive one or more of the remaining Big Four over the brink of collapse.

The next of the Big Four to fail would take down the entire Big Audit structure, in a cascade of network failures, disintegrations and risk-averse market withdrawals. A three-firm system cannot survive, under the pressures on the remaining firms caused by the limited range of client choice, partnership instability and regulatory stress.

Liability-driven, the global accounting networks would disintegrate. Their separate national practices, already distinct legal entities under the requirements of their local laws, would act to protect their local partners and franchises, following the course taken in 2002 by the speedily unraveled Andersen global network.

Publicly-held companies would then be out of compliance with their securities regulators' requirements for audited financial statements. A single auditor's opinion on the consolidated financial statements of global companies would no longer be available, from any source or at any price.

In the United States, the SEC requires every corporate registrant of significant size — "large accelerated filers," defined as registrants with securities having public float of more than $700 million — to file audited financial statements within 45 days of its financial year-end. But this would not be possible post-collapse, because there would be no audit network capable of delivering the required report.

For companies typically having a calendar year-end, the bureaucrats' 45-day deadline could fall on Valentine's Day. But as would be known well before that dire day, the SEC and the stock exchanges would — despite their understandable bureaucrats' distress at the prospect of comprehensive noncompliance — be forced to yield to the world's insatiable appetite for access to capital on a basis that is constant, liquid and seamless. The demands for uninterrupted daily trading would be a force too strong to consider denial.

Instead, market pressures would prevent regulators from restricting the right to trade in the securities of the world's largest companies — as was the case in 2001 with the destruction of the World Trade Center towers on September 11, which kept the New York Stock Exchange closed for only three days.

Customer pressure on the governance of the Big Board would impel it to brush aside the absence of a one-page regulatory filing as a minor nuisance. The stock exchanges would find a way to remain open for business on February 15.

From that day forward, investors would inflict a new form of risk premium on the capital costs of companies whose noncompliant financial statements left their doubts unsatisfied. They would continue the search, already well started today, for new forms of reliable assurance on financial information, to supplant the present low-value product.

And the fragmented accounting organizations that managed to survive the breakup of their global networks — having withdrawn from the statutory assurance market altogether — would have the opportunity to adapt, respond and reinvent themselves.

But for the evolution of the Big Four to redesign and evolve their services for the sake of survival, the present constraints of "independence" and the life-threatening liability exposures that currently inhibit the development or use of new and innovative reports would have to be lifted or dramatically modified. Only then, to avoid exposure to a further apocalypse of litigation, would the survivors deem it even remotely attractive to return to the assurance market.

With Big Audit leadership presently lacking visible participation in the search for a holistic and sustainable model for the future, the only alternative may be the obligation to design new forms of reporting and assurance after the collapse of the entire Big Four structure — itself the inevitable consequence of the disintegration of any one of them — a grim but real prospect almost too disruptive to contemplate.

Regulators along with the rest of the players would face a new future — where market influences would determine the content, value and pricing for new forms of financial reporting.

Perhaps the most comprehensive change would occur in the executive suites and the boardrooms. Corporate chief financial officers and audit committees would have new and critical roles. Today they are the *best* available resources from which to obtain company financial information. In the future, they may well be the *only* ones. They would have the responsibility to assemble and issue the best available assurance, with the assistance of the surviving national and niche accounting practices to emerge post-collapse.

In short, although until now it has been neither recognized nor openly discussed, a fundamental reordering lies ahead.

LESSONS FROM BIG AUDIT'S EARLY HISTORY: THE GREAT WESTERN RAILWAY — MR. DELOITTE'S FIRST AUDIT REPORT[12]

The origins of the learned professions are hidden in the mists of prehistory. There are no records of the activities or the identities of the first doctor or priest, lawyer or architect.

We can, however, come very close to fixing the birth date of the independent audit. On February 8, 1850, William Welch Deloitte, Accountant, opined on the half-yearly accounts of the Great Western Railway for the period ended December 31, 1849.

Great Western Railway.

GENERAL STATEMENT OF RECEIPTS AND PAYMENTS TO THE 31st DECEMBER, 1849.

Audited and approved, 8th February, 1850.   W. W. DELOITTE, Accountant.

Deloitte's assurance that the railroad's accounts were both "Audited and approved" may not have been the world's first report by an independent auditor.[13] But if not, this report by one of the profession's pioneers comes near enough to be worth close attention.

As cannot be done for the origins of law-making or healing or spiritual ritual, the birth of Big Audit and the very beginning of its history can be seen on one printed page, from which have followed over eight score years of practice in the assurance of financial information.[14]

For context, the roles and services of both accountant and auditor have supported commerce since the dawn of trade. The earliest known forms of writing are not romantic poetry or odes to military heroism, but inventory records, etched on clay tablets to document counts of livestock and measures of grain.

Accounting conventions were required as soon as transactions evolved beyond the most primitive and elementary. A simple agreement from before the time of recorded human history — "I will give you this stone axe today, for which your brother will give me a lamb in the spring" — implicates agreement on policies and principles involving timing, revenue recognition, transaction and credit and currency risk.

Assurance — the work of auditors — was also required early. Tax collections on behalf of king or pharaoh involved verification of crop yields, herd sizes and slave holdings. Some trusted functionary was needed, to do the counting.

Matters remained straightforward if evolving for centuries. Kings and princes in Europe financed their political and military ambitions through lenders in the Mediterranean city-states, sitting at their benches — the *bancs* — hence the modern term. And whether by ship or caravan, foreign trade ventures were one-off undertakings with simple bookkeeping. Promoters would sponsor and outfit the voyage. If it returned, pay off the crew, sell the goods and divide the profits. If it failed, take the write-off and absorb the loss.[15]

Came eventually the great works and ventures of the early Industrial Age — the landscape-changing railroads, mines, toll roads and canal companies with their voracious needs for access to investor capital.

Great Western was organized in 1835. In 15 years it had grown to an enterprise showing half-year revenue of £13 million and share capital of £8 million, with its locomotives logging 900,000 miles in the second half of 1849.

As had become typical for the early limited liability companies, its accounts were prepared in accordance with the requirements of the recently enacted Joint Stock Companies Act 1844. These had initially been scrutinized for the benefit of its proprietors and commented upon by "auditors" selected from among the shareholders themselves. It was then an entirely sensible governance proposition — although today questionably superseded as quaint and naïve — that an examiner holding a direct financial interest was best motivated to provide the most scrupulous achievement of useful assurance.

The two worthy shareholders of Great Western who performed that function, Messrs. John Dickinson and Richard Atkinson, have retreated into obscurity, but for their outreach to engage the assistance of the youthful Mr. Deloitte.

Deloitte's opinion on the 1849 accounts — "Audited and approved" — was terse and to the point. Not for him the ambiguities or equivocation that would creep into later years, of "true and fair" or "in all material respects," or "in accordance with generally accepted standards."

And his audit scope, as recorded in the corporate minutes, was comprehensive: "Every item has been minutely examined by the Auditors, the vouchers and receipts have been inspected, and the purpose to which the payments were applied has been ascertained."

Again, notions of sampling, judgments as to scope of work, or limitations based on cost or effectiveness did not enter. Auditors in the earliest years really did count the stuff, and all of it.

As for the agonizing modern debate on the responsibilities of auditors to observe on systems of internal control, reflected in the significant costs and debatable benefits of Section 404 of the Sarbanes-Oxley law of 2002, Deloitte spoke directly on both the existence and the efficacy of Great Western's systems. As he put it, the auditors not only "authenticated the accounts," they "expressed their general commendation of the system itself, and the mode in which it has worked."

There is both good and bad news in the ability to trace the origins of Big Audit all the way back.

Deloitte himself was in the forefront on two issues of acute modern relevance. He was an innovator on both the form and content of financial statements themselves, and he argued in favor of a legislative framework under which corporate reporting would be required — a result of which was the 1867 English legislation leading to the routinizing of railroad reports. As the legibility of his work to a modern reader makes clear, he would need only a short seminar to be updated on the proliferation of financial complexity and professional vocabulary, to be at home in today's reporting environment.

But suppose a prospective investor in a modern-day English company, doing due diligence by reading its accounts, were to encounter Deloitte's opinion, "Audited and approved." Unless told its date of origin, no reader today — with the possible exception of a few professional insiders — would recognize it as anachronistic, or balk at the Great Western disclosure if dated in the 21st century.

What are the implications, that a document of such a venerable age would be so familiar as to arouse page-turning indifference?

For the historical context of Mr. Deloitte's pioneering report — Queen Victoria, age 30, had been on the English throne for twelve years. Charles Darwin was back from the voyages of HMS *Beagle*, although publication of his work on evolution was still a decade in the future. The discovery of gold in California was inspiring a rush of both prospectors and capital-intensive infrastructure investments, transforming the North American continent and reordering the world's economies.

Mr. Deloitte's contemporaries in other fields, whose industries have mutated and evolved beyond all recognition, would be utterly lost in today's world. Consider their dislocation:

- A Victorian train engineer, in the cockpit of a space shuttle.

- A typesetting pamphleteer, updated to CNN's global newsroom or a Facebook page or YouTube link.

- A telegrapher, confronting Skype or Twitter, Instagram or Snapchat.

- A surgeon, knowing neither anesthetics nor X-rays, beholding the tools of CAT scans or laser surgery.

While the transmutations wrought by science and technology mean that nothing else from the early Victorian era would be recognizable in today's culture of commerce, there are reasons to find it unsettling that Mr. Deloitte's work might still appear current.

Since then, railroads and the telegraph have begot commercial aviation and the computer, satellite communications and the Internet, cloud computing and drones and big data. In a globalized world, products and entire industries change beyond recognition in cycles measured in months.

No one would wish to go back. It would be a foolish and sentimental yearning, for the time of the slave trades, suicidal cavalry charges, and 30% infant mortality. But neither can time's arrow be deflected. Evolution cannot be stopped.

But mutation is subtle. Even while the last generation of dinosaurs disported around the tar pits, furry little mammals were multiplying, under foot and out of sight. So too, Detroit's Big Three auto makers took no notice while the Japanese and German carmakers were evolving from small-engine entry-level machines to leading positions of innovation, quality and market dominance.

The world's securities exchanges — global high-volume algorithmic electronic trading platforms spawned from the open-outcry bourses of the 19th century — are consolidating under collaborative systems of intergovernmental regulation. Newspapers are either dying off or migrating their business models to the world of the web and the smartphone. Blogs and videos, Pinterest and Instagram have displaced broadsheets as the information vehicles of popular choice.

Darwinian evolution means not just the survival of the fit, but the correlative extinction of the obsolescent. When the accounting profession successfully lobbied the American securities regulators in the 1930s to control the franchise of financial statement assurance, an unappreciated consequence was the acceptance of a regulatory straitjacket. With the form of reporting essentially unchanged since that crafted by Mr. Deloitte and his pioneering fellows in the 1850s, mutation adaptive to changing conditions has been stifled. Today's handcuffed auditors could not provide a more timely or valuable form of report even if they wanted to.

The tectonic plates under the auditors' franchise within Big Audit continue to shift, with ominous speed and expanding risk that the participants are barely able to acknowledge. The auditors themselves have little control over their most immediate threats. They can muster only limited attention, respect and influence among critics, politicians and regulators, leaving them hostage to the uncertain assumption of their continued survival into the future.

Big Audit and the measure of its value to investors must change no less than the rest of the world of business. But down the road, it is unknown what financial statement assurance will look like, or who will provide it. The large firms that emerged under the leadership of Mr. Deloitte and his contemporaries have called for dialog on the need for a fundamental reengineering, toward a model of reporting in real time and utilizing the availability and power of "big data," and opening the prospects for a redesigned form of assurance.

They assert that the accounting profession is ideally poised to lead and participate. But that position rests more on historic inertia than on presumptive necessity. The auditors have no more guaranteed tickets to survival than did the dinosaurs or the steam locomotives. Being under assault from regulators and shareholder plaintiffs does not *ipso facto* confer either virtue or a right to relief.

The challenge may be put this way: In the world of commerce and the capital markets, large-company assurance is essential. Its delivery by the Big Four is not.[16]

Entrepreneurial as he was, William Welch Deloitte would take pride that his work has survived virtually intact across this span of decades. But he would also be among the leaders sounding the call for Big Audit's redesign and renewal.

HP VERSUS AUTONOMY: HOW BIG AUDIT MIGHT SURVIVE THE FALLOUT

One hundred and sixty-one years following Mr. Deloitte's opinion on Great Western, a partner in the Cambridge office of the Big Four firm bearing his name and legacy signed the firm's report dated February 22, 2011, on the 2010 financial statements of UK-based software company Autonomy.

Autonomy was acquired the following October by Hewlett-Packard, for $11.1 billion. A year later the deal imploded — on November 20, 2012 — with the announcement by HP's CEO Meg Whitman of an $8.8 billion write-off, of which $5.5 billion was attributed to massive accounting irregularities.

As one of the many real-world examples that provide the building blocks for this narrative, a lesson in the many perceived shortcomings in the current financial reporting and assurance model of Big Audit lay under the toxic cloud of charges and counter-charges:

- Whitman's claims of pervasive accounting fraud were derided by critics as a mask for HP's faulty due diligence, gross over-payment and post-transaction mismanagement, and have been vigorously denied by Autonomy's ex-CEO Mike Lynch.[17]

- Lawsuits followed promptly — by HP's shareholders against the company for its self-inflicted wound; derivatively on behalf of HP and by shareholders as a class, against the entire range of usual targets including Deloitte as Autonomy's statutory auditor in the United Kingdom and KPMG in its due diligence role for HP; and by HP itself against Autonomy's leadership — the last a UK-based suit, said to be one of the largest individual claims in the history of the British courts.

The dust-settling process will be years in coming — including the eventual litigation exit price that would predictably be paid by Deloitte when trans-Atlantic teams of lawyers concluded their inevitable settlement negotiations[18] and finalized the allocation of responsibility around Autonomy's revenue accounting and HP's due diligence.[19]

As to the implications for the Big Four collectively, pointed questions arose that go to the structural heart of the traditional auditor-client relationship:

- Floyd Norris in the *New York Times*, November 29, 2012: "'Where were the auditors?'...They were everywhere."

- Francine McKenna, *Re: The Auditors*, December 1, 2012: "'To the victor's auditor go the audit spoils'... is not how the Big Four audit industry is played now that consulting is again King."

- Tom Selling, *The Accounting Onion*, December 2, 2012: "If Autonomy's accounting practices were too aggressive, would Deloitte's staff have had the gumption to push back given the stakes?"

Meaningful confrontation of these questions, which have evaded resolution for decades, includes two essential issues:

First, because Autonomy's accounting and reporting and Deloitte's issuance of the standard commoditized auditor's report were targeted as unsatisfactory, just when critically most important, the question was raised yet again:

> "What good are models having the appearance of utility, only up to the point of their unexpected exposure as insufficient, when suddenly they seem not to have worked at all?"

Second, the finger-pointing at Deloitte's business alliance relationship with HP and the scope of its nonaudit services for Autonomy raise again the unresolved obsolescence of the notion of "appearance of independence."

Regulators have long had the large accounting firms' expansion of nonaudit services in their sights. For example — at the AICPA's SEC-PCAOB conference in November 2012:

- Then-SEC Chief Accountant[20] Paul Beswick: "I question whether accountants' expanding practices into areas unrelated to their primary competencies weakens public trust."

- PCAOB Chairman James Doty: *"Audit practices have shrunk in comparison to audit firms' other client service lines — not all of which are schooled in, or depend upon, the fundamental exercise of skepticism. This threatens to weaken the strength of the audit practice in the firm overall."*

To much the same effect, PCAOB member Lewis Ferguson, quoted at a press conference in April 2014, on the auditors' rapid expansion into the applicability of Big Data to the practice of auditing, called it "a source of great concern to all regulators around the world," and "rais(ing) serious concerns about differential levels of profitability in these businesses, differential rates of growth, where the economic incentives are and to what extent does audit quality *suffer* as a result" (*emphasis added*).

The accounting profession may survive what would otherwise be another generation under this radioactive rhetorical cloud; to make it so, fundamental adjustments are in order.

A priority would be a robust defense of the "client-pays" model. However much criticized, it dates to the invention of independent assurance in the 1850s, and is the *only* approach ever to stand the test of actual adoption and use.

"Client pays" being irreconcilable with "independence in fact," however, the HP-Autonomy fiasco is a reminder of the profession's long-standing inability to articulate intellectually stable support for "independence in appearance."

For which, it is worth anticipating here in summary (*see* Part II) the reasons why the sacred cow of auditor independence should be led off and humanely put out of its misery:

- The concept of auditor independence does not serve the interests of investors.

- Audit performance — and more immediately, the survival of the large firms to serve their global clients and the capital markets — would be better achieved if the current independence requirements and constraints were scrapped altogether.

- Auditors should be free to provide their clients with any services within their skills. The only thing that should be required is comprehensive disclosure of all relationships, to be evaluated and decided by the voting power of the marketplace.

At the same time, clearance of the radioactive debris of independence inhibitions would free the Big Audit marketplace from the entire sterile debate over permissible services by auditors.

The community of financial information users is capable of defining, engaging and valuing the scope of services available from its gatekeepers — whether bankers, lawyers, rating agencies, or auditors.

The public users' trade-off — to release the large accounting firms from the constraints of a system that has long lost its value — would involve a downward reassessment in the asserted value of their traditional core product. That would only acknowledge a reality long suppressed or denied in any event — an exchange that would be worth making.

	Deloitte	EY	KPMG	PwC
Sidebar: Counting the Beans — Facts and Figures on Big Audit				
Global revenue ($ billions)[a]	36.8	29.6	25.4	35.9
Global personnel (thousands)	244	231	189	223
Global partners	11,122	11,599	9,843	10,803
Practice line revenue ($ billions):				
Assurance	9.4	11.3	10.1	15.3
Tax (and legal)	6.9	7.8	5.6	9.1

	Deloitte	EY	KPMG	PwC
(Continued)				
Advisory/consulting[b]	20.5	10.5	9.7	11.5
Profit per partner (UK) (£thousands)	837	662	582	706

[a]Global figures are from the 2016 annual reports on the Big Four's global websites. UK partner profits are from their audited UK accounts or news reports. Global growth rates reported for 2016, year-on-year, are: Deloitte + 9.5%, EY + 9%, KPMG + 8%, and PwC + 7%.
[b]Includes consulting practices variously described as Transaction, Financial and Enterprise Risk.

For context and comparison with the Big Four's global revenue — all together some $128 billion — the latest available combined annual total revenue of the next six largest networks, associations and alliances, reported by those organizations or the International Accounting Bulletin, totaled some $28 billion — a *total* amount falling roughly between the size of the two smaller of the Big Four:

BDO ($ billions)	7.6
Grants	4.6
RSM	4.6
Praxity	4.5
Baker Tilly	3.8
Crowe Horwath	3.5

Examples of the Extent of Large-Company Audit Concentration

United States

Of the large companies comprising the Dow Jones Industrial index, all 30 were audited by the Big Four in 2016: Deloitte — four, EY — six, KPMG — five, PwC — 15. All but a handful of the companies in the S&P 500 index are likewise Big Four audit clients.

The Big Four today

United Kingdom

In the United Kingdom, according to the report of the Financial Reporting Council in July 2016, the Big Four audited all but two of the FTSE 100 companies — a list significantly dominated by PwC's 37 engagements. As reported, the Big Four also audited 228 of the next FTSE 250 companies.

As measured by Adviser Rankings Ltd., of the UK public companies audited by the top ten firms, the Big Four audit more than 98% by both market capitalization and profits.

Under rules in the United Kingdom issued by the Financial Reporting Council and the Competition Commission starting in late 2013 — discussed at more length in Part IV — the United Kingdom has experienced a flurry of audit tenders — including some retentions of incumbents and a larger number of replacements.

While issues of limited auditor choice and cost and inefficiency of the re-tender process continue — as ancillary challenges to the still-unproven proposition that lengthy audit tenure is somehow causally related to audit quality — those who advocate auditor replacement as a means of advancing increased competition from the smaller audit firms confront the evidence that *none* of the announced FTSE 100 switches in the United Kingdom has involved replacement of a Big Four firm with a firm outside that quartet.

France

France is the single large country that follows the practice of joint audits. Of the companies in its large-company index, the CAC 40, all use at least one Big Four firm, and 27 use two. No CAC 40 company uses two audit firms from outside the Big Four.

Of the companies in the CAC 40 headquartered outside France, and free to follow the French practice of joint auditors, none does so — each chooses to use a single Big Four firm.

Germany

All of the large companies comprising the DAX 30 index are audited by the Big Four — 18 are clients of KPMG, and nine use PwC.

As an indicator of the uneven geographic distribution of audit resources even among the Big Four, KPMG's dominant position in Germany is contrasted with the fact that it holds only eleven audit mandates under the joint-audit regime applicable to the CAC 40 in France, edged out by the 13 mandates held by the Mazars firm, a member of the Praxity alliance and the single player outside the Big Four in the French large-company market.

NOTES

1. Arthur Andersen's leaders made two branding decisions in the firm's last year. First, they shortened the global name to "Andersen" — a convention followed here unless context requires otherwise. They also chose to replace the long-familiar "Doors" logo, modeled on the mahogany entrance to the firm's original Chicago office, with a red-and-orange ball of uncertain provenance. Leadership at the time lacked the perspective, now provided by hindsight, to appreciate that those decisions, separating the firm from its historic roots, were symptomatic of deeper issues at the core of the firm's values.

2. *Arthur Andersen LLP v. United States* (2005).

3. Meanwhile, the remaining shell of the Andersen organization used what was left of its resources to wind down its litigation inventory. As a

defendant in the WorldCom civil litigation, for example, in which a group of investment banks agreed to settlements totaling over $6 billion, Andersen eventually contributed the relatively paltry sum of $103 million.

4. From there the stock has bumped up and down, to 215 p in October 2016 — just before the outbreak on November 7 of a massive hacking of customer accounts at Tesco Bank that sent the stock reeling afresh.

5. The tumultuous finale to the 2017 Academy Awards ceremonies caused by the Best Picture envelope mix-up put PwC and its responsible partner under the harsh spot-light of an avoidably ill-managed process. While the partner lost his role for the future, the firm will retain its 83-year relationship with the Academy, and there is little prospect that PwC's greater reputation among clients in the global-scale professional services market will be affected.

6. Ben Affleck's eponymous star turn in 2016's hit summer film *The Accountant* only proved the rule — operating as he did out of a seedy strip mall and an Airstream trailer, not as a large-company statutory auditor, but with a unique solo practice combining tax, forensics, and deadly force.

7. George Bernard Shaw, *Major Barbara* (1905).

8. *Financial Times* (September 28, 2005).

9. The large accounting firms have engaged in sustained competition, to the astonishing degree that active price-cutting still survives from the days of the Big Eight. But the idea that one firm should emerge triumphant, as happens in those great spectacles of American college sport, the NCAA basketball tournaments, is beyond contemplation. As will be discussed, the uneven concentration of resources and the constraints on client choice are already disruptive. Because a three-firm system is unworkable, the next Big Four failure would bring down the entire structure. The slang of a basketball tournament has provided a label that is colorful but inapt. The better if ominous gaming metaphor is "Russian roulette."

10. Because of reference from time to time to the "standard" auditor's report, included as appendices are both the pioneering report of William Welch Deloitte dated February 8, 1850, on the financial statements of Great Western Railway for the half-yearly period ended December 31, 1849, and a modern version — the report by EY on the 2016 financial statements of Apple Inc. — whose market capitalization as of late-spring

2017 of over $800 billion pairs it with Alphabet as America's largest public companies. Readers might readily find language identical to EY's by digging out a version from one of the annual reports forwarded from their brokers — assuming they had not immediately been tossed into the trash.

11. While the audit opinion language in the United States has borne the compliance-oriented qualifier, "in accordance with" accepted accounting standards, the early English reports originated the plain language of a "true and fair view." That distinction is now essentially lost, with the British use of the International Financial Reporting Standards; it is in any event looked on by users, if at all, as a distinction without a difference — inconsequential to the investing public and of academic interest only to those counting the number of angels on pin-heads.

12. Presented in an earlier form as a paper for the American Accounting Association's August 2008 meeting, Anaheim, California.

13. Although an affirmative claim of primacy is always subject to discovery of an earlier example, diligent inquiry with historians of the profession has so far not yielded up a competitor for the position.

14. In the sprawling modern complex of Britain's National Archives, in the suburb of Kew on the outskirts of London, documentary history spanning a thousand years is directly accessible to the interested civilian, through a beguiling combination of highly automated data retrieval and manual techniques that would be familiar to medieval clerks and scriveners. A researcher picks up a reader's card. "Pencils only in the reading rooms, sir — no pens or highlighters allowed." Into a locker go all banned and dangerous instruments of potential defacement. Intensely earnest scholars and amateur family genealogists pad around in appropriately hushed and reverential attitudes. Research librarians help refine searches and log in requests. A staff of helpful clerks fetch a stack of Victorian-era ledgers and minute books. There are indeed needles to be found in this vast field of haystacks.

15. Incidentally, if the ship sank, investors resorted to another recently developed trade-based sector, lodging their claims under maritime insurance policies written with the specialists tracing their new activities to the 17th century gatherings at Edward Lloyd's coffeehouse in the City of London.

16. Nor should the inhibitions on the Big Four's innovation capabilities be a surprise. Uber was not the invention of taxi fleet owners eager to

redesign the industry by destroying the value of their portfolios of medallions; Airbnb was not the brainchild of the hotel chains, nor Amazon of the bricks-and-mortar bookstores.

17. At this writing it is premature to assess the impact or eventual outcome of the November 2016 criminal indictment in California of former Autonomy CFO Sushovan Hussain, on federal fraud charges for conduct designed to manipulate Autonomy's stock price.

18. In the spring of 2015, HP and Deloitte signed a "standstill agreement" — a convention suspending the effect of statutes of limitations that would have fixed a deadline by which HP would have been obliged to sue Deloitte — a means of preserving amity between the parties and an almost-inevitable signal that the ultimate resolution will be at a level modest enough to be inconsequential.

19. Largely peripheral to the story here, except for its impact on the remaining legal maneuvers in the United Kingdom, HP's own litigation exposure took some peculiar turns. In the summer of 2014, the judge supervising shareholders' suits against HP in San Francisco rejected a proposed settlement, under which HP would have paid nothing, but would have engaged the very firm of *plaintiffs'* lawyers who brought suit against the company, to migrate the pre-trial record they had built against HP itself over to support for HP's claims against Autonomy's former executives. In June 2015, a settlement was announced under which HP would pay $100 million in resolution of shareholder claims — an outcome including the typical language, that "While HP believes the action has no merit, it is desirable and beneficial to HP and its shareholders to resolve [to] settle the case as further litigation would be burdensome and protracted."

20. At the time, Acting Chief Accountant, and since departed for the private sector.

II

THE PRESENT STATE OF BIG AUDIT

HOW BAD IS IT?

What Is Expected? What *Should* the Auditors Do?

Before going into the details, it is worth pausing to ask, what should be realistically expected of financial information, for the smooth and well-informed functioning of commercial society?[1]

At a high conceptual level, information is required that is sufficiently current and reliable to enable the effective commitment of resources to support the enterprise: capital as put at risk by all sources, including proprietors, investors and lenders; company personnel from governing boards and executive management through the entire workforce; suppliers and customers whose relationships rely on both trust and credit.

Since the origins of trade, the need for accounting and reporting conventions has been accompanied by some form of assurance — to provide the levels of confidence and reliability necessary for the management and governance of commercial enterprises, and also for government to fix and collect taxes, to deploy public resources for political, diplomatic and military ambitions, and to support institutions of social welfare, such as public works, education and health and welfare.

Reflecting the increasing complexity in the structures of commerce, from early in the Industrial Age the involvement of an outside third party — the independent auditor — was deemed effective to provide a satisfactory level of trust and confidence in company information, in aid of the needs of those charged with governance such as directors and audit committees, as well as the proprietors, the investors and all other stakeholders.

In addition, that function must also serve the needs of information users to evaluate the performance of executive leadership in their ultimate task — namely to manage, lead, innovate and produce — at the same time assessing the risks of the enterprise and safeguarding its resources for the sake of the interested parties.

By contrast, it should be perceived as a misalignment of interests, and a failure of legitimate expectations, to reward management for their skill in manipulating the processes of financial reporting and assurance for the sake of parochial incentives — the bending of judgmental accounting principles beyond all recognition, the incentivizing of selfish and self-serving compensation schemes or the relentless pursuit of a trivial advantage in the reporting of short-term results.

On such fundamental principles, the present state of Big Audit needs examining in a comprehensive way — a candid look at its weaknesses, shortcomings and limitations, exploring the attitudes and behaviors of all the players in the system while avoiding the temptation of narrowly focused finger-pointing.

The Big Four Won't Be Here At All — The Next Collapse Goes "Four-to-Zero"

When Reality Bites, It Will Bite Hard

Even before Andersen was dragged into the federal court in Houston for the shredding of its documents relating to Enron, the destructive rules of Wonderland were in full force. As the Queen of Hearts explained to Alice, "Sentence first — verdict afterwards."

"Afterwards" had already arrived. The jury's guilty verdict on the single charge that Andersen obstructed justice by destroying material related to its work for Enron had absolutely no effect on whether or how the accounting firm would be broken up. The flight of its clients and personnel, and the deals made by the surviving Big Four for bits and pieces of Andersen's global business, had already taken care of that, long before the lawyers began their arguments in the June 2002 criminal trial in Houston.

Andersen's demise made two things clear: the first is the global-scale damage that a deathblow in a single major country would wreak on an international accounting network. As passionately as Andersen and the US government fought to make their points at the trial, the short-term Five-to-Four restructuring of the large-firm sector of the profession was already playing out.

The second is the fundamental structural fragility of an enterprise whose primary value rests on the stability of public trust in its franchise.

For what else did the Andersen partners "own"? Along with a short-term stream of client accounts receivable, they had a roster of salaried employees, a portfolio of leased offices, short-lived libraries of methodology and technical support, and their collective accumulated years of professional experience — all of which, in an intense burst of dissipated credibility, the marketplace showed itself unwilling to buy.

The long-term consequences of Andersen's collapse remain ominous. Well before the day of its indictment, Andersen's global organization was fatally wounded. The same fate stalks the Big Four today.

The challenges to these global networks of private partnerships are daunting. Unlike a typical corporate enterprise, the accounting partnerships are exposed to the worst kind of discontinuity:

destructive liability that is asserted globally against the networks, but inflicted locally against individual practices and their partners.

Multinational companies require and obtain accounting services in dozens of countries. Their typical needs include regulatory compliance in each country where their securities are listed, statutory reports on the local results of their significant subsidiaries, and a single auditor's report on a top-level set of global consolidated financial statements. In response, each of the Big Four networks delivers client service under a unified brand, pursuing integrated worldwide strategies including advertising, communications, methodology, training and personnel deployment.

But on the ground, country-by-country, the Big Four's audit work is done locally, by individual professionals licensed and authorized to practice only in single countries, and belonging to separate firms whose legal structures and operating franchises are confined within that country's borders.

Occasional arguments are made that the challenges of multinational service demands could be solved, or small-firm delivery could be achieved, by flying SWAT teams of headquarters-level audit personnel into locations lacking an officially compliant local practice. These however would be promptly refuted by the defensive acts of local regulators and licensing authorities, protecting their own interests by the invocation of their laws prohibiting foreigners' attempts at unlicensed professional practice.

Integrated global corporations can open new territories on a test basis. They succeed or fail, and they later can isolate and close off their unprofitable experiments. Examples include the 2014 withdrawals from China of whole product lines by both Revlon and L'Oreal.

Multinational corporations do so through their compartmentalized subsidiaries and affiliates. But they rely on interlaced networks of accountants to make sure they stay within the bounds of their various jurisdictions.

European-based as they are, for example, Daimler AG and Diageo PLC and Royal Dutch Shell PLC all have audit requirements in the United States. When Tata Motors of India bought Jaguar and Land Rover from Ford in the United States, along came the need for British-based auditors.

Is there really a need for the global Big Four, if clients could cobble together a virtual network for each job? There are good-quality local firms in most developed countries, but — for good reasons — they have a negligible share of the big-company global work.

Post-Andersen, it *might* have come to that — but did not. The increased costs, inefficiencies and failure rates would have been so horrific that local enthusiasm, hard to imagine, never emerged.

Accounting principles vary across borders, and their reconciliation requires massive investment in knowledge transfer. At the same time, cross-border audit work means cross-border legal liability. That double whammy explains the absence of new global delivery models: the local practitioners know where their risk thresholds lie, and evolution does not run in reverse.

Before Andersen's indictment, the flight of its departing clients included such US-based global enterprises as FedEx Corp., Delta Air Lines Inc. and Merck & Co. As the stream became a flood, Andersen's non-US firms stood to lose all that inbound revenue, even ahead of the later departure of their own home-based clients. The stress on the integrity of the globally organized Andersen structure quickly became unbearable.

As Andersen proved, a geographically crippled accounting network cannot operate *anywhere* if it cannot operate *everywhere* — at least, everywhere that matters.

The disintegration of the Andersen network was a reality check on the global cohesion of the large networks. Previously, able and willing to provide and obtain mutual support in prosperous and happier times, the ex-US Andersen firms refused under stress to participate in the defense of the US firm, which would have required the stabilizing long-term commitments necessary for their mutual credibility and survival. There were to be no IOUs written against the local partners' future earnings, by which to bankroll defense costs, settlement payments, possible appeal bonds or potentially massive final judgments. Instead, they exercised their local self-interest and swiftly made their own deals.

Isolated by and from its global support system, Andersen's US firm was in no position to sustain the defense of claims arising from Enron's $67 billion bankruptcy.

Without fundamental restructuring of the current risk environment, in which legal exposures and obligations clash with both professional standards and the accountants' ability to deliver, the conditions for a replay of Andersen's fate remain. The vagaries of courtroom calendars will determine which of the Big Four will have the next turn on the billion-dollar bull's-eye. Each is burdened with nightmarish worst-case exposures, any one of which would be enough to overwhelm a single country's practice. As may be worse, each also carries an inventory of other claims, viewed as "small" only by comparison but onerous enough in sum to drain their partners' capital in multimillion-dollar gulps.

As will be expanded in the next section, the fate of the Big Four may indeed be determined by a singular, exceptional "black swan" event. This hazard was updated in October 2013, when Deloitte's US firm settled its potentially catastrophic $7.5 billion exposure in the Florida case brought by the bankruptcy trustee of Taylor Bean & Whitaker, the mortgage lender that collapsed in 2009 under a hail of fraud charges that led to prison sentences for its principals, and again in August 2016, when PwC's US firm endured three weeks of trial before settling claims of $5.5 billion, brought by the bankruptcy trustee of the same TBW and relating to PwC's audits of the failed Colonial Bank.

Both those settlement amounts were confidential and remain undisclosed today, but the litigation outcomes at their worst would have far exceeded the breakup threshold of either firm.[2]

The Problem of Available Choice

In April 2006, with concern growing over the shrinkage to four global accounting networks, a report by the Oxera consulting firm in the United Kingdom was released under the sponsorship of the Financial Reporting Council and the Department of Trade and Industry.

The issues were then in high relief, as the accounting regulator in Japan had suspended the audit practice of PwC for two months in connection with five years of falsified accounts at the cosmetics group Kanebo.

The regulators' suspension of PwC over Kanebo was not extended, however, to its work done for Japanese companies or subsidiaries to comply with the laws of other countries — for example, to satisfy the requirements of the SEC in the United States. PwC got a life-saving break, sparing it the fate of Andersen, whose clients had abandoned it in droves after the firm's 2002 indictment over its work for Enron.

Even so, two unpleasant prospects confronted some 2300 Japanese companies: the cost, disruption and limited choice in finding a new auditor, or the risk of not having one at all.

That Kanebo could have triggered the disintegration of another Big Four firm — what Oxera called the "Four-to-Three" scenario — could not have been discounted. But the consultant's overly tempered view was that this scenario would only "exacerbate problems around auditor choice" — an example of British understatement on a scale not seen since King George III was told that the colonials in Boston were falling a bit behind in their taxes.

Four years after the Oxera study, the American Antitrust Institute's January 8, 2010, paper *Financial Reform and the Big 4 Audit Firms* forthrightly recognized that:

> "*With pending claims totaling billions of dollars, the Big 4 audit firms face serious threats to their survival .... (L)iability exposure substantially exceeds the combined partner*

*capital of the Big 4 firms ... (They) contend that liability
limits are necessary to prevent the loss of another Big 4
firm, which would throw the global financial system into
chaos (footnotes omitted)."*

The AAI's politically unworkable "solution," however, was to
be a legislated trade-off: "government incentives to break up the
Big 4 into smaller, more competitive firms" — namely a liability
cap conditioned on a firm divesting itself of, say, 20% of its
domestic revenue and the personnel serving the surrendered
clients.

The AAI deserved credit at least for recognizing the completeness of the Big Four's market dominance — auditing "nearly *all* of
the world's public companies with annual sales over $250 mil-
lion" (*emphasis in original*) — with even tighter limitations on
auditor choice in such industries as metals and mining, energy, air
transportation and financial services.

The death threat to the large auditing firms was and remains
not only a matter of reputation, as with PwC in Japan, but financial. The precedent, updated to a much larger version, was the
1989 litigation shipwreck that sank the midsize Philadelphia-
based firm of Laventhol & Horwath. The same mortal litigation
blow awaited Andersen, had it not been for the quicker death
inflicted by its post-Enron indictment.

Oxera cited the two familiar limits on clients' choice of auditors
already existing in a four-firm world. First, regulatory constraints
prohibit an accounting firm that provides whole ranges of consulting, tax or advisory services to an enterprise from also serving as
its auditor. Second, the limited geographic and industry coverage
of the middle-tier firms effectively disable them as alternatives.

In the United Kingdom, back in 2006, the Big Four audited all
but one of the FTSE 100 and more than 240 of the 250 next-
largest corporations — a dominance extended to all large markets,
as summarized in the *Sidebar* in Part I. With auditor choice so

severely restricted across the board, Oxera noted that in such sectors as banking and insurance, large companies could have no alternative to their present auditor even if they did wish to change.[3]

Oxera posited that a solution to the paralysis of losing another firm would be conflict waivers by the regulators. But such a screeching U-turn would be politically inconceivable, after the protracted demonization of the accounting profession for its supposed conflicts and loss of virtue.

And by limiting the scope of its inquiry to Britain, Oxera missed the point that large-firm audit dominance is at least as great elsewhere in Europe, but with different firms in leading positions. Where PwC audits the lion's share of big companies in Britain, EY is the leader in France, in Germany it is KPMG, and in Spain it is Deloitte. Because of that uneven distribution of personnel and expertise, loss of any one of these networks would eliminate auditor availability for a significant population of global companies.

The Attitude of the Regulators

Consider this question: What might happen when one of the Big Four disintegrates?

Regulators around the world have been squeamish to the point of denial. The best observation managed by the Financial Reporting Council, the regulator for corporate reporting and governance in Britain, is that the current limitations on auditor choice would be "exacerbated" if another major firm left the market. In the United States, the departing chairman of the PCAOB, William McDonough, said in the fall of 2005, "none of us has a clue what to do if one of the Big Four failed."

Taking McDonough at his word — and his successors have never said otherwise — why are regulators so timorous? Two reasons:

- It sticks in a regulator's throat to admit that a problem is outside his scope of influence or competence.

- And the politically minded have a reflex to pass off an intractable problem to a successor.

The problem is that regulators routinely provide passionate but sterile endorsements of the importance of the audit function — reiterated and reinforced by those speaking for the profession itself. But the reality facing auditors and their audiences of information users is otherwise. Since regulators cannot solve these problems, they avoid confrontation with them. The problems will not go away, and treating them as only incrementally more difficult than the *status quo* does not lead to productive examination.

What should be examined instead is the case why a three-firm universe is unsustainable:

- Auditor choice, which is already limited by conflict-of-interest rules and other "good-governance" measures, would be so reduced that many companies in significant industry and country sectors would be unable to find auditors.

- The combined demands of geographic coverage and depth of professional expertise mean that alternative suppliers could not emerge from among the smaller networks of auditing firms.

- When a majority of corporate issuers would be out of compliance with financial statement filing requirements for extended periods, the incentives for the surviving large firms to continue to issue their opinions on the statutory accounts that are now primarily litigation magnets would disappear.

Beneath the central question posed above, several other related questions follow:

Under the effects of life-threatening lawsuits, official hostility and their own fragility, it should be both reasonable and prudent to anticipate the possible disintegration of one or more of the Big Four by the end of the decade.

In the current state of concentration, perhaps 25% of the world's largest companies could then be unable to replace a failed audit firm. So how realistic is it to assume that a surviving Big Three — or fewer — would find it an attractive business proposition to maintain that service?

The facts dictate the implausibility of large-scale competitors emerging from the AAI's suggested divestiture program:

First, an abundance of small practices already exist. Why they have not coalesced into global-scale practices is a long-familiar story of limited geographic scope, limits on available expertise, realistically limited risk appetite, and hesitance in the readiness to invest.

Second, as a practical matter, how else would global-scale competition emerge? If a Big Four network were to hive off a small geography-based practice, that newcomer would suffer handicaps of capacity and expertise no different than those of today's smaller firms. If a large firm were to shed an entire industry practice, that would add no new competition to serve that industry. And if instead, it were to divide a viable large-scale practice, then each of the two sub-practices would be burdened with shortages of expertise, personnel and the capital strength necessary to build to scale and withstand their risks.

Anticipating that the traditional audit report on consolidated financial statements may no longer be available for large companies, what might be done now to design both the model of the future and a legal and regulatory framework for newly organized audit service providers? That is the subject of Part V.

Finally, what would the audit of the future look like if the industry were made up only of fragments of the Big Four?

Specifically, to split the large firms along industry lines would not increase choice. A Big Four firm depleted of its global-scale expertise in a complex sector — say, insurance or communications or defense contracting — would have no more motivation or access to resources for a restart than the current mid-sized firms — which already show their lack of appetite for the risks and challenges.

Yet the alternative — surgical bifurcation of existing teams of talent — would devolve onto new firms, now smaller and weaker, all the existential challenges looming today over the Big Four themselves, along with the added burden of cost and management diversion to build duplicate centers of technical, industry, quality and risk management competence.[4]

It must be concluded, then, that the business reality is not Four-to-Three, but Four-to-Zero. Imperiled as the Big Four audit franchise is, the regulators and politicians have no lifeline to offer the accounting profession. If the next big network goes over the cliff, there is nothing to break the fall of the entire Big Audit model, all the way to the bottom.

So if the now-standard auditors' report were suddenly not to be obtainable from any source, who would miss it?

Regulators and politicians would have convulsions, to be sure. But the stock exchanges could not be closed, just because a Big Four failure meant that one-quarter of the large listed companies lacked an audit report. Unthinkable, that those companies' securities could be barred from trading. Out where capital really flows and trade is actually engaged, the world's markets would shrug, start the process of designing new forms of assurance from a blank page, and move on.

The splintered pieces of the former Big Four could — and desirably would — provide the building blocks for a new assurance structure. Again, that will require a vision of the future — for which, see Part V.

The Financial Fragility of the Big Four — The Tipping Point

"Predictions are difficult. Especially about the future."
— *Variously attributed to a Danish proverb,*
or to physicist Niels Bohr

Here is the issue: The deadly bullet for Andersen was not its indictment, but its litigation exposure. And that has grave implications for today's remaining Big Four.

What is the size of the litigation hit that would disintegrate one of them?

The question requires scrutiny and attention, because reactions of regulators, politicians and the public in general to any proposal for serious adjustment to the potentially fatal auditor liability regime range from lukewarm to downright hostile. Those antagonistic views are based on the disbelief and denial that there could be another collapse — which, in turn, is based on the persistently erroneous view that the disintegration of Andersen in 2002 was caused by its Enron-related indictment by the US Justice Department.

The answer matters, and the communities of financial information users should care — although it can be easy to ignore this gloomy topic in a combination of indifference, unease and denial — because the collateral damage caused by the loss of that next firm would be the collapse of the entire structure of privately provided assurance on the financial statements of the world's large companies.

I have visited this question over the years, even as the Big Four have continued to show growth and prosperity — their latest fiscal-year figures showing total annual global revenues approaching $128 billion.

Quantifications of the litigation "tipping points" that would leave the world's large companies unable to procure the audit reports necessary for listing and regulatory compliance, from any source and at any price, have never been disputed — ominous and shockingly small as they are — nor have other alternative models or estimates ever been offered. Nor is there anywhere in sight any credible claim that a political or regulatory solution is achievable.

The Model and Its Assumptions

For background: In September 2006, a report by the consulting firm London Economics to then-EU markets commissioner Charlie McCreevy modeled the threshold limits of financial pain that would become intolerable to a Big Four partnership in the United Kingdom. As had actually happened at Andersen in 2002, the model quantified the level of personal sacrifice, beyond which the owner-partners would lose confidence, withdraw their loyalty and their capital, and vote with their feet.

Unlike large public companies with their access to investor capital, the Big Four must fund their litigation settlements out of future partner profits — the insurance industry's readiness to contribute having long since been outstripped by twenty years of massive escalation in the size of the "worst" cases.[5]

The London study observed that the viability of the Big Four firms, and their ability to retain clients and personnel, would be hostage to the effects of a highly charged crisis environment, as dominated by the reputational pressure and hostile publicity of a massive adverse litigation result. Using a variety of scenarios and assumptions, it concluded that critical numbers of partners would defect, so as to put a firm into a death spiral, if faced with the financial commitment of an individual personal profit reduction of 15–20% and extending over three or four years.[6]

The Grim Reality of the Calculations

Bearing on the model, but poorly appreciated, if at all, is that the private partnerships that make up the Big Four operate with razor-thin levels of capital. That is for three reasons:

- Their major working capital needs — employee salaries, space costs, and technology and methodology investments — are financed out of the short-term cash stream of client-derived revenues.

- The income tax codes of the largest economies are cash-based for partnerships, creating a powerful incentive for the firms to distribute substantially all their current profits out to the partners, speedily and timed to match with their immediate tax liabilities.

- And, there being no alternative need or opportunity for the deployment of excess capital or outside investment, under the firms' current business models, idle cash would serve only to whet the appetites of the litigation sharks circling in the feeding tanks.

Extending the UK breakup assumptions of the London Economics model to the Big Four at the global level, the "tipping point" amounts range from about six billion down to about four billion dollars.

But this is only a first step. To emphasize, those are worldwide numbers, which assume that a Big Four network under deadly threat could maintain its global integrity and the ongoing support of its members around the world. To the contrary, as illustrated by Andersen's rapid disintegration in 2002 with the flight of its non-US member firms, cohesion of the international networks under the strain of death-threat litigation, or the extended availability of collegial cross-border financial support, not only cannot be assumed — the contrary should be expected.

It must be recalled that with its American firm bleeding personnel and clients, and facing ruinous liability exposure over the implosion of its premier Houston client, Andersen's leaders were unable to negotiate a transaction by which its American practice could be amalgamated into any of the other members of the then-Big Five.

The prospect that the Andersen practice would, as a merger partner or buyout target, come with the freight of its pending litigation legacy was a burden too great for any of the other firms to take up — either domestically or globally.

So current calculations must be made on Big Four results for the Americas only — the United States being still the world's most hazardous litigation venue. If left to their own resources, as was Andersen's firm in the United States, breakup numbers for the US practices of the Big Four today, as calculable under the London model, shrink to a range from about three billion down to a truly frightening number below one billion dollars.

As a brief but critical parenthetical, these calculations also make plain that the Enron-inflicted litigation blow falling on Andersen was mortal. In 2001, the firm's worldwide revenue was $9.3 billion. Andersen confronted lawyers for the Enron shareholders who claimed that the case would be the first against accountants to reach a billion dollars in actual recovery. The crippled firm was already dealing with claims involving Baptist Hospital, Waste Management and Sunbeam, and it was about to receive the incoming bombardment of WorldCom and Qwest, among others.

So those who blame Andersen's death on the Enron indictment miss the point. The firm was like a patient on late-stage life support, already terminal and residing in an intensive care unit, who happened to catch a fast-moving infection: Its demise was imminent, and inevitable. By indicting Andersen, the Justice Department only pulled the plug.

And the Cause for Optimism?

Is there a persuasive case that it won't happen — especially in the face of the empirical evidence of Andersen's collapse, that it can? The answer, with regret, is negative.

First, neither the template's assumptions nor the output of this inquiry have ever been challenged. A public discussion would be illuminating, but Big Four financial fragility is a "third rail" topic for the profession's leadership. Little wonder that the only available validation is on deep background — reluctantly given at that — which never rises to a position on the record, but suggests that if anything the cited numbers are too large.

Second, what can be made of the record of recent years? Optimistic surveys indicate that the recent volume of investor litigation against the accountants has moderated compared to earlier periods, and Big Four settlements of credit-crisis cases have been modest indeed.

It is the case that, in the aftermath of the financial crisis, the large accounting firms enjoyed remarkable success in disposing of huge litigations for remarkably modest sums, all well within their financial tolerance. Examples include KPMG resolving Countrywide for $24 million and New Century for $45 million, Deloitte settling Washington Mutual for $18.5 million, and EY settling private investor claims in Lehman Brothers in 2013 for $99 million and wrapping up its exposure in 2015 by agreeing to pay an additional $10 million fine to the New York Attorney General.

But multibillion dollar settlements have become all too common, in claims relating to the financial crisis, the sales of mortgage securities and LIBOR and FOREX rate-fixing. Data gathered by the Boston Consulting Group show that the total in fines paid by the large banks for their crisis-era conduct has reached $321 billion — led by Bank of America's agreement in August 2014 to an additional subprime-mortgage settlement of $16.9 billion.

Single-company examples included JP Morgan Chase's busy period beginning October 2013: its record-setting $13 billion settlement with the Justice Department, its $4.5 billion settlement the following month with its mortgage-derivative customers, moving on to January 2014, and its $2.6 billion in settlements of claims relating to its lucrative client, Ponzi scheme Bernard Madoff.[7]

Outside the financial sector, the list of complex mega-settlements includes:

- The still unknown final total for BP arising out of the Deepwater Horizon oil well catastrophe — $20.8 billion to date in fines, penalties and damages paid to federal, state and local governments, plus some $13 billion to pay claims for loss by businesses, individuals and local governments.

- Fines, penalties and customer claims payments exceeding $24 billion, agreed by Volkswagen as part of its settlements relating to its diesel emissions "defeat devices."

- Such investor settlements as Enron ($7.2 billion), WorldCom ($6.2 billion) and Tyco ($3.2 billion).

Those settlements and government fines were only payable, it must be emphasized, because they could be funded out of the investor-supported balance sheets of the publicly-held corporations contributing to the results. By contrast, the Big Four as networks of private accounting partnerships simply do not have access to the resources of third-party investor capital.

Making the point with stark clarity are the examples, already noted, of the settlements by Deloitte in October 2013 and PwC in 2016 of the claims against them relating to Taylor Bean & Whitaker Mortgage Corp. and Colonial Bank.

Those amounts remain undisclosed, but must have included some level of pain, given that the worst-case exposures exceeded their breakup threshold capability.

Cutting sharply against the flawed assertion, that "it *can't* happen, because it *hasn't*," history offers horrific examples of the flawed inductive assertion that recent experience provides a satisfactory basis for prediction — frequently grounded on blind overconfidence, too-short history and biased incentives.

Among the masters of the universe who fell during the 2007–2008 financial crisis, such as Jimmy Cayne, Dick Fuld, Angelo Mozilo and Jon Corzine, the attitude of their fraternity was perhaps no better displayed than by Citigroup's Chuck Prince in July 2007, while his upcoming ouster was still unforeseen, that "As long as the music is playing, you've got to get up and dance. We're still dancing."

The partners of the large firms are not indentured, nor on-call hostages to the unexamined assumptions of the politicians and regulators of the world's large economies. If put under enough stress, they will act to protect their interests.

As the catastrophic impact of "black swan" events makes clear, it only takes a single event. In context of this Damoclean reality, reduced claim volumes and short-term "average" settlement amounts lose their meaning.

Third, given the continued vitality of the myth that the Big Four are protected by insurance, it must be noted that these numbers are net of whatever cover may in fact be available. Which is neither good news nor especially relevant.

That is because — as addressed in Part III — the effective absence of the commercial insurance sector from coverage of the large firms at the current and greatly expanded catastrophic levels, and the limited protection of the Big Four's own self-insurance by way of loss-shifting to the future generations of their younger partners, is one of the underappreciated sidebar factors in this entire calculus.

To use the illustrative off-the-record metaphor of an expert industry source, not only is the Big Four's patchy insurance blanket far too small to cover the liability bed they have chosen to lie in, but also — as a consequence of large and growing deductions and retentions — it is thin, frayed and full of holes.

The fickle cyclicality of the commercial insurance market means that even today's ragged capacity would ill-protect against the chilly horrors of the inevitably recurring new litigation nightmares.

At the same time, there have recently been build-ups of reserves held by the captive insurance companies operated by each of the Big Four. But access to those international network resources by a failing national firm would be hostage to the survivability of the cross-border financial commitments of the network's other members. Again, that optimistic assumption proved illusory in the speedy collapse of Andersen's global network in 2002 — appearances of its members' ostensibly robust and mutually enforceable contractual commitments notwithstanding.

As one of the authors of Andersen's uniquely cohesive but ultimately fragile worldwide organization puts it, "the structure was at best a treaty. And as a treaty, it was only as stable as the continued trust and commitment of all of the separate country practices."

Finally, and perhaps most important, loss of another Big Four firm would throw the entire system into chaos — for lack of auditor choice and readiness among the survivors to stay in an unbearably risky business.

It cannot be assumed that — just because the surviving Big Four were able to absorb the clients of the failed Andersen back in 2002, along with the staff necessary to serve them — a Four-to-Three scenario is also viable today.

In fact, the Big Four are already down to their critical minimum. The uneven concentrations of personnel, market share and industry expertise around the world's largest economies, the politically imposed restrictions on auditor choice due to outmoded concepts of independence, and the post-Andersen fragility of the large firms' networks combine to show that a four-firm structure is irreducible.

One more down, and likely they all go down. To survive, the stability of the entire wobbly structure rests on the continuing survival of all of them, including the weakest.

The Big Four Accounting Firms Are Down to Critical Mass, Said the *Financial Times* — So It Must Be Official

In the country where independent audit was invented back in the Victorian era, the *Lex* column in the *Financial Times* for November 2, 2010, finally gave recognition to the fragility of the global franchise of private-provided assurance — "The Big Four are down to critical mass."

This marked a subtle but real shift in language, more candid and direct than the usual euphemisms of the regulators, that another large-firm failure "could disrupt the market," as put in the vacuous prose of the European Commission's Green Paper of October 13, 2010, *Audit Policy: Lessons from the Crisis*.

As put more forthrightly by the salmon-pink London paper:

> *"It is vital to work out how to deal with a repeat of the Arthur Andersen/Enron affair, because* four is the minimum number *of global accounting groups needed for a healthy industry. Many companies employ one firm for internal audits, another for the external audit and a third to offer consulting advice. The fourth player picks up the slack when a change is needed. Neither regulators nor customers would want to see the Big Four turn into the Big Three (emphasis added)."*

The next small and agonizing step, which the *FT* was on the very verge but did not take, would have been the explicit realization that an unsustainable three-firm model would go into immediate collapse — not least because the survivors after the next disintegration, which would occur in another Enron-like spasm of recrimination and finger-pointing, would have neither the appetite nor the resources to pick up the wreckage.

The *FT* came close, but was not there yet — because still fixated on either of two non-achievable approaches:

> *"If that happened, regulators would be left with two unappealing options. First is a forced split-up of the remaining accounting groups — a plan that would meet vehement opposition. Second, an ambitious smaller outfit could take over the ailing giant, roughly as Nomura took on Lehman Brothers' European operations. But any non-Big Four auditor would face a huge challenge doing this, since these firms rarely work with big or even*

midsized companies; they audit only 5 per cent of the
UK's FTSE 350."

Opposition aside, not only is there no legal authority anywhere
for cleaving the Big Four into smaller bits. As a practical matter
such a split would have to be done in all the major global financial
jurisdictions — none of which has a regulator or legislature capable of conceiving such an idea alone, much less in concert with
dozens of others. In any event, as noted, the result would only be
a group of smaller and weaker firms, with unevenly distributed
personnel, industry expertise and capacity for execution.

If the *FT*'s writers had done their sums, they would have faced
the reality that — good as they may be — the smaller firms lack
the scale, coverage and execution ability ever to play at the level
of the world's global-scale companies.

Accounting Standards Convergence — Nobody Knows Where *They* Are

For years the world's accounting regulators have kept up a complex charade — a choreography of pretense that the varying models for accounting, reporting and auditing corporate financial
information will converge to a single set of global standards.

It has been like watching a carnival performance of dancing
bears — notable not that they're so slow and clumsy, but that
they dance at all.

If the final turn around the dance floor has not been taken, it
was at least signaled in August 2014. In a speech in Singapore,
Hans Hoogervorst, chairman of the International Accounting
Standards Board, issuer of the International Financial Reporting
Standards (IFRS) that are applied in more than 100 countries but
conspicuously not the United States, said of the failed effort to
converge on a standard for financial instruments:

"It's a pity. Convergence would have allowed the US to make the ultimate jump to IFRS. But nobody can force it to do so .... But IFRS moves on — we have a large part of the world to take care of."

Hoogervorst's assessment was echoed in an exchange in April 2015 between Sir David Tweedie, his predecessor at the IASB from 2001 to 2011, and Bob Herz, who from 2002 to 2010 had been the chairman of the Financial Accounting Standards Board, the body in the United States responsible for issuing Generally Accepted Accounting Principles (GAAP).

In a public dialog at Baruch College in New York and quoted by the *FEI Daily*, Tweedie put it that "We (the convergence process) are at a low point now ...."

And Herz expanded:

"For good or bad, the US has moved away from the (convergence) idea ... In the US we have become very comfortable with the idea that we will have two global accounting standards, US GAAP, and if there are things in IFRS that we like, or the market likes, we will consider adopting those, but no systematic program to converge at this point ... A two-GAAP world from the US perspective seems to be a comfortable notion."

These two alumni of the convergence maneuvers continued their commentary in a joint interview reported by *Accounting Today* on May 20, 2015, with Herz underlining that "there's no systematic program to further converge at this point."

Which was echoed by Tweedie, "these sorts of conditions don't exist at the moment."

For a brief look back over the recent years of depleted energy and resources:

Convergence had first been seriously sounded in the 1990s with the work of the FASB and the International Accounting Standards

Committee, the predecessor to the IASB. These discussions were brought forward in October 2002 with the so-called Norwalk Agreement, named for the FASB's hometown — a memorandum of understanding aimed at formalizing the "commitment" to convergence of the two bodies.

The argument made by the partisans of convergence was and has stayed consistent — that the use of common standards promotes strong globalized capital markets, supports investor comprehension and confidence, and fuels economic growth.

But with all the cheerleading, the background had changed since the time the Americans had been setting the tone.

In the early days, corporate listings were migrating to the New York Stock Exchange; the Euro-to-be was denigrated as a regional form of play money, rather than a legitimate new currency with global-scale influence and credibility; and the extensible hegemony of accounting principles as issued in the United States was taken for granted. Little wonder the Europeans were mostly unenthusiastic wallflowers at the party.

And then — still shadowed by the darkening gloom of the Enron era, the American-led scandals around executive options and subprime mortgages showed the limits on its capacity for regulatory detection and deterrence. London became the center of the IPO market, and the Euro powered up to an exchange rate of €1 = $1.59.

Europe ascendant had its mis-steps, of course. The French-led opposition to unqualified EU endorsement of the standards for derivatives accounting showed the resilient survival of its parochial difficulties.

And although the subprime contagion of 2007–2008 started in and primarily affected American markets and institutions, it extended from the regional German banks to the funding of villages in northern Norway; the Bank of England stubbed a toe against the collapsed mortgage lender Northern Rock, and UBS showed the storied competence of Swiss bankers to be as holed as its cheese.

The SEC had announced in November 2008 that it would start to accept the financial statements of non-US companies, as prepared in accordance with IFRS — only without the reconciliation to US standards that had been so costly, disruptive and questionably useful.

Next followed EU internal markets commissioner Charlie McCreevy, with a symmetrical plan for American companies to list their securities in Europe using accounting principles generally acceptable in their home country — good and familiar US GAAP.

Then came the December 2008 announcement by the PCAOB that starting in 2009, its inspections of non-US audit firms would move toward fuller reliance on the inspection and enforcement regimes of that agency's counterparts in other countries. Inputs from the US Chamber of Commerce and the SEC's Advisory Committee extolled the necessity of integrated global standards and principles.

Back in the United States, while the London bankers took market share from their New York counterparts, the SEC's readiness to accept IFRS-based financial statements — half a decade after passage of Sarbanes-Oxley in 2002 — rang as an effort to protect against market-share erosion. And fair-value accounting became the target of choice for blame-shifting to evade the dysfunctions of the bankers' black-box valuation models.

At the same time, the PCAOB's readiness to "increase its level of reliance on non-US oversight systems" stumbled against the reality of foreign law prohibitions and the limited resources and experience of authorities in 86 other countries.

The long-dated estimate for convergence to a single set of global accounting standards then focused on the meeting of the G-20 countries in Pittsburgh in September 2009 — the context for a leaders' statement, calling for completion of a convergence project in 2011 — a date also targeted for the SEC's decision whether to require IFRS adoption.

But the chorus for convergence did not sing in unison, and the reluctant Europeans continued to have their way. As the *Financial Times* reported on September 28, 2009, Henri de Castries, chief of French insurance giant AXA, viewed the local setting of standards as "a matter of political sovereignty," and Christine Lagarde, then the French finance minister before her move in 2011 to head the International Monetary Fund, put it to EU commissioner Charlie McCreevy to "'ensure the safeguard' of European public interest."

Disparate nationalistic players in Europe showed their ability to evade, frustrate and maneuver around attempts at cross-border unification and cooperation at many levels. The conspicuous examples were the French bankers, abetted by no less an accounting expert than President Jacques Chirac, who led years of lobbying to prevent the applicability of a single international standard on derivatives accounting.

Which sounded like political cover for the European capacity for protracted refusal to yield up national autonomy — foreshadowing a *de facto* continuation of country-based "mark to management" accounting, however superficially enthusiastic were the leaders' pronouncements in favor of convergence.

Add in the politically motivated local vetoes retained by the likes of the recalcitrant French, exemplified by the spirit of M de Castries and President Chirac, and reflected in the measurements of European progress over spans of geological time: the deeply embedded antagonisms and resistance recall the lesson from high-school geometry, that parallel lines only converge at infinity.

After the G-20's declaration in Pittsburgh that global standard-setters should complete their convergence project by June 2011, the SEC gave itself the entire following year even to be *positioned* to *consider* a determination *whether* to give more support to convergence, much less when or how. Depending on a new staff-level

Work Plan that was to supplant the famous "Roadmap" of 2008, during the last year of the tenure of Chairman Christopher Cox, the SEC projected that then-undefined steps in implementation *may* be taken no earlier than 2015 or 2016.

It was a fair question, concerning the SEC's position as set out in its statement of February 24, 2010, *In Support of Convergence and Global Accounting Standards*, whether personnel at that agency really believed in a highly uncertain timetable that at its most optimistic extended more than halfway through the decade.

So on one side, the Europeans showed their ability to jawbone the convergence process for as long as it suited — while the SEC's manifest uncertainties only pointed distantly down the road, far past the tenure of any present office-holders. Which meant that the absence of accomplishment half-a-decade in the future would become the responsibility of a whole new set of map-readers.

Move along they did, as Chairman Cox[8] passed the poisoned chalice. His successor, Mary Schapiro, in May 2010 brought to an annual conference of the chartered financial analysts a major tilt at what she called the "myths" about the SEC's lukewarm attitude toward GAAP/IFRS convergence and globally merged accounting standards.

Whether or not the agency's own "commitment to international standards has flagged," Schapiro was unable to reconcile the implacable international antagonisms to convergence that her agency lacked the ability to resolve or overcome.

An eloquent concession of the "convergence gap" was Schapiro's own admission that "US GAAP and IFRS are currently not converged in a number of key areas," including "the accounting for financial assets (the very types of securities at the center of the financial crisis), revenue recognition, consolidation principles, and leases."[9]

It was not necessary to believe Schapiro to have been malign in her intent, or to fault the *bona fides* of her commitment to the "fundamental principle" of "comprehensive and neutral accounting standards." Because on the prospect of core-level GAAP/IFRS convergence, she could be presumed to have been firmly committed.

In the same way, however, so were the pre-Copernican astronomers committed to the "fundamental principle" of an earth-centric solar system. Which only shows that while good-faith belief is fine, eventually it must yield to reality.

In assessing the parochial attitude of America's chief securities regulator, it would have helped to keep at hand a glossary of trans-Atlantic euphemism. That is:

- When a Frenchman says, "We need to be pragmatic," what he means is, "Agree to do it our way — or there's no deal."

- When an Italian says, "You don't understand how things are done here," the unspoken message is, "You have no chance — cut your losses and head for home."

- And when Schapiro's typical gung-ho American attitude gave way to her concession to *understand the importance* of process to a successful conclusion (*her emphasis*)," it meant that "We know we're at an impasse, so we'll kick the can down the road and try to sell it as success."

Next in this chronology was the pre-retirement bequest in April 2011 of outgoing IASB chairman David Tweedie, to his successor: an agreement with Leslie Seidman, then his opposite number at the FASB, to extend by "an additional few months" the already elastic June 1 date for completion of the decade-long aspiration to converge international and American accounting standards.

The continued slippage in this always-distinct possibility — hardly deserving the credible label of "target," much less "deadline" — continued to recede into the distant future. Which was inevitable, for two reasons:

First was the still-unfinished workload on the four large pending priority projects. The individually challenging topics of leasing, revenue recognition, financial instruments and insurance had long been recognized as impossible of accomplishment within the resources of the two bodies and the politicized obligations to their antagonistic constituents — even presupposing that there had been agreement between the bodies themselves, which on these highly complex subjects, there was not.

Second and more fundamentally, the repeated proclamations of convergence commitment had consistently served as screens behind which lurked the divergent interests of the Americans and the Europeans. (Recall, for context, that the SEC was still uncertain as to whether, if ever, that agency was even going to confirm a date certain on which to decide *if* to weigh in or not.)

There was, in effect, a two-level fantasy in the dialog: the IASB, the FASB and the SEC all pretended to believe in the desirability of fully converged accounting standards, and the community of financial statement issuers and users pretended to believe them.

So, Tweedie and Seidman, having picked their low-hanging fruit, were left to confront the reality of a tree too tall to climb.

Moving onward, the SEC staff's July 2012 report on International Financial Reporting Standards conspicuously did *not* include a recommendation on whether, when or how the United States should get on board.

But an interim signal of the end of the convergence effort was the statement by newly arrived FASB chairman Russ Golden, on the occasion of that body's 40th anniversary celebration in September 2012, limiting his aspiration for the relationships to "evolve," in an environment where standard-setters would "co-exist and cooperate."

In straight talk, realistic prospects for convergence were over.

The Standard-Setters Finish the Job

Just in case reinforcement of the end-state of futility were needed, an outburst of ambiguous rhetoric came on October 16, 2013, when — by coincidence — Golden and Michel Prada, Chairman of the IFRS Foundation Trustees, made speeches on the subject before audiences in, respectively, Tokyo and Frankfurt — presentations that were worlds apart both literally and substantively.

The two speakers' obligatory statements of respect for converged global standards clashed with their nuanced acceptance — whether reluctant or sincere — of the reality of pressure for nonconforming local versions.

In Japan, Golden saw "four basic principles" in a "new, decentralized, multilateral approach" (*emphasis added below* to illustrate the tensions on display):

> "*It is in the best interests of the world's major capital markets, including Japan and, I believe, the United States, to work* toward *a common set of global accounting standards.*"

> "*Fully participating in the standard-setting activities of the International Accounting Standards Board is an important way that we can* promote *this process.*"

> "*As we work toward developing more converged global standards, it is critically important that we* also maintain and improve *the high-quality of our national accounting standards, including JGAAP and US GAAP.*"

> "*There are likely to be occasions when preserving the integrity of our national business cultures* requires *us to* maintain some differences *in national accounting standards.*"

While in Frankfurt, Prada referenced the "dangers of drifting from IFRS as drafted by the IASB, such as when individual nations grant 'exceptions' from IFRS as part of their national endorsement process of particular standards .... resulting in a return to European accounting standards becoming many sets of standards, instead of one set of standards ...."

In Reality, Convergence Doesn't Matter

Intelligent exegesis of the language on convergence from the standard-setters is impossible, as made plain by the rhetorical gymnastics of Hoogervorst, Tweedie, Herz, Cox and their fellows. To slice the baloney fine enough for public consumption would require a blade finer than a butcher's.[10]

In the end, beneath the unending and fruitless wrangling over the relationship between generally accepted accounting principles in the United States and the International Financial Reporting Standards, the convergence discussion that persists as insoluble need not be resolved, for a most compelling reason.

Which is this: It just doesn't matter. The entire convergence debate is greatly distracting and a thorough waste of time, energy and resources. Even if, by whatever name, "convergence" were desirable, it is not achievable.

There are actually two reasons that render illusory any realistic sense of cross-system transparency or comparability.

First is the guidance of those deeply versed in the accounting literature. Experts with world-class credentials provide a crystal-clear message that the many complexities and range of judgmental decisions *within* either of these sets of standards are so extensive as to give issuers ample opportunity for self-service and manipulation, beyond the capability and competence of regulators and gatekeepers.

A generation ago, one of my colleagues — then as now the world's expert on accounting for complex financial instruments — maintained a list, on which he always included one entirely fictitious product. His standard wager of a partner's full-year bonus was that even a knowledgeable practitioner could not find the bogus item. And he never found a taker ready to accept the challenge.

In practice today, he says that there is already so much slack and flexibility, judgment and overnight obsolescence in the tough issues of recording and reporting, even within single systems — whether the best-in-class among the major countries' local GAAP or under IFRS itself — that the prospects for true convergence at any level of detail will remain perpetually elusive.

The world of financial reporting is long past the point, in short, that anything in quality of standards can be gained through the wrenching process of forced amalgamation of the two.

Second, on the pure politics of convergence — whether by SEC adoption of IFRS or otherwise — the simple truth is that the American regulators lack the will, the skill and the patience to navigate the path.

The SEC's proposed "roadmap" to convergence is yellowed and brittle with age and disuse, while the speechmakers' superficially supportive platitudes fail to offer any substantive indication of actual progress down the road.

There are more than enough divergent and antagonistic interests competing in the accounting standards "debate" to drive the conclusion that reconciliation will not ever occur, even if deemed desirable by all those of good will and genuine *bona fides.*

In the fresh air of reality, the global markets should decide — US GAAP or IFRS, or other frameworks able to compete for attention and adoption. The energy and intelligence currently being expended might better be deployed to goals worthy of the attention of the participants and realistically susceptible to beneficial solutions.

Sidebar: Convergence and Postponements

There is an observation that is both striking and pertinent to the endlessly postponed aspirations for accounting standards convergence, which comes out of the academic studies of breakdowns and failures in large-scale strategies.

Which is that once a project starts to go over time and budget, each of the successive series of further delays and overruns is typically longer and more costly than the last.

Sketched out in Nassim Nicholas Taleb's incisive but frustrating and much misunderstood book *The Black Swan* (Random House, 2007), the proposition is readily illustrated by public works projects, diplomatic initiatives and military actions.

Public works projects are notorious:

- The Sydney opera house was completed in 1973 for A$102 million, nine years late and 15 times over its initial A$7 million budget.

- Finally completed four years late in 2003 for $14.6 billion, Boston's "big dig" harbor highway tunnel tripled its initial estimate.

- The Eurotunnel was a happy contrast, only one year late in 1994 and a mere $3.6 billion over budget.

Military and political conflicts are equally instructive:

- President George W. Bush's May 1, 2003, speech under a "Mission Accomplished" banner, two months into the conflict in Iraq, is now approaching a decade-and-a-half and counting, even while that troubled land threatens to revert to total collapse.

- The continuing escalations of American commitment in Vietnam for a victory supposedly just around the corner still have tragic resonance.

- The broken promises of peace in the land of Abraham's children date not just to the founding of Israel in 1948, but go at least back to the Balfour Declaration of 1917.

In Joseph Heller's darkly comic 1961 war novel *Catch-22* (Simon & Schuster, 1961) — still the best manual in print on the absurdities of dysfunctional organizational management — the sycophantic lieutenant Scheisskopf secured his reputation and his promotion by the strategy of announcing that the regularly scheduled and much-despised weekend parades would be postponed and not held.

Commentators, regulators and standard-setters may continue to assert that there are real mileposts down a possible road to GAAP/IFRS

> convergence. But the never-ending postponements and impediments suggest otherwise — there is neither such an achievable prospect nor any visible end to the road.

"In All Material Respects" — The Auditors Don't Say [11]

Auto mechanic: *"Your car's ready. I've repaired it in all material respects."*

Job applicant: *"Offer me the position. I can do the work in all material respects."*

Pulmonary oncologist: *"Congratulations. Your lung X-rays appear normal in all material respects."*

Nowhere in the world of uncertain and judgmental decisions, from the trivial to the truly significant, would these forms of advice be considered satisfactory. Yet every day, investors make highly consequential decisions, arguably based on the auditor's standard report, that "the financial statements present fairly, in all material respects, the financial position of the Company."

Whatever weight it actually carries, this elliptical and ambiguous assurance language, from an auditor, would be unacceptable if issued by any other provider of professional advice. Investors put up their life savings with less probing inquiry than given to their dental hygienists or their travel agents, and then behave like insulted victims when a stock price that had rocketed up has the audacity to go down.

The question has been timeless since the 1940 problems with the accounts receivable of McKesson&Robbins. It took on new significance in the decade of tumult that began in the fall of 2001 with the third-quarter results reported by Enron.

Time and again, investors have professed outrage, crying, "Why weren't we told?" Companies and their auditors, in lame self-defensiveness, assert with as much conviction as they can muster, "But it wasn't material."

It all brings to mind the 1943 classic film *Casablanca*, and the famous and much-cited exchange between Rick, the outwardly cynical club owner played by Humphrey Bogart, and Claude Rains, playing Captain Louis Renault, the local front-man for the occupying Nazi forces:

> Rick: *"How can you close me up? On what grounds?"*
>
> Louis: *"I'm shocked — shocked — to find gambling is going on in here!"*
>
> Croupier: *"Your winnings, sir."*
>
> Louis: *"Oh, thank you very much."*

The investors' bargain on materiality with companies and auditors is the same as that between Louis and Rick about the roulette wheel in the back room: We won't ask, and you don't have to tell us.

The deal works — but only until it is disturbed from the outside. In the film, Major Strasser of the Third Reich shows up at Rick's saloon to search for a fugitive underground leader, pulling back the curtain of hypocrisy and denial to expose the hidden secrets.

In real life, the exposure is of corporate malfeasance — whether in artificial off-balance-sheet entities, abusive corporate governance or executive looting.

The basic bargain needs to evolve, across the entire community of financial statement issuers, auditors and users: What amount of information can be conveyed as meaningful and valuable? What level of assurance can reasonably be provided, and at what cost to issuers and risk to auditors?

The standard report flies a warning flag that should be unmistakable: fair presentation "in all material respects" leaves a hostage to fortune that is open ended. Who decides how big is "really" big? And under what criteria?

The literature of the professional standards on materiality is opaque, and its logic strictly circular — as illustrated by the language of the venerable *Statements on Auditing Standards*, adopted wholesale by the PCAOB in the United States:

- AU Section 312, *Audit Risk and Materiality in Conducting an Audit*, declared (¶ 312.03) that the phrase "'*in all material respects*' ... *indicates the auditor's belief that the financial statements taken as a whole are not materially misstated.*"

- But the circular loop of both language and logic closed in the very next paragraph (¶ 312.04), and never reopened: "*Financial statements are materially misstated when they contain misstatements whose effect, individually or in the aggregate, is important enough to cause them not to be presented fairly, in all material respects.*"

And the circularity came around again with the updating in 2010, as Auditing Standard # 8 (Release 2010-004, August 5, 2010), reaffirmed (¶ 5) that "*The risk of material misstatement refers to the risk that the financial statements are materially misstated.*"

The standard-setters have long resisted imposing requirements to quantify what is meant by "material." For good reason — in a stable, mature enterprise with a dependable operating history, the likelihood of material error in the major operating accounts should be minimal. And normally, the level of required audit work is set accordingly.

But the discovery that a chief financial officer has deliberately bent the rules beyond their limits, or falsified things even by "a little bit," ought to figure very large, since it opens the prospect that he has concealed a really big problem somewhere else. In that case it is back to "how big *is* big?" And how to write those rules.

One way is to change the basic nature of the bargain. A suggestion would be a footnote along the following lines:

> *"Management has prepared the company's financial statements, and the auditors have planned and conducted their examination and issued their report, on the basis that events and transactions the aggregate effect of which is less than $XX million, or YY% of the Company's total assets, are deemed not material."*

> *"In addition, in conducting their examination and issuing their report, the auditors have not addressed, examined or searched for events or transactions individually smaller than $ZZ million."*

Companies and their auditors already have the responsibility to set and apply thresholds of materiality. This disclosure would be consistent with the obligation of corporate officials to attest to the fairness of the resulting statements.

The capital markets can as well handle and evaluate materiality disclosures. Informed in detail, for a change, about what is covered and what is not, shareholders and lenders would no longer have the ability to second-guess the handling of "the small stuff." But as a trade-off, if uncomfortable with the agreed levels of audit scope and reporting, users could force onto CFOs and audit committees a recalibration of those thresholds, influencing the scope of the auditor's work and its associated cost.

If so, share prices would reflect the level of investor comfort with a company's materiality disclosure, right out in the open, enabling companies and their auditors to adjust their performance and be evaluated on the results.

Investors have lived like Captain Renault. In good times they have closed their eyes and taken their winnings. Under pressure, they have professed shock at the presence of the roulette wheel and stalked away, even while holding a ticket in the shareholder litigation sweepstakes.

In a newly righteous era, all parties would change these rules — lest the nightclub and the gaming table be closed down completely.[12]

Non-GAAP Metrics — What Does "Generally Accepted" Really Mean?

Reinforcing the serious doubts about the legitimacy of the conventional and traditional modes of financial reporting, much of the year 2016 saw a fixation among public companies, analysts, investors and regulators with financial reporting metrics other than those compliant with Generally Accepted Accounting Principles (GAAP).

As Den Howlett put it on his blog:

> *"Non-GAAP reporting has largely superseded GAAP reporting as the focus upon which management wishes analysts to pay attention. Many of those same analysts have happily fallen in line if that means the stock price can be pumped upwards."*

Companies urging non-GAAP metrics on their followers included Brixmor, Herbalife, Apple, the New York Times, FedEx, GE and Microsoft — while a roster of regulatory functionaries were wringing their collective hands, including SEC Chairman Mary Jo White, Commissioner Kara Stein, chief accountant James Schnurr, and PCAOB chairman Jim Doty.

Howlett made the point, both noteworthy and unsurprising, that non-GAAP measures have the unsettling tendency to favor an issuer's desired reporting goals — the inevitable gaming of financial reporting being a human trait as old as the systems themselves.

To which, Francine McKenna blogged on the futile issue of attempting to limit choice:

> *"The proliferation of non-GAAP metrics and the thou-sands of versions of each has made [users'] life a night-mare. It's like standing behind the person in the Starbucks line who orders their coffee with seven different variations."*

Because consumers *will* be served, the hard question was as put in a May speech by Hans Hoogervorst, chairman of the IASB,

> *"whether IFRS Standards provide sufficient criteria by which performance can be judged by users of financial statements."*

As for actual cases of abuse, the regulators' ability to deal as best they can was bound to be spotty. The SEC's Division of Corporation Finance issued its "Compliance & Disclosure Interpretations" on May 17, and established a special task force. But in practice, its review of non-GAAP filings is generating uneven results.[13]

From a broader perspective, to confront the non-GAAP conun-drum requires timely attention to this proposition:

> *If decision-making by the broad population of information users is now so focused on non-GAAP measures, does that not essentially challenge the adequacy, sufficiency and legitimacy of GAAP itself?*

In other words, even though ill-founded herd behavior based on "conventional wisdom" is based on proximity, convenience and inertia, it still compels reexamination of GAAP's basic utility — all the more so because *even* a position both long-established and intellectually robust is not immune from rejection or displacement.

Examples range from the trivial to the profound of beliefs that are "generally accepted." Nothing abstract compels a driver approaching an octagonal red sign — the expected **STOP** is "generally accepted." No written code obliges the congregation to stand for the bride when her father walks her to the altar.

Yet beliefs evolve. It was long held that the earth was the center of the astronomical universe, a position "generally accepted" by the world's best thinkers from the time of Ptolemy, even as the model's complexity of deferents, epicycles, eccentrics and equants become unwieldy to the point of breakdown — eventually to be consigned to history's dustbin with the contributions of Copernicus, Keppler and Galileo.

Social policies supported by coercive legal systems throughout history included the "general acceptance" of such inhumanities as child labor, chattel slavery and exclusion of minorities — all of them to be swept away in more enlightened eras.

As for the future of GAAP under its current challenges, theoreticians in the development of knowledge teach that the displacement of long-held paradigms happens only when two conditions are met:[14]

- The necessity must come to be recognized even by those with interests in preserving the *status quo.*

- An alternative paradigm must be available to which to migrate.

So if as suggested, the dialog as to non-GAAP metrics has indeed engaged the attention of a quorum of the key players, there are two next steps in the process:

- The actual if reluctant acceptance of the need to explore the supplanting of GAAP itself.

- And the convening of a far-reaching discussion of the structure by which non-GAAP measures can be identified, articulated and codified with sufficient clarity to be integrated into a reporting and assurance structure by which investor needs can be truly served.

No part of this challenge lies beyond the reach of those leaders among the community of interests that comprise the Big Audit model.

Auditor Independence — Appearance and Reality

No Value — No Point

The drubbing that fell upon Andersen over Enron was captured in January 2002 with the ill-mannered attack on David Duncan, that "Arthur Andersen provided the get-away car and they say you were at the wheel."

It was effectively a no-win subject for the auditors: "By which are you more corrupted — your breadth of client relationships, or your fee levels in general?"

A central reality at the heart of this story is the obsolete and overvalued concept of auditor independence. The subject is infected with denial and misunderstanding, but cannot be avoided. As put by the American writer Dorothy Parker, who never shied from afflicting the comfortable:

> "If you can't say something nice — come over and sit by me."

There is nothing more sacred in the auditor-client literature than the notion of auditor independence, dating from the emergence of a professionalized service in the 19th century.

According to the self-congratulatory atmosphere among the regulators of the world's securities markets, the problem of dubious corporate accounting would be fully solved by strictly limiting the kinds of services that auditors can provide to clients. Yet with each of the surviving Big Four burdened by the weight of a litigation list of cases large enough to be fatal, this unexamined burden has become yet another millstone.

To be both blunt and unconventional — it is time to stop making nice, and to discard this 165-year-old piece of conventional wisdom. The concept of auditor independence does not serve the interests of investors.

Audit performance — and more immediately, the survival of the large firms to serve their global clients and the capital markets — would be better achieved if the current independence requirements and constraints were scrapped altogether. Auditors should be free to provide their clients with any services within their skills.

Some will be scandalized by the suggestion. But there are compelling reasons why it should be done.

Regulators confess to being clueless about what will happen if the next of the Big Four disintegrates under the combined pressures of hostile law enforcement and overwhelming shareholder litigation.

Those tempted to think it can't happen are reminded not only of Enron and Andersen, but also of the near-death $456 million fine over questionable tax shelters paid by KPMG in 2005 to escape indictment. The game is Russian roulette out there, and the gun is full of bullets.

The purest argument for driving the profession back to audit-only basics has always been that as clients pay the fees, for services of any type, auditor independence is inevitably subject to compromise.

But that thought requires finishing. If such a system is presumed to be so inherently subject to corruption, auditors should never take any fees from their clients. So then, who should pay? Inserting a government-run structure would amount to nationalizing the audit function — an idea that figures nowhere in rational dialog. And there are no other volunteers around.

Likewise, the argument that the consulting fees paid by Enron corrupted Andersen's audit behavior was always stretched. Heady as that stream of revenue was, it was the money itself, not the source. It could be said, in fact — and the proposition surely should be examined — that auditors who depend on audit fees alone are under even more pressure to accommodate a client's wishes.

And whenever that accommodation has turned ugly — Andersen's travails with Enron being only an egregious example — it has been the firms that pay. But as history shows, they have neither the reputation nor the capital to bear the terrible cost.

The auditors have been garnering neither respect nor liability protection by complying with the enforced codes of independence. They, and their clients, would achieve better value if audits were based on a comprehensive understanding of and involvement with the business. In other words, auditors need to be *closer* to their clients, not further away.

Who better to advise the public, that the financial statements of an enterprise are free of material error, than the professionals who design, install, operate and maintain the system that records and accounts for its transactions — the very services from which today's auditors are barred?

This does not dismiss the importance of accountability or of oversight. Regulators have their place — as do the enforceable legal requirements for public companies to issue financial statements that are fairly stated — but only under systems of liability that address the reality of today's deadly threats.

Advocates for the *status quo* argue that the code, rules and constraints of independence are worth preserving as "the very essence of what the auditors are selling."

But here lies the heart of the problem, and the unacknowledged secret within audit's very design: The auditors' core product — the one-page report with its "pass/fail" opinion that financial statements are fairly stated and free of material error — is no longer providing value to investors or other users. No one reads it or pays attention to it. If not for the deeply embedded compliance

requirements of the securities regulators, no rational audit committee or chief financial officer would engage outside auditors to
produce it.

The presumptive value of the independent audit report, which
has come down to us from a simpler era long past, has been one
of those Jeffersonian verities — manifest, unexamined, and
immune from critical challenge. But the evidence of its irrelevance
is compelling.

The Auditors' Real Clients — Time to Reassess

> "Ahh, but the strawberries — that's where I had them.
> They laughed at me and made jokes, but I proved beyond
> the shadow of a doubt and with geometric logic that a
> duplicate key to the wardroom icebox <u>did</u> exist, and I'd
> have produced that key if they hadn't pulled the Caine out
> of action."
>
> — Capt. *Philip Francis Queeg (Humphrey Bogart)*,
> *"The Caine Mutiny"* — 1954

Comprehensive review of the scope and language of the standard
auditors' report has long been overdue. As taken up in Part III,
the initiatives of both the PCAOB as the American audit regulator
and the IAASB as the source of international standards are welcome, although with measured enthusiasm.

It falls under the rubric of "auditor independence," however,
that high on the list of barriers to clear thinking and potentially
constructive evolution is the persistent canard, renewed by
PCAOB member Steven Harris at its June 21, 2011, public meeting, that auditors "must fully embrace the concept that the company paying their fee is *not* their client."

This proposition is confusing in logic, wrong in history, and
malign in its influence. Until snuffed out, it will continue to deflect
and distract from the task of reengineering a role for outside

auditors that brings real value to the community of financial statement users.

Since the middle of the 19th century, when Mr. Deloitte and his pioneering colleagues were first engaged to assist the "auditors" of Victorian-era public companies — themselves selected from among the body of corporate shareholders, to advise their fellows in their shared financial interests — the auditor/client relationship has been contractual, consensual and private.

The *appliqué* of "public interest" has been allowed not only to stick, but to become an incrustation on the auditors' appropriate functions. Fostered since its infancy by the newly invented profession itself, not always to its credit and lately to its mortal threat, the label did fend off — if only temporarily — the prospect of government-provided assurance — but at high cost and under the now-realized hazard of exaggeration and misapprehension of its capacities.

One prop for the shaky structure on which Harris bases his claim, that "the ultimate client of an auditor of any publicly traded company must be investors," is the 1984 decision of the United States Supreme Court in the case of *United States v. Arthur Young*. There, perpetuating the unfortunately long tradition of judicial misappreciation of the auditors' role, Chief Justice Warren Burger invoked the inapposite image of the "public watchdog" — that "the accountant maintains total independence from the client at all times and requires complete fidelity to the public trust."

As a matter of jurisprudence, Burger's gratuitous *dictum* was unnecessary to the Court's holding in that case, that the Internal Revenue Service could by subpoena compel the accounting firm's turnover of its tax accrual working papers.

And as a matter of unexamined rhetoric, Burger defied the logic of canine behavior, that even the most vigilant guardian might bite the very hand that feeds it. In his judicial remove from reality,

the Chief Justice missed the compelling folk maxim, "I'd trust my
dog with my life — just not with my ham sandwich."[15]

Events have now shown that on such a tenuous rationale, the
bulky but fragile edifice of constrained client service and "appearance of independence" cannot stand.

Critics such as Harris of the "pass/fail" audit report model
have much to complain of — but there will be no solutions in
shooting at the messengers, who continue to deliver this outdated
and devalued commodity product.

Instead, history provides many examples of the dangers that
lurk in broadening the distance that separates the payor of fees
from the subsidized interests ostensibly served:

- Raising the limits on depositors' insurance incentivized the reck-
  less behavior of the American savings and loan institutions in
  the 1980s, underlying their ruinous boom-and-bust.

- Lodging the management of American health care cost reim-
  bursement decisions with self-interested insurers only opened
  the doors to the waste, abuse and misallocations in the pricing
  and delivery of medical services.

- Requiring an issuer-paid rating agency's report as a "green
  light" to sell complex derivatives was a central element in the
  inflation of the subprime-mortgage driven crisis that plagued
  the financial markets in the years still counting since
  2007–2008.

None of which is to say that the "agency problem" of close
auditor relationships with corporate boards and managements can
be addressed successfully by the further intrusion of government.
The prospect of government-run audits — that an audit regulator
could take on and satisfy the task of providing even today's outdated "pass/fail" assurance — is beyond Panglossian fantasy or
imagination.

Rather, hope for progress lies in a realistic reframing of the results that can reasonably be expected from the auditors, in an environment where legitimate and valuable new forms of assurance can be designed and delivered.

Which requires putting aside inflated language, moderating unrealistic expectations, and nurturing the profession's acknowledged and considerable expertise.

Those who pine for the days when an auditor earned broad professional respect by detailed examinations of the distinct items in corporate accounts are entitled to mourn. What they cannot avoid, however, even through the best-intentioned sentimental wishes, is the inevitable evolution that has taken the profession to the brink.

As taken up in Part V, valuable forms of financial statement assurance remain to be created and brought to market. What form the profession will take that will do so remains a vital question. The only certainty is that the structure will be different from the one that exists today.

Lost among the Mixed Messages

At the AICPA's Washington conference on SEC and PCAOB developments in 2010, the then-Chief Accountant of the SEC, James Kroeker (who has since moved to Norwalk as a member of the FASB), advocated "a change to our collective vocabulary.... (D)ont use the word 'client' to refer to the management of companies under audit .... (I)t is time to give serious consideration to changing the perceived 'client' in audit relationships."

Among the many pernicious effects of Sarbanes-Oxley has been a multidimensional degrading of the auditor/client relationship. From an advisory role to one of adversarial compliance-checking, it has become so forms-and-process based that young professionals no longer have a working environment in which to learn and absorb actual client business. Under ongoing stress on revenues and profitability, the firms' clear imperative to their staff is to complete the work needed to issue another commodity report, "on time, within budget, and without making waves."

The dynamic for an eager but career-sensitive young professional is no better put than by a senior-level expert: "If you raise a problem, then by definition *you* become the problem." No wonder, then, that "client satisfaction" — the long-popular mantra across the spectrum of professional services — readily elides to "client capture."

Kroeker's former agency might, of course, advocate for a nationalized audit function carried out by civil servants. But if that were to happen, it would be revealed quickly enough how the community of financial information users would compare the value of today's archaic and obsolete report with an equivalent document delivered by federal agencies distinguished by their inaction during the post-crisis years of tumult in the capital markets.

Until then, it requires recalling that it has been a basic premise since the 1930s passage of the American securities laws, when the profession lobbied successfully for private control of the assurance franchise, that the company under audit does the hiring and pays the bills.

Indeed, the disregarded malign consequences of migration away from that plain election, over to an ambiguous definition of "client," are amply shown in the vast amount of time and energy devoted to the intellectually ineffective attempt to define with precision what constitutes an "appearance of independence," in light of the contractual and economic linkage of direct auditor engagement.

It is also readily recognized that important rights and obligations arise outside the strict confines of a provider-client relationship. Concepts based on agency, trust and fiduciary duty are familiar — as is legislative authority to create duties based on extra-contractual reliance and expectations, whether for investors, consumers or even innocent bystanders.

As I try to instill in my graduate-level law and business students in Risk Management and Decision-making, the guidance is still relevant, as laid down by 18th-century lexicographer Samuel Johnson, that "sloppy language is a mark of sloppy thinking."

It does no favors to the complex challenges to evolve a valuable and sustainable audit function, to blur the lines of accountability with careless invocation of an ill-defined shift in "client" identity.

Whether Independence Has Value — Two Cases Suggest Otherwise
Because the model of Big Audit has been so long and deeply embedded in the operation of the modern capital markets, the opportunities have been limited to identify "alternate realities" — that is, to inquire and observe "what if" the conditions were otherwise.

Two cases are available, however, that support the proposition that the amount of value placed by investors on the independence of the auditor is at best minimal — based on the absence of a negative share price reaction to the withdrawal and extended absence of independence-compliant audited financial statements.

The EY/Ventas Affair — In the End, Who Really Got Bonked?

> "When I married an accountant, I always thought his eyes would go first."
>
> — *"Same Time Next Year"* — 1975

In Bernard Slade's poignant Broadway play and later film, at least, romance originating on an audit engagement could include a touching laugh line.

Less so today — taking a look at what the SEC delicately called the "close personal and romantic relationship" between the chief financial officer of Ventas, Inc., the Chicago-based REIT, and an audit partner on the team at Ernst & Young LLP.

Both were sacked in July 2014 when their affair became public. EY's opinions for the two prior years were withdrawn, and it was replaced by KPMG. The SEC's penalties imposed in September 2016 included censure of EY, required disgorgement of $3.2 million in fees plus interest and added a civil penalty of $1 million. The package of sanctions also includes fines of $25,000 each and SEC practice bans on the CFO (one year) and the EY partner (three years), with a similar ban on her superior to boot.

All enforcement proceedings aside, the point here is to note forthrightly the investor community's clear indifference to the entire Ventas affair, including a lack of concern with bedrooms as compared with boardrooms or audit rooms.

That is, between EY's withdrawal of its opinions in July 2014 and the September 4 filing of the company's amended 10-K with a fresh opinion by successor KPMG — in other words, while the company lacked audited financial statements — the company's stock price actually *increased* by 3%.

Of possible impact were fawning reports on the company by Fitch and Motley Fool — although flipping to the period that followed, after KPMG's opinion became available to relieve any investor anxiety about the company's noncompliant status, its stock price went into a brief but sharp *decline*, not recovering its early September price until October 17.

In brief — no stock price punishment for the absence of an independent auditor, nor any reward for reachieving a state of virtue either. *QED*, the complex of rules regarding "auditor independence," is delivering nothing on which investors place value.

It can well be said based on Ventas, and the demonstrated readiness of the stock-buying public to ignore an independence violation so flat-footed as to leave the company without reliable audited statements, that the entire anachronistic edifice of "appearance of independence" rests on shifting and unstable sands, and deserves to be washed away with the tides of modernized assurance performance.

KPMG, Herbalife's Stock Price and the Blame Game

Earlier, it had spoken volumes about the question whether investors really place value on the independence of outside auditors, in
April 2013, that two trading days after KPMG's April 9 withdrawal of its audit reports on the financial statements of its Los
Angeles clients Herbalife and Skechers, because of inside information shared illegally by its engagement partner Scott London —
who had been promptly sacked and criminally charged — the
stock price of both of those stock had actually risen![16]

The consequences of London's illegal passing-on, to the mil-
lion-dollar benefit of his golfing pal Bryan Shaw, were swift and
nasty:

- Ratted out by Shaw, London cut the fastest plea deal the prosecutors offered — ultimately drawing a prison sentence of 14
months, of which he served eight, while Shaw for his cooperation received and served only five.

- KPMG committed to the costs incurred by its ex-clients to
obtain replacement auditors — Herbalife selecting PwC and
Skechers going with BDO.

Meanwhile, plaintiffs' lawyers with claims of harm — despite
the stock price upticks — spun the long-running spat over
Herbalife between raider Carl Icahn and short seller Bill Ackman,
and the pyramid claims of the Federal Trade Commission — settled by the company in July 2016 for $200 million — into share-
holder class action claims, starting an exercise of legal maneuvers
that ran until dismissed in November 2015.

London's downfall framed this top-level question, heretical as it
may seem:

> *"What value to the operation of the capital markets — if
> any — is actually delivered by the entire structure of audi-
> tor independence?"*

London's professional position was destroyed, and his liberty taken away, not because he violated the elaborate dictates of the auditor independence rules, but because of his multiyear violations of the insider-trading prohibitions of the American securities laws.

And on the other hand, despite KPMG's immediate and apologetic resignation and report withdrawals, the stock market gave credence to the assertions that the substantive content of the Herbalife and Skechers financial statements were unaffected (even given the charges hurled in the Icahn/Ackman dust-up).

In short, the indifference of equity investors to the state of KPMG's independence was fully demonstrated.

As dealt with above, under the "client pays" business model for financial statement assurance, invented back in the Victorian era, the accounting profession has gained nothing positive for years, by way of reputation, stature or risk and exposure mitigation, from the intellectually unsatisfactory edifice of "appearance of independence."

The stock price nonevent of Scott London's misadventures equally showed the converse — that investors impose no downside price penalty on even a slam-dunk independence violation.

From these two examples, then, may come this reasonable conclusion: the time, energy and cost of maintaining the outmoded and anachronistic structure of "independence" should be redirected to the long roster of topics legitimately worthy of the effort.

Limits on Big Audit's Ability to Innovate

Apologists for the capability of the large accounting firms to innovate their way out of their survivability predicament are entitled to much sympathy. But not much credit or credibility. That is because under examination, their optimism is seen to be entangled in the paralyzing web of intersecting and conflicting interests.

A summary is offered here. Fuller treatment, one element at a time, will come in Parts III and IV.

It is argued that an audit firm might differentiate its value, to both issuers and users, through the use of "big data" analytics or application of psychological factors to the detection and prevention of fraud and other financial irregularities.

But serious threshold issues arise immediately.

Skepticism is needed, to start, about the ability to screen and identify the white-collar fraudster or the financial manipulator — before his conduct rises to the level of the eruptions of Bernie Madoff or Jeffrey Skilling, or defrocked credit-crisis CEOs such as Chuck Prince of Citigroup, Jimmy Cayne of Bear Stearns or Dick Fuld of Lehman Brothers. "Forensic" assessment after the fact has advanced, to be sure. But the psychologists' catalog of personality and behavior factors identifiable with the classic white-collar criminal — big ego, narcissism, seductive personality, unwillingness to accept criticism, dissent or bad news — are no less characteristic of the standard-issue chief executive at any large global company, or indeed of politicians at the highest level of elective office.[17]

Next — developments in data analysis will surely transform the process of auditing as it becomes possible to capture and assess *all* of the financial information of a large company, making obsolete the historical approach to assurance through sampling. But the rapid spread and sharing of those techniques will quickly disperse and eliminate any early-mover advantage — leaving the large firms still on the same level playing field in their futile search for differentiation.

Also — the heavy hand of regulation will be felt. Regulatory constraint imposes the commodity language of the SEC-compliant standard auditors' report. However motivated they might be to pursue evolution in both the processes and the reporting on their assurance, both issuers and auditors are trapped in an economic model where the cost of the "pass-fail report" comes first — eating up budgets that if freed from the requirements of the securities regulators could be more productively deployed elsewhere.

The degree of Big Audit commitment to innovation must, regrettably, be assessed with a skeptical eye. Recent revenue growth among the Big Four — notably in their nonaudit practices under the evolved label of "Advisory" — suggests at least that their ready continuation of profitable practice using the current model occurs under the bindings of golden handcuffs.

In addition, with the PCAOB able both to set the standards for auditing in the United States, and to judge with hindsight the extent of compliance of US auditors with the standards it sets for itself, fear of regulatory second-guessing will operate to stifle initiative.

Also in play is the inhibition on innovation imposed by scale — namely the barrier to entry presented by size alone.

That is, inapposite examples abound where transformative developments in technology and process could be incubated at small scale, on the margins of the marketplace, before erupting to overtake and obsolesce the old order. Small cars evolved in post-war Japan, mini-mills displaced the giant steel works, Bobcat earthmovers and Dyson vacuum cleaners appeared under the radar. All were able to work out their growing pains in the shadows.

Not for nothing does the business-school case model of the birth of Federal Express emphasize the fact that when founder Fred Smith picked up his first package and flew his first plane in 1973, it was only after years of work to establish the infrastructure by which every link was in place in a network of sufficient critical mass for a holistic, fully networked launch.

No such opportunity exists, for a niche technology-based audit upstart — since the audit of a large global enterprise requires physical presence, locally licensed personnel and industry expertise in dozens of countries.

Perhaps the most compelling aspect of the skepticism that must attach to the notion of advanced fraud-detection capability concerns motivation and opportunity: advocates of supposed "fraud audits," under whatever vocabulary, have singularly failed to explain why — if such techniques actually existed in forms superior to present practice — they are not already fully deployed.

That is because the large firms are not lacking in reasons or motivation to apply their very best efforts. The adverse judgments and settlement costs of litigation are burden enough. The added weight of legal fees, management time and energy, insurance premiums and reputational loss provides a further stimulus amply sufficient to spur any management to utilize the best efforts at its command.

Whether "the best they can" rises to the level of "good enough" is, of course, a central question in the necessary dialog. But the same coin has two messages etched on its flip side:

The *first* is the necessary recognition on the part of the profession's critics that the Big Four partnerships are made up of men and women of good faith, concentrated energy and professional expertise — who put their entire financial fortunes at personal risk behind the opinions they sign.

And the *second* is that any complex system of human design and operation is subject to the nonzero likelihood of breakdown and highly consequential failure — invoking the necessity of norm-setting and compliance mechanisms on the part of lawmakers and regulators that are within society's tolerance to bear the intrusions and taxation costs of oversight and enforcement.

Legal Standards and Public Expectations

The Big Four's Unsustainable Liability Exposure

The accounting firms are bleeding capital and talent. Their permissible scope of professional services is under attack, while their exposures are expanding. The cost of resolving multibillion dollar claims continues to escalate, with billion-dollar settlements now expected in the largest cases, as was reportedly Andersen's pre-collapse exit price in Enron.

As set forth as long ago as 1969 in Judge Henry Friendly's decision in the *Continental Vending* case,[18] there is no "safe harbor" for auditors. A firm's demonstrated compliance with professional standards is not an effective defense, even to criminal liability. The American legal system does not practically differentiate between deliberate manipulation and aggressive use of permissible professional judgment, when judged with the hindsight perspective of an emerged scandal. In the attitude of juries, a significant stock-price shock means that *ipso facto* something has gone seriously wrong, and blame is to be imposed.

Because "recklessness" plus hindsight satisfies the fraud-based standard for liability under the US system, defendants who may wish to go to trial are exposed to the vagaries of the jury system and the hired testimony of the experts. This combination — plus the death-blow potential of a worst-case jury verdict — renders the mega-cases untriable and requires settlements instead.

Meanwhile, in countries other than the United States, mostly lacking a mature body of jurisprudence and actual trial experience, examples are emerging of cases on unappealing facts and under the clouds of political and media attention, which are being settled for eight- and nine-figure amounts.

Accounting firms are obliged to settle their big cases, whatever the cost, since their leaderships cannot afford to risk an adverse jury verdict in a dispute large enough to be fatal.

Examples include BDO's May 2015 settlement of $40 million related to the Ponzi scheme of Allen Stanford;[19] the October 2013 agreement by CliftonLarsonAllen, to pay over $35 million in settlement of claims relating to the $53 million defalcations by the controller of the city of Dixon Illinois; the agreements by Deloitte in 2013 and PwC in 2016 to settle their exposures of $7.6 billion and $5.5 billion relating to Taylor Bean & Whitaker and Colonial Bank; and PwC's 2017 agreement to settle its exposure in MF Global rather than carry its on-going trial to a conclusion.

Under the American standard for fraud, including recklessness, and the inevitable use by juries of hindsight in situations of corporate fraud or failure, the firms are hostage to a "zero-defects" performance standard.

But the accounting profession has never achieved "zero-defects" performance, and cannot do so. The limits of human behavior plus the demands of the market prevent such a level of performance. Audit quality is constrained under the limitations of scope and sampling, especially in the context of accounting standards requiring the application of client judgment and permitting the application of client pressure.

Also, despite available litigation experience and lessons going back over forty years, the profession has not shown an ability to improve its performance to a level that would eliminate *completely* its life-threatening failures and litigation claims, and thereby enable real confidence in survivability.

At the same time, the commodity nature of the audit report inhibits the profession's ability to pursue a model of either pricing or quality based on differentiated client perceptions. Clients do not want and would not pay for a "zero-defects" audit, even if achievable.

Finally, the requirements of regulators and the profession's own commitment to sell an undifferentiated assurance product — the standard "pass/fail" report — means that the accountants could not design, sell or furnish an audit that is "guaranteed defect free" — even if a firm were inclined to attempt one.

Escalated Public Expectations — The Firms' Responsibility
The profession itself bears a major share of the responsibility for the mismatch between user expectations and performance capability.

The modern accounting profession is unique — unlike doctors, lawyers and other service professions — in that its evolution, structure and regulation did not occur over the centuries through changes in culture, social institutions and science and technology.

Rather, the assurance function was a creature of government regulation, starting with the requirements for financial statements under the English Companies Act of 1844 and the emergence of the independent audit in the following two decades, and extending through the American securities acts of 1933 and 1934. The large firms now represented by the Big Four emerged and evolved accordingly (*see* the *Timeline* following the *Appendices*.)

Unfortunately, the tensions and ambiguities caused by this close linkage with government oversight are seldom acknowledged, and have never been fully accepted or resolved. The large firms' practice expansions of the 1990s — into technology-based consulting, legal practices, investment advising and other areas — assumed that any conceivable service could be delivered consistent with assurance. But the expansion strategies were never grounded in a revisiting or successful demonstration to the public of the validity of that original concept.

The firms pursued the work and revenue that they saw being enjoyed by the bankers and the lawyers, but misplayed the interrelationship between those practices and their public accountability for the limited-value audit product. Unable to free themselves to deliver a truly multidisciplinary practice and revenue model, the firms lacked the political savvy and historical perspective to overcome local political and regulatory animosity, for which they have now paid an enormous price in the loss of the scope-of-services debate.

Neither Regulatory Nor Market Solutions Are Viable

Defenders of the profession, who argue passionately about the basic ethics and good faith of its personnel, miss an essential point: No matter how much good work is done, the bad cases deliver the bad impacts.

As comparable examples, each year the airlines safely convey millions of passengers, and doctors successfully treat whole populations without incident. But even as air travel and doctor visits are routine parts of daily life, the rare catastrophic crashes and the isolated instances of horrific medical malpractice shape both the public criticisms and the adverse consequences.

Oversight and sanctions are *post hoc*, and are therefore not effective for either behavior change or deterrence. Sarbanes-Oxley has not been a deterrent to doubtful corporate behavior.

The catalog of the post-enactment examples includes such situations as HealthSouth, Ahold, Shell and Fannie Mae; the personal stock trading activities of Sam Waksal of ImClone and Martha Stewart; the rogue trading of Jérôme Kerviel at Société Générale, Kweku Adoboli at UPS and JP Morgan Chase's "London Whale"; the outbreak of executive options pricing backdating; and the consistent availability of unqualified audit reports up to the failure date of such crisis-era collapses as GM, AIG, Lehman Brothers and Merrill Lynch.

Precisely apposite is the maxim invoked by every well-meaning but bewildered spouse in the tangles of fraught domestic life or a glitch in marital relations:

> *"When I do well, nobody remembers — when I do bad, nobody forgets."*

Sidebar: A Case Study — Standard & Poor's in the Gunsights

The US Justice Department filed a $5 billion lawsuit on February 3, 2013, against credit-rating agency Standard & Poor's (S&P), over its ratings of mortgage-backed collateralized debt obligations lying at the heart of the last decade's financial crisis.

After the filing, S&P ran a publicity campaign proclaiming that the government was retaliating for its 2011 downgrade of the US sovereign debt — a tactic that had no more likelihood of success than the attempt, criticized by Mark Twain, of trying to teach a pig to sing:

"It wastes your time, and only annoys the pig."

Pre-filing settlement talks had broken down, over S&P's reluctance to admit to fraud charges. The case ground along toward a possible trial, until — so much for S&P's posturing — the Department of Justice's press release of February 3, 2015, announced S&P's agreement to pay $1.375 billion — to be shared between the federal government and attorneys general of 19 states plus the District of Columbia as additional plaintiffs.

Of concern here, rather than the litigation itself, is the broader comparison of the roles, relationships and exposures of the two sets of gate-keepers — the ratings agencies and the auditors — ambiguously deemed by society to be critical to the functioning of the global capital markets.

Consider the menu of their common attributes:

- A standard, commoditized report, without which financial products cannot be brought to the investor market.

- Providers not engaged by or in direct contact with investors, but competing to be engaged and paid directly by the issuers.

- Elaborate assertions of "independence" — despite being paid by the clients — widely criticized as resting on the shaky platform of "appearance."

- Severely constrained choice among providers to large issuers, from a number of providers limited to the low single-digits.

- Barriers to new competitive entry based on market demands for global scale, competence and resources — although tightly regulated, the provider cartels are not constrained by limits on government licenses or other franchise restrictions.

- Claims that, broadly speaking, the reports reasonably reflect reality, most of the time — except under highly stressed conditions, when they do not — a position not unlike the claim that the lithium-ion batteries in the Samsung Galaxy Note 7 or the Boeing 787 worked reasonably well, most of the time — except when they caught fire or exploded.

- Provider claims to have adjusted and improved methodologies and process in light of recent criticisms — proclamations echoing those of an era before political correctness, that "nice college girls don't do those things — and besides, the grass was wet."

- Finally, the standard document noted at the head of this list, explicitly couched in the language of an "opinion" — as if, despite the construction of an elaborate and expensive pyramid of supportive analysis and procedures, the result was intended as no more than a *like* on Facebook or an amateur diner's review on Zagats or Trip Advisor.

Up to the last, this list of attributes would apply equally to the three dominant ratings agencies — S&P, Moody's and Fitch — as to the accounting tetrapoly of Deloitte, EY, KPMG and PwC.

Except, that is, for the dissonance at the "Expectations Gap." There the Big Four face potentially catastrophic litigation exposure for each large-company audit report they sign, while the ratings agencies have — until now at least — successfully wrapped themselves in the armored blanket of free-speech protections under the First Amendment.

The government's suit against S&P may portend a realignment of the exposure realities. A new era of litigation risk may confront S&P as well as its brethren — as may be reflected in Moody's agreement in January 2017 to pay fines of $864 million to settle Justice Department claims that it contributed to the financial crisis of 2007–2008 by inflating credit ratings of subprime-mortgage bonds.

But from the Big Four's perspective, any temptation to *schadenfreude* would be hazardous — because of the speed and vigor with which the slightly guilty pleasure taken at another's misfortune could turn to ashes.

Especially if there should be a contagion effect.

NOTES

1. In organizing these themes, I thank Duane Kullberg — my friend, partner, and first boss at Arthur Andersen when I arrived in 1982 — only the firm's fifth managing partner since its founding in 1913.

2. The exigencies of a publishing deadline prevent more than passing reference to the results of PwC's March 2107 trial date in New York, where it was defending against claims of more than $3 billion relating to its work for MF Global, collapsed in 2011 under the management of former Goldman Sachs partner and ex-politician Jon Corzine. The consequences of that outcome — a confidential settlement only after three weeks of actual trial — reprise PwC's unhappy experience in the Colonial Bank litigation, and re-emphasize the ever-present exposure of the Big Four to threats on an existential scale.

3. Unresolved at this writing are two global-scale challenges in auditor replacement. BT Group in the United Kingdom — its search to replace PwC after a 33-year tenure accelerated by the emergence of a £530 million hole in the accounts of its division in Italy — had relationships with each of the other Big Four that either were outright disqualifying or required stand-downs by way of "cleansing," while no smaller firm appeared capable of stepping in.

And in Japan, scandal-ridden Toshiba — having sacked EY in 2016 — released third-quarter results without a report and was threatened with de-listing, due to unresolved disagreements with successor PwC — while Deloitte and KPMG reported business-based conflicts and no available second-tier candidates appeared qualified and willing.

4. Cries by the uninformed to "break up the Big Four" have never been supported by a workable plan to do so. The reality is that to

isolate and distill the components of a Big Four network into separate viable portions would be no more practical than the challenge to re-create pure tomato, celery, and carrot juice from a vat of Campbell's V-8.

5. Examples include Enron's $67 billion bankruptcy in 2002, and the €20 billion hole in the balance sheet of Parmalat, revealed in 2003 — both years ahead of the far larger collapses of the long roster of failed global-scale financial institutions from 2007 onward.

6. In the calculations were assumptions as to the impact on the revenue and profitability of a firm under litigation and reputational threat. Actual per-partner profitability data were and are available from the annually published financial statements of the UK firms — components of the global networks large enough to provide a metric that can reasonably be extrapolated.

7. Further showing the breadth of the mega-settlements were:

- The fines of $2.5 billion agreed by Credit Suisse in May 2014 in connection with its guilty plea over the concealment of American tax evaders.

- Rate-fixing fines ranging from $1.5 billion agreed by UBS in 2012 as the first large bank to settle, to the $2.5 billion agreed by Deutsche Bank in April 2015.

- The $8.9 billion fine finally agreed by BNP Paribas in June 2014, after the exceptional intervention tactics of the French government officials.

- The $5 billion in federal and state fines packaged in the five-bank set of guilty pleas to antitrust violations and rate-fixing — Citigroup, JP Morgan Chase, Barclays, RBS and UBS — announced on May 20, 2015.

- The mortgage securities-related fines of $5.1 billion, $3.2 billion, $7.2 billion and $5.3 billion, agreed in January, February and December 2016 by, respectively, Goldman Sachs, Morgan Stanley, Deutsch Bank and Credit Suisse, with an outcome still to come in the Justice Department's targeting of Barclays.

- The record-setting total of some $3.5 billion, largest ever under the Foreign Corrupt Practices Act, agreed in December 2016 by

Brazilian conglomerate Odebrecht and its petrochemical unit Braskem, under charges in the Petrobras scandal of conspiracy, bribery and corruption.

8. Later, in a speech in June 2014, by then well away from the SEC and out of the spotlight of authority but able to put a zing of blame upon IASB chairman Hans Hoogervorst, ex-Chairman Cox declared his apostasy after years in office as a cheerleader for convergence, stating that "the prospect of full scale IFRS in our life-times has ceased to be," and proclaiming convergence to be as dead as Monty Python's famous parrot.

9. Of the four, the nearest ever to an accomplished goal was the set of converged standards on revenue recognition issued by the two bodies in May 2014. But as reported in the *Journal of Accountancy* on April 1, 2015, the FASB announced a one-year deferral in implementation, later joined by the IASB's own announced adjournment — suggesting the applicability in standard-setting as elsewhere of baseball philosopher Yogi Berra, that "it ain't over till it's over."

10. Any attempt to stay current is doomed to frustration by the endless issuance of bureaucratic blandness. One late entry was the July 5, 2015, speech by the SEC's then-chief accountant, James Schnurr. Surveying his "considerable time ... researching and discussing IFRS," Schnurr opined that "FASB and IASB should continue to focus on converging the standards" — a position derided by blogger Tom Selling in his *Accounting Onion* for the next day as "converging two sacks of mush."

Among the latest as of this writing, Schnurr's successor at the SEC, Wesley Bricker, was part of a trio issuing the expected platitudes in their speeches on December 5, 2016, at the AICPA's annual hoe-down (*all emphases added*):

> Bricker: "*On the question of* possible *use of IFRS for domestic users, I believe that at least for the foreseeable future, the FASB's* independent *standard-setting process and US GAAP will continue to best serve the needs of investors and other users.*"

> Hans Hoogervorst: "*Even though the US does not permit domestic use of IFRS standards, you have a great deal invested in our success.*"

> Russell Golden: "*I believe that working* toward *the development of more comparable global accounting standards is important to reducing complexity in financial reporting.*"

11. Adapted from the original in the *International Herald Tribune*, December 7, 2002.

12. As will come in Part V, modest steps toward progress are detectable in the revisiting of the standard auditors' report language by the PCAOB and the IAASB, and the roll-out of expanded reporting requirements in the United Kingdom under the Financial Reporting Council's guidance issued in the fall of 2013.

13. As of the end of 2016, the SEC's comment letter criticisms had induced Valeant Pharmaceuticals to re-vamp its process of stripping from non-GAAP results such apparently normal recurring expenses as restructuring and legal costs, and to persuade FedEx Corp. to add extensive additional disclosures and to revise its reconciliation of GAAP and non-GAAP numbers. On the other hand, the SEC apparently gave a pass to GE, although as reported by Dow Jones on November 15, "the agency contended that the company's disclosures could be unclear or confusing to investors and that its metrics may have excluded some costs they shouldn't have."

14. *See* Thomas Kuhn, *The Structure of Scientific Revolutions* (University of Chicago Press, 1962).

15. The metaphor was treated with more care and respect in the early English cases. As Lord Justice Lopes wrote in *Re: Kingston Cotton Mills Co.* (1896):

> "*An auditor is not bound to be a detective, or, as was said to approach his work with suspicion, or with a forgone conclusion that there is something wrong. He is a watchdog, not a bloodhound.*"

16. Skechers' stock price was stable in the $20s into the fall of 2013, then went on a run to peak at $54 in August 2015, before falling off sharply back to the low $20s as of late 2016. Herbalife, a different and complex story, wandered from the high $30s at the time to a spike above $80 in January 2014 and has since bounced around widely between the $30s and the $60s.

17. See Ramamoorti, Morrison, Koletar & Pope, *The ABC's of Behavioral Forensics* (Wiley, 2013).

18. *United States v. Simon*, 425 F.2d 796 (2d Cir. 1969).

19. The large-firm frustration and futility with the necessary dynamics of settlements was caught in the plaintive tone of the BDO spokesman, quoted by *Accountancy Today* on May 26, 2015, that "BDO audited an affiliated company whose financial statements are not alleged by plaintiffs to have contained any material misstatements. However, after almost four years of litigation and the likelihood of more to come, this settlement makes the most sense for our partnership ...."

III

A TAXONOMY OF THE NON-SOLUTIONS

PREFACE: THE AUDITORS — MISSING FROM THE FINANCIAL CRISIS

> "A conventional wisdom is gradually developing that the audit is largely irrelevant to the investment process today."
> — *PCAOB Chairman James Doty, January 9, 2013, speaking to the AICPA National Conference on SEC and PCAOB Developments, Washington, DC*

The Big Four, who audited every one of the institutions contributing to the worldwide financial crisis that began in 2007, not only were absent from visible influence on the catastrophe, but also have largely been spared the *postmortem* recriminations and accountability.

The simple reason is that their core product had been judged irrelevant. The standard auditor's report is an anachronism — having lost any value it may once have had, except for legally required compliance.

If that single "pass/fail" page disappeared from corporate annual reports, no candid user of financial information would admit to missing it. Nor, offered the choice, would any rational audit committee or chief financial officer pay the enormous fees required to obtain it.

The regulators' mantra that audits have a "critical role" rests on the unexamined and self-reflexive assumption that audit reports will simply and always *be there* — like water at the tap or electricity at the switch. To the contrary — if one of the Big Four does trip into disintegration, nothing within the capacity of any regulator on earth will be able to put the shattered networks back together again, or compel the delivery of audits when there is nobody left to perform them.

There are at least these issues:

As examined in Part I, the financial structure of the Big Four partnerships must be recognized as too weak and limited to sustain their current exposure. Unlike the banks, their franchise is not "too big to fail." The question is whether there is a better cliché than "too weak to survive."

Next, it is time to put closure to the unachievable structural "solutions" to the Big Four's complete dominance of the large-company global audit market. None of these can happen — whether growth to competitive scale of a Five or Six, breakups to restore a new but even further weakened Big Eight, new insurance or outside capital, liability limitations, mandatory rotation or re-tender, or government takeover of the entire function.

Then, as a message to Big Four leadership, who should have no choice but to get out in front, the private sector must acknowledge that no help will be forthcoming from government. Legislators and regulators — whose essential DNA bars them from any activity other than belated overreaction — cannot be counted on for anything other than interference.

Worse, coordinated official strategies are impossible at the global level — witness the floundering over GAAP/IFRS convergence as a simple example. While in the United States, where political leadership orients either to populist activism or to small-government retreat, neither end of the ideological spectrum is about to provide relief to a white-collar profession perceived to be overpaid and underperforming.

So there is no falling back upon the fallacious assumption that "'they' won't let another firm fail." There is no "they" — no regulator or politician with the vision, interest or authority to prevent a debacle.

To address these issues, consider the following:

This Part III reviews the regularly advanced "non-solutions," each of which is unachievable under constraints of the market itself — having to do with the very nature of the Big Four networks' organizations, structures and interplay with the systems of law and regulation under which they function.

Part IV then explores some of the attitudinal and behavioral limitations shown by the array of other players, whose interests and activities are so often in antagonistic conflict, but whose candid and intelligent cooperation would be essential to any long-term and sustainable progress.

THE UNACHIEVABLE "MAGIC BULLETS"

Insurance — To Save the Auditors

An important part of the necessary landscape-clearing exercise is to eliminate the misapprehension that the commercial insurance market would provide any meaningful protection against the catastrophic disintegration of one of the surviving Big Four.

The full version of the insurance story has several pieces: the notion of issuer-specific "audit insurance," the issuance of specially designed "catastrophe bonds," a realistic view of the truly modest value of the accounting firms' own guaranties of the value of their work, in light of their severely limited financial resources, and the limited scope of government-based insurance of last resort.

To start — as part of the debate over the future of Big Audit, Joseph Nocera floated a proposal in his *New York Times* column of July 16, 2005:

Corporations would buy optional "audit insurance," which insurance companies would issue on receipt of a new and separate form of audit report. This new coverage would, in Nocera's notion, protect shareholders from losses resulting from faulty auditing.

An entertaining idea. But a few questions required exploring:

First, are there accounting firms available to do this new work? The SEC and other regulators have shown no willingness to surrender their requirements for the standard "pass-fail" audit reports, so companies would have to find a second firm with the skills and resources to perform this new form of audit. That, by definition, means another member of the market-dominating Big Four.

The problem is that the large clients of the Big Four — after eliminating their current auditor and any firms of which they are consulting clients — will find there is at best only one other firm eligible to bid for new work. This had already been shown the year before Nocera birthed his idea, when Fannie Mae had nowhere to go but Deloitte after firing KPMG. The range of choices, already poor, threatens to become irreducible.

Second, what about personnel? Although always hungry, the Big Four firms have been operating flat out, to the point of staff abuse, and they are hiring workers as best they can to replace those they chew up, waging what with curious bellicosity they describe as the "war for talent." It is not a recipe for success to think that they could ramp up further to perform a newly designed, high-demand service, with foot-soldiers recruited from the next lower level of education and professional competence.

Third, if the current audit firms took on this new role, what kind of additional work would they do? Auditors today already put their reputations and their survival on the line by issuing opinions that financial statements are free of material error. There simply is no more or different work they are competent to do — either to bolster that opinion, to manage their overhanging catastrophic litigation exposure or to entice the insurance companies. Because if there were, in both business logic and pure self-defense, they would already be doing it.

Fourth, would the numbers work out? As Nocera recognized, the problem is one of scale. Audit insurance would never cover a debacle the size of Enron or Lehman Brothers or Colonial Bank — namely, investor losses from a bankruptcy scaled in the multibillions. But in positing that the new coverage would be more than enough to cover shareholder losses linked to bad audit news, he missed two key points.

Initially, in the American legal system a defendant auditor can be held liable for 100% of all investor losses, even in a large-scale debacle like Enron or Lehman. Moreover, whether or not a shareholder suit ever comes to trial, the escalating size of the pretrial settlements — on the order of those paid by the banks in Enron and WorldCom — would overwhelm the modest capital accounts of the accounting firms' partners.

In other words, incremental addition of insurance, at the small-scale level that is all that the insurance market could make available, is a proposed solution for the wrong problem. It is the mega-cases, like Enron itself or Taylor Bean & Whitaker — the ones threatening to kill the Big Four — that would run amok through the current legal system and its puny array of defenses.

Fifth and finally, why would the insurers want to play? The popular perception is that insurance industry capital is a rainbow pot of infinite size. The truth is that the role of insurance as a risk-spreading intermediary is constrained by competing demands on its limited capacity. The insurers, burned by a generation of bad experience with the debacle of the American savings and loan associations in the 1980s, had already looked at the auditors' exposure and were devoting their resources to more predictably quantifiable disasters — like hurricanes and airplane crashes.

As will be discussed in Part V, the Big Four can in theory bring assurance services of real value to investors — but only with realistic and achievable standards, at higher cost, and with tolerable liability limits. The chances of getting there, with the cooperative participation of all the necessary players, may be as unlikely as an invasion of aliens. Today, for all Nocera's good intentions, the process has yet to begin.

Catastrophe Bonds for Auditors — An Idea That Refuses to Stay Dead
In the summer of 2008, during the increasingly antagonistic drama around the global capital markets, George Washington University law professor Lawrence Cunningham addressed the threatened collapse of Big Audit by proposing an alternative to caps on auditor litigation liability.

Namely, as he proposed, the firms should instead issue high-interest "catastrophe bonds" — whose principal would be callable to cover massive litigation awards. His analogy was to the now-familiar "cat bonds," that are triggered to fund losses from hurricanes, floods and other natural disasters. In that sector — a great success in the insurance industry's capacity for invention — the aggregate value of catastrophe bonds outstanding in 2016 approximated $26 billion.

Not that it was wrong for Cunningham to be skeptical of the Big Four's ineffective advocacy in favor of liability caps, as they have continued to resist calls for the financial transparency essential for any credibility on the subject. But he missed the broader public policy issue. The nontrivial likelihood of a disruptive "worst case scenario" continues to extend well beyond the personal cost to its partners of the next Big Four failure — it is also about the reverberations in the capital markets that would follow from the cascading failure of the entire franchise.

The problem in the policy debate has been that the weaknesses in the Big Four's messages do not make viable the alternatives. Although the critique of Cunningham's proposal by insurance expert Kevin LaCroix on his blog, the *D&O Diary*, for September 11, 2007, should have laid its ghost years earlier, it still stirred to life. A brief tour on the basics of insurability shows its lack of feasibility:

Diversity: The essence of real insurance is the spreading of risks — whether life insurance for a broad human population or hurricane bonds across the broad geography of the Caribbean. No life insurance underwriter could survive, that served only insureds from a single hospital ward of the terminally ill. Just so, the concentrated and homogeneous Big Four audit market is exposed to every major corporate collapse anywhere in the world.

Predictability: Dangerous as it is, the annual hurricane season is measurably limited by both calendar and geography. While the Caribbean is exposed, as its natural geographic region, there are no hurricanes in Paris or Chicago. Effective modeling of Mother Nature's habitat gives a confidence level in the expected volume and severity of claims.

By contrast, the Big Four's risks extend across every one of their clients large enough to generate a billion-dollar claim. And the presence of globally recognized names in their litigation inventory illustrates the pervasive nature of their exposures. Models of frequency and severity are simply ineffective to measure and set prices for the extremes of unpredictable events arising out of glob-ally dispersed but isolated cases of human malfeasance.

Independence of Cause and Impact: Mother Nature does not generate hurricanes in order to trigger claims against available insurance or cat bonds. A storm surge will take out a levee, whether it is insured or not. Here Cunningham went astray in his assertion that auditor cat bonds would not "attract suits against auditors because they fund only catastrophic losses, upwards of $500 million."

How could these large sums not be incentives to the plaintiffs' bar? Did anyone ask those advocates for investors whether money talks or not? American lawyers representing shareholder classes or bankruptcy trustees have never shied from auditor liability cases on a multibillion dollar scale, and the existence of a ten-figure honey pot would be well publicized and irresistible — both commercially and as a matter of the ethical obligation of the plaintiffs' lawyers to provide zealous advocacy for the causes of their clients.

Still, the most telling evidence that auditor cat bonds have no pulse is that in recent years the innovators in financial services — whose nose for invention leaves no source of securitization unexplored, and who even now, a decade and counting after exotic mortgage-backed financial derivatives threatened the very stability of the world's capital markets — are back with multi-tranched securitizations of portfolios ranging from student debt to auto loans to single-family rental homes. Even these financial engineers have shied away from taking a flyer on the insurability of auditor performance.

Put another way, if the idea were viable, the bankers and insurers would have been there by now. The combination of greed and ingenuity that transformed portfolios of subprime mortgages and other doubtful debt into the multilayered mountains of toxic financial waste spread across the capital markets was readily transferable. Extending that creative venality, to the cobbling up of an "auditor cat bond," needed only to breathe the life of profits into the body on the laboratory table. And it has never happened.

It is of passing interest that in Bram Stoker's 1897 original, the eponymous Count Dracula was actually able to live and move about in the daylight. But as Supreme Court Justice Louis Brandeis put it more elegantly in a 1913 magazine essay, "sunshine is said to be the best of disinfectants." So illuminated, the idea of catastrophe bonds for auditors deserves its place, tightly closed up in a dark box with the lid nailed shut.

Government-Backed Insurance as a Trade-Off
Blogger Tom Selling suggested in his *Accounting Onion* for June 25, 2008, that there could be a reincarnation of the old "Big

Eight," if "the government could offer to share the litigation exposure from each of the Big Four's prior audit engagements in
exchange for [their] splitting up into two completely separate
firms."

Well, maybe. But anyone thinking that large-company audits
would be helped by hacking up the large firms should consider the
application of Occam's Razor, the tool of logic named for the
14th-century English friar and logician, William of Occam, whose
rule of succinctness stated that all things being equal, the simplest
solution is preferred.

Beyond the purely political issue that auditor liability reform
has forever been an officially toxic topic in Washington, and the
absence of any legal foundation for such slicing and dicing, there
are some practical issues:

First, unless the Big Four were to bifurcate their industry teams,
no new competition would emerge. That is, if a current Big Four
practice serving health care or insurance were spun off as a whole
into one new firm, while its technology or energy practice stayed
intact but went to another, the range of auditor choice within the
group of companies comprising an industry sector would not be
expanded.

And the glacial and ineffective pace of change within the profession itself makes it unlikely that senior experienced audit personnel would have the incentive or take the initiative to retool their
expertise from one industry over to another.

On the other hand, in any fashion that the Big Four firms might
be broken up, it would not reduce the complexity or resources
needed to audit a large global company. For example, each half of
a firm's split-up banking industry practice would still require a
full-bore set of technical and regulatory expertise. With the loss of
economies of scale, duplicating such competence would reduce
efficiency and increase rather than reduce the cost of large-client
engagements.

Second and relatedly, on the issue of performance quality, Selling suggests that the Big Four may have grown "too decentralized to control." But to serve global companies, any Big Four practice cleft in two would still need a serious presence in all the dozens of countries where its clients require service. That challenge of scope, scale and resources has not been solved today by the Big Four's smaller and structurally noncompetitive brethren — and would present an immediate quality challenge to any Big Four offspring.

Which asks the question whether division would be desirable beyond the United States, in countries deemed to be low risk. Are there any such candidates? Significant litigation has originated in engagements or companies as far-flung as Italy, the Netherlands, Russia and South Korea. So countries attractive for audit firm mitosis may be few indeed. And with one or two of the Big Four typically dominant in the larger non-Anglo countries, division of the firms only in the United States might well have perverse effects on concentration elsewhere.

Third, as for the economics of a bailout, leave aside the political improbability that any government would assume an insurance role to insulate a firm from a litigation exposure that might be easily estimated to exceed $100 billion. True, the cost of a rescue would be small change compared with the taxpayer burdens that loomed over such rescues as Fannie Mae and Freddie Mac. But public passions would be even less aroused for auditor salvation than for the country's dominant home mortgage institutions.

The idea is a nonstarter for other reasons, starting with the impracticality of doing a "one-off" solution. That is because protecting the Big Four from *today's* catastrophic litigation threats does nothing for the future. Any new mini-firm would, post-split, still be exposed to the next generation of new cases that — based on half a century of experience — would inevitably arise.

And it would not bode well that smaller, capital-challenged new firms would have only half the financial resources they do now, when today's firms are already facing litigation-driven extinction.

There is one positive glimmer in the heart of Selling's idea — a stand-alone government assumption of the large firms' catastrophic exposures.

Today the Big Four are forced to settle their biggest cases. They lack either insurance or partners' capital robust enough to take the nontrivial risk of going to trial and incurring a punishing adverse outcome.

It cannot be imagined that politicians would create a $100 billion honey pot for the investor plaintiffs and their lawyers to dive into. But there could indeed be created a government-under-written catastrophic reinsurance mechanism or "litigation trust" — which as a form of contingent capital would enable the firms to litigate their cases without fear of a death-blow verdict.

If such a lifeline were available, it could obviate the viability threat. So simplified, the very reasons for the otherwise impractical Big Four split-up could go away. The firms in their current form could then address their twin goals of quality and relevance, without the distractions of imminent overhanging bankruptcy proceedings.

Using Occam's Razor to pare away the parts that fail to benefit audit quality delivery effectiveness, the Selling proposal suggests a financial buffer worthy of consideration. That idea would logically be housed in the proposal outlined here at the end of Part V — for a government-sponsored chartering of firms doing audits of publicly traded companies.

The Auditors' Own Financial Resources — Insignificant Protection
The problem with children, the writer and social critic Fran Leibowitz has said, is that they are seldom in a position to lend you a truly interesting sum of money.

That is the problem with a guaranty of any kind: It is worth no more than the resources standing behind it. And one of the problems with financial statement assurance is the fragility of the private accounting partnerships — whose resources, compared to the risks they undertake, are not material, much less truly interesting.

It is all very well to ask such a question as, "Is there enough competition?" The accountants naturally see themselves as competitive central players. But the imperiled state of the Big Four and their highly concentrated audit franchise sidesteps a crucial issue: Do the Big Four have the wherewithal to stay in the game at all?

A comparison of the resources of the Big Four to the ostensible value of their opinions is one way to assess the basic question of who can and should provide the assurance of the future.

The value of reliance is capped by a guarantor's limits. In the entire credit industry, exposures are linked to ability to pay: the maximum size of a properly underwritten home mortgage is measured by the collateral value of the house; credit card ceilings are tied to payment history; even casino markers are designed to be collected, by means legitimate or not.

The ability to deliver against expectations is questioned everywhere. Bail bonds require sureties. Stock traders have collars on their portfolio exposures. Insurance policies are written with defined risks and fixed limits.

Think beyond the business world. An athlete's pre-game swagger is immediately tested by the scoreboard. The power and protection of multinational diplomacy depend on the strength of the available military and economic forces. Consider — nobody seeks a mutual defense pact or a trading partnership with Zimbabwe or Somalia.

So what is an audit report really worth, to global companies whose individual market capitalizations dwarf the resources of their auditors?

The revenues of the ten largest companies in the Fortune 500 ranged in 2016 from $146 billion for ATT up to $482 billion at Walmart. For comparison (see Part I), the calculations of the liability "tipping points" that would take down one of the Big

Four range globally from three to six billion dollars, and in the United States alone from three to less than one billion — amounts that hardly register against either the size of the companies they audit or the damages that can arise from large claims overhanging the firms themselves.

Those modest amounts effectively limit the amount of "audit insurance" that a large-company purchases to be in compliance with the rules of the securities regulators that require those audits.

Given all this, would it not be rational — not to say normally expected — for an audit committee or a finance director or chief information officer to think this way:

> *"What are we really getting in exchange for our audit fee? A report that nobody reads or values, and insignificant protection in the event we suffer a large-scale financial or audit problem.*

> *"Would it not make more sense to ask our own internal information managers, or our outsourced information systems providers, for assurance on the quality and integrity of our systems and our reporting? They are the ones who design, own and operate the systems, so they are the most informed and best positioned — unlike the outside auditors who perform only a sampling function anyway, and who are constrained by obsolete requirements of independence from immersing themselves deeply in those very systems.*

> *"If only the regulators did not require us to commission and pay for these low-limit, effectively worthless audit reports, we could hire the same outside accounting firms to design and perform work that both we and our investors and bankers would really value."*

No Big Four chief executive could face his partners by admitting the acuity of those messages, and they lack the support of the capital markets to seize the initiative and redesign their business models. But on their behalf, there is a clear message for regulators in Washington and Brussels and London: In a world of globalized capital flows, ready to migrate away from regulatory excess, it is evident that the current system of financial information assurance is not working, and that the best a company can expect in a financial statement disaster may be no more than a billion dollars of auditor support. Absent fundamental redesign, the large companies would — offered the opportunity — logically declare it irrelevant and simply opt out.

On these issues, even Leibowitz would have echoed Groucho Marx: "A child of five would understand this. Send someone to fetch a child of five."

Government Involvement with Big Audit

Could a Government Agency Assign Publicly Financed Audits?

"Full many a flower is born to blush unseen,

And waste its sweetness on the desert air."

— *Thomas Gray, 1751*

Attention by mainstream media to the structural challenges of Big Audit is — for the most part — sporadic, superficial and uninformed. Fully in that mode was the *New York Times* editorial of August 15, 2014, calling for "a revamped system in which audits are paid for not by company management, but by fees that companies pay to a public entity for the purpose of financing audits."

There were three good reasons to be both optimistic and thankful that the *NYT*'s misguided views failed to achieve traction. These were, in ascending order of significance:

First, any print release at the absolute nadir of the annual news cycle, on a Friday in the dog days of August — and on the widely observed holiday of the Feast of the Assumption at that — was bound to be ignored as inconsequential.

Second, two key people were distracted and not listening. Through her tenure, the then-chairman of the SEC, Mary Jo White, had shown no more interest in the accounting profession than her predecessors, Christopher Cox and Mary Schapiro. In any event, White was herself teetering on her back foot; as the *NYT* itself only two days earlier had put it, "she has disappointed a wide swath of would-be allies ... whose opinions of Ms. White's performance range from dissatisfied to infuriated."

While over at the PCAOB, Chairman James Doty had been fully tied up with deciding whether or not audit partners should sign opinions for their firms or in their own names — as discussed later in this part, a long-perplexed but basically trivial matter not worth the years of effort.

The diminished measure of the influence of the agency Doty leads can be seen over the years 2015–2016, when the PCAOB reached auditor inspection protocols with the authorities in Hungary, Greece, Luxembourg and Italy. Pleasant enough countries, these, but so modest in the global capital markets that Hungary has only six PCAOB-registered firms in all, while Greece has seven and Luxembourg has four.

For comparison, the PCAOB's website also shows where its global aspirations remain stymied — listing the issuers "whose PCAOB-registered firm is located in a jurisdiction where obstacles to PCAOB inspections exist." This list is headed by the 43 registered but uninspected firms auditing public companies in the massive economy of China — where successfully evasive politics continue even now to be as slippery and entangled as a bowl of ramen — and most significantly includes issuers based in Hong Kong with mainland Chinese operations, and extending to such otherwise civilized jurisdictions as Belgium, Ireland, Poland and Portugal.

Third, the *NYT*'s endorsement of government-administered audit assignments reflected either naïveté or a lack of understanding of the audit services market — one continuing to operate exclusively on the "client pays" model, as it has since privately provided assurance was invented in the 1850s.

Not that the accountants were or should be free from critical scrutiny. Examples of then-pending legitimate concerns included:

- The very acceptability of the accounting by Lehman Brothers and its auditors, EY, cited by the *NYT* editorial itself.

- The personal conduct of a very small handful of large-firm partners — who in the preceding year had been charged with, and in some cases jailed for, activities across the spectrum of misconduct from misappropriation of firm funds and insider trading, to child abuse and a partner's inappropriate romantic liaison with a client's CFO.

- The settlement announced on August 18, 2014, between the New York State Superintendent of Financial Services and PwC, imposing a $25 million fine and a two-year ban on certain consulting for New York-regulated banks, summarized by the *NYT* as based on the firm's "watering down" of a report on money transfers for blacklisted companies by Bank of Tokyo-Mitsubishi.

The large-company audit market continues under the near-total dominance of the Big Four — whose aggregate 887,000 personnel in fiscal 2016 generated $128 billion in global revenue for their 43,000 partners. For a government agency to assume the administration of the greater part of that sector of professional services — hardly a mere "revamping," as the *NYT* would have it — would present a catalog of challenges unexamined by the *NYT* and unaddressed by even the profession's most rabid critics:

- What single-country government agency could evaluate and compare the global competence, resources and freedom from conflicts of auditor candidates in every one of the several dozen countries where a global-scale company operates and would require audit services?

- What costs and disruptions would the audit networks have to incur, to tender their credentials and proposals to such a government body? And how would their business model mutate, by way of talent and audit performance, if forced to deploy their resources to such a business-seeking process?

- Because government agencies are by their very DNA unable to resist political pressures, what would be the impact of the inevitable lobbying on behalf of small and minority audit firms, lower-tier accounting school graduates and population groups underrepresented in the profession?

- What would be the choice and allocation method? Would auditors bid for appointments? While tempting to politicians, for the revenue-raising impact on an agency's budget, the impact on perceived "independence" would be immediate; so, what pricing mechanism could be functional to provide transparency and integrity?

- Or would engagement assignments be dispensed like government permits? If so, what public confidence could be reposed in light of historical experience with the awards of broadcast licenses, mineral exploration rights, and cable and mobile telephony franchises?

- It would be a significant understatement to observe that the government-contracting industries are pervaded with issues involving change orders, cost overruns and the dynamics of reimbursements. With the multidimensional impacts of delays, impediments and appeals, how would these influences be reconcilable with the need for audit engagement modifications in light of judgmental decisions to expand or adjust audit scope?

- How, if at all, would a regime of government-assigned audits be influenced by the overhanging and overlapping systems for both liability exposure and government oversight and discipline? Put another way, why would the large firms find the risks of such a regime tolerably appealing, without structural modifications sufficient to free their networks from exposure to life-threatening claims and judgments?

In light of these and a host of other questions, how could a government-run process of auditor proposal, selection and monitoring possibly function on a schedule that would enable the delivery of audit reports both timely and informative to the community of interested users?

In short, what possible public legitimacy could an agency achieve, operated under the aegis of a government that has inflicted on its citizens such administrative monstrosities as the Internal Revenue Service, FEMA and healthcare.gov?

A robust public dialog has long been needed on the future of privately provided large-company audits. But it was neither started nor assisted by the *New York Times*.

Audit by Government — More Heat in the Kitchen — And Less Light
If, as just examined, it is impractical to look to government to furnish an agency-based selection and allocation of audit engagements, what might it take to kill off the persistently advanced idea that audits actually performed by government employees could provide value to the world's capital markets?

Like Banquo's ghost in Shakespeare's *Macbeth*, this gruesome specter keeps stalking the discourse on the troubled state of privately provided assurance.

In search for a metaphor with an edge sharp enough to the task, consider — does anyone choosing a restaurant ever give a single second's thought to the local health inspector's report on the state of the kitchen?

Never did a restaurant owner welcome diners or execute a menu with the least consideration of the requirement to pay a nuisance fee, just in order to post on his back wall the same ticket of compliance issued to everyone else — whether a tea shop or burger joint or elite purveyor of haute cuisine.

Nor does that annual documentation provide any significant customer comfort.

Whatever that irrelevant certificate may say, competition applies relentless quality pressure in the narrow-margin food service business. A chef has ample incentive for the sake of survival to conform to the standards generally accepted among his peer group — whether running a gyros wagon or a three-starred temple of gastronomy. With ready access to reviewers' critiques and customers' word-of-mouth — Michelin and Zagats and Trip Advisor — a clientele will quickly vote the extent of their satisfaction and loyalty with their feet.

So, irrespective of the commodity language of the inspector's report, quality and value will quickly reach equilibrium.

On the other hand, the narrow limits of an inspector's box-tick are illuminated by the commentators with inside knowledge. The celebrity ex-chef and international foodie, Anthony Bourdain, in his *Kitchen Confidential: Adventures In The Culinary Underbelly* (2000), exposed to the point of hilarity the nasty secrets of professional kitchens — fully compliant with regulations as they are:

- Never order fish on Monday, because it was likely carried over the weekend.

- The best chance for freshness is the chef's daily special, because of the high volume and extra attention.

- And for salmonella's sake, keep distance from the salad bar, never knowing who or what has been rooting around in it.

Bourdain makes it clear that a restaurant inspector's annual pass-through gives customers no information about what lurks beneath the grease trap or inside the meat cooler — consigning their reliance instead to the combination of peer influence and managerial attention to reputation and survival.

Which should validate the preferability and efficacy of market dynamics, compared to further regulatory intrusion over the audit sector: restaurants, like corporate issuers, fail for multiple reasons, but above a minimal level of legitimacy, not for lack of code compliance.

Just as a health inspector is in no position to assure the quality of a dining experience, audit by government agencies would be helpless in the search for financial statement assurance of any real value — too little, too slow and far too late behind the speed of creative private enterprise.

Government audits could be imposed, of course — especially in the event of a Big Four disintegration. But the impulse would be political, expedient and superficial — primarily under motivations of cover for legislators and secondarily to serve the self-interested bureaucracy that would quickly become entrenched.

And the results would be much like the other models for agency-enforced compliance. Effectiveness would be measured by easily measured inputs rather than defects exposed. Think of the numbers of grandmother pat-downs reported by airport security, or inspections conducted by the PCAOB — neither of which has a record of detection or deterrence for all their effort, disruption and expense.

Other examples abound. Consider drivers' licenses. Above a minimal threshold level, anyone can get one — only to support a large and costly administrative structure interested primarily in its own perpetual existence — while delivering a compliance certificate offering no assurance on the quality of the holder's ability behind the wheel.

The entirely justifiable public dissatisfaction with the institutions at the heart of the financial crisis — Bear Stearns, Lehman Brothers, Merrill Lynch, AIG, Fannie Mae, Freddie Mac,

New Century, Countrywide, Washington Mutual, as the start of the US list; plus endless examples elsewhere that would include banks in the United Kingdom and across Europe — rightly challenges the utility of the current financial reporting model and the performance value of privately delivered assurance.

But great care and caution are required before speculating that the deficiencies of an existing model would be relieved by trashing it for another of uncertain and highly doubtful capabilities.

Or as a percipient restaurant critic might suggest — the leap from a well-seasoned but encrusted frying pan may be into an unknown and far more dangerous fire.

If the Banks Were Nationalized — Why Not the Auditors?

Blogger Francine McKenna had a tart message in October 2008 at *Re: The Auditors* for then-Senate banking committee Chairman Christopher Dodd (D-Conn.):

> *"Demand PwC be fired as AIG's auditors, and get rid of Fannie Mae and Freddie Mac auditors* (Deloitte and PwC, respectively). *Have the PCAOB audit them directly."*

Take Francine's position for discussion, without necessarily agreeing, that the Big Four should have been stripped of their engagements for the large financial institutions subject to government rescue or takeover. At the heart of the concern would have been this problem: with all of the Big Four carrying death-penalty litigation mega-claims, there were no available private alternatives.

Her view was that with Fannie and Freddie taken over — and with the government's controlling position in AIG and its investment in nine of the country's largest banks — its interests and those of taxpayers were best looked after by a government-run audit function as well.

Expand the PCAOB's current remit, she said, or create a new form of "audit inspector general."

Despite a skeptical first reaction, could this have been a plausible path to a reengineering of the model of private assurance — which, as seen in Part I, would be inevitably necessary in the event of a litigation-driven collapse of the Big Four themselves?

There are causes for concern. Here's why:

First, Francine would see no problem in building a federal audit agency. Reality intrudes. In its 2017 budget, the PCAOB aimed to hold its budgeted employee head count steady at the 2016 level of 876 warm bodies. Whereas, to build a remotely credible capability, it would have to multiply by many orders of magnitude, at all experience levels and in worldwide locations — noting that today, the Big Four deploy a total of some 43,000 partners overseeing 887,000 employees.

A hiring pool might be available, of course — the wave of crisis-related failures, bailouts and mergers drastically reduced the population of surviving institutions, so the net loss of clients among the Big Four would have put whole cadres of employees into the job market.

It does require noting, however, that any such hiring would be of those unable to reproduce their big-firm stature and compensation by moving about in the private sector. Staffing a government audit function with the superannuated and the second-rate would not be a recipe for staying ahead of a set of mind-bending problems. And it is depressing to think of the creation of yet another such vast government bureaucracy.

Second, it also bears asking, how the concepts of independence and avoidance of conflicts could be squared with the appearance of one agency of government auditing the investments of another. But because any intellectually sound argument for "independence in fact" gave way decades ago with the rationalized acceptability of "client pays," it would be a short if facile step to condone a cross-Washington audit function.

Third, as for the questionable value in the market place of a report both by and for the government, the current one-page "pass-fail" audit report is already a no-value anachronism, useful only for statutory compliance but failing to show its worth to investors. So it could as well be done by a collection of civil servants, with the diminished level of attention and respect it would deserve.

Government assumption of audit responsibility for the bailed-out financial institutions would, however, have opened this tempting door:

Even under state ownership, these huge and complex financial institutions would still have undiminished future needs for sophisticated and specialized assurance — in such areas as financial product design and evaluation, process execution and operational soundness — which the Big Four should be both able and enthusiastic to design and deliver.

Freed from delivery of low-value but litigation-exposed statutory audits, they should in reason be evolving their services — but, if and only if, under contractual terms unburdened by the threat of investor claims.

To be sure, for the sake of transparency and accountability of public funds, these large financial institutions themselves might well choose to share with the outside world the reports they would obtain from the Big Four (or the niche providers which could arise by spin-off or new growth) — but they would be prudent and risk-sensitive enough to do so only under strict limitations of warranty and liability.

Both the potential stream of new revenue and the liability relief offered under such a model could be heady stuff for the Big Four, who might well see the potential to extend such a model across the entire spectrum of public companies.

In practice, they could tender to a new government audit agency the keys to their now-outmoded franchise — thereby finally unshackling themselves from its unsustainable burden. By evolving into sources of real user value, they would escape the looming fate of catastrophic collapse.

Senator Dodd's retirement from political leadership was pending, it is true. But when he did not give Francine the courtesy of a response, it seemed a little ungracious, for a politician savvy enough about the new media to run his own blog and subscribe to an instant message platform.

Especially when she had lit the fuse on an issue ripe for political leadership.

Unified Structures — Could the Big Four Think Local, But Act Global?[1]

The American humorist Jean Kerr, paraphrasing the much-quoted advice in Rudyard Kipling's 1895 poem — "If" — wrote that "if you can keep your head when all about are losing theirs … it's just possible you haven't grasped the situation."

Which may explain why one very good idea's time has not yet come.

Observers of the continuing troubled state of the Big Four have urged that these aggregations of local-country entities should evolve into truly unified worldwide partnerships. It hasn't happened yet. Might it?

There is need and desire at the global level for consistent, high-quality accounting advice and audit services. Large companies have widely dispersed locations, suppliers and customers, and increasingly, outsourcing of all kinds — all of which can pose material threats to their operations and their financial results.

Global lenders and agencies — such as the World Bank, the International Monetary Fund, the regional development banks and the Organization for Economic Cooperation and Development — have loan portfolios and other undertakings in countries whose accounting and reporting standards range from primitive to nonexistent.

Yet, while the large accounting networks defend their common branding and integrated breadth of services as responsive to their clients' calls for one-stop delivery, their critics charge that standards, practices and quality vary widely across borders.

All participants in the conversation about quality decry the fragmented national systems for regulation and standard-setting. And the history of locally required oversight should lack force in today's world. With globalized communications, knowledge-sharing and enterprise structures, parochial regulation should be no more than a speed bump on the road to unified audit structures.

There is, after all, a model — or at least there used to be. Over its history back to the 1970s, the Arthur Andersen organization uniquely demonstrated that the economic fortunes of its worldwide partners could be tied closely together. The cost-sharing structure of the Andersen Worldwide Société Coopérative, a Swiss form of partnership in which the individual Andersen worldwide partners were members, meant that both the profits of each local-country practice and the coverage of losses necessary to build a practice in a new country or to carry through a temporary economic slump were direct and immediate pocket-book issues for each Andersen partner.

The most cohesive of the then-Big Eight global networks, in both its governance and in the shared and highly profitable financial fortunes of its partners, Andersen had addressed with success the perceived barriers of local regulation. Its legendary culture of discipline and consistency — subject to the constant tensions of distance, language and culture — had a great run.

The surviving Big Four firms have done some regionalizing of their global structures: EY, for example, organizes its country practice entities in the Americas, Europe and Asia (except Japan), and Africa, under separate coordinating and governance entities — at the same time disavowing that they engage in client services or control or manage the local firms. And in the fall of 2016, Deloitte announced the combination of its firms in nine countries, to form "Deloitte North West Europe," headquartered in London.[2]

But no large network has achieved the financial and organizational unity that marked Andersen's best days. There is a simple reason.

The flaw in Andersen's achievement was exposed in the dynamics of its disintegration in the winter of 2002. Effectively a set of treaties, it was a structure brilliantly engineered for success, with a level of financial prosperity the envy of the profession. But a trust-based structure was no match for the destabilizing pressures of litigation on the modest capital base of a group of private partnerships.

As mightily as the Big Four strive today to firewall the liability exposure of their individual practices, they are caught by the unavoidable demands of multinational practice. To provide assurance for global clients, they must cross borders with their people, their working papers and their opinions. Examples of the multinational demand: part of the engagement responsibility of PwC, the auditor for Ford in America, was the need to audit Jaguar and Land Rover in Britain — an obligation handed over to Deloitte in Mumbai when those marques were later sold to Tata Motors, its client in India. With its engagement based in Turin to audit Fiat SpA, EY had to be on the ground in the United States as the company absorbed Chrysler.

The Andersen model showed that shared prosperity was a powerful sustaining force for a cohesive global partnership. Unfortunately — proving yet again that in organizational as well as accounting terms, debits always equal credits — the unacceptable prospect of sharing the global litigation exposure due to Enron was enough to smash the Andersen organization into shards no bigger than a single country.

In Kipling's Victorian world it could be urged with a virtuously straight face that those twin impostors, Triumph and Disaster, should be treated the same. Today, the price tag for worldwide partnership loyalty is too high. As Andersen showed, nobody is willing to stick around and pay it.

Outside Capital — What Money Can't Fix[3]

Billy Rose, the legendary Broadway producer of the 1920s and 1930s, offered a maxim to anyone hoping to replicate his success: "Never invest your money in anything that eats." Rose was referring to showgirls and racehorses, but his admonition could apply equally to accountants and auditors.

In a report released in March 2007, the US Chamber of Commerce, trade group and lobbyist for American business, advanced the notion that client service by the Big Four would be better provided if the accounting firms could bring in outside investors, sourced from private equity or the venture capitalists.

The Big Four are stretched to their limits by their expansion ambitions, the corporate governance reporting requirements of Sarbanes-Oxley, and the threats and realities of multibillion dollar litigation liability. Cash infusions, the Chamber argued, would either support survival-level insurability, or encourage the creation of new firms to lighten the load and provide competition.

The business group's report — part of the growing body of commentary bemoaning the erosion of American competitiveness in world capital markets — did make some good points. It called for cooperation among domestic and international policy makers, and suggested that US-based auditors of public companies might better operate and be regulated under national government charter, supplanting the current patchwork of state-level authority.

But on the issue of outside capital, for several reasons, the report was wrong. Outside capital is not a solution.

For starters, what would be the real role of venture funding or private equity in a global accounting partnership? The Big Four business model is that the firms are capitalized by their partners' collective contributions, with the partners sharing the profits. So funded, the firms already manage and run their global operations today on the modest working capital provided by their individual partners. Simply put, they have no need for outside money.

And since no capital comes cost-free, individual Big Four partners would have to vote away major portions of their current personal profits to pay the handsome return on investment that outside investors would demand.

If the idea is that fattening the firms' balance sheets would cushion a huge litigation charge, then it is doubly perverse. If increased capital acts as a form of self-insurance, a simpler solution is immediately available: New insurance companies *might* provide the Big Four with high-limit coverage that is not available today.

The trouble is, the business case goes the other way: Insurance coverage at the multibillion dollar level is not available to the Big Four, at any price. As already discussed, rational insurance industry decision-makers have long ago seen the accountants as effectively uninsurable, at levels high enough to be meaningful to their survival.

And for the other perversity, exposing any additional capital to the hazard of litigation claims of investor plaintiffs would only feed the beast of litigation. The economics are basic: prices rise to eat up available subsidies. If dog food costs $1 a can, and for public policy reasons a subsidy of $1 is made available, the consumers' cost immediately becomes $2.

The same goes for litigation settlements. Andersen's defunct US unit eventually settled its litigation with Enron's shareholders for $72.5 million — the most the plaintiffs could get out of the dry husk of this once-great enterprise. But prior to Andersen's disintegration in 2002, plaintiffs had hailed the pending agreement-in-principle by Andersen relating to Enron, anticipated to be the first billion-dollar settlement payment from an audit firm — an outcome frustrated only by the death of the Andersen global structure, the goose that laid those golden eggs.

The Chamber's other argument in favor of outside capital was to finance new competitors to the Big Four. But studies from 2006 by two consultancies, London Economics and Oxera, concluded that creation of a Big Fifth or Sixth would require talent, funds and risk appetites that simply did not exist, nor could be available to be built or bought at any price. Shrinkage to the critically small quartet has followed a natural, inevitable and irreversible evolutionary course. There is neither incentive nor authority to expand — not among the Big Four, their smaller brethren nor the clients — and certainly not with regulators.

Finally, despite Billy Rose's caution, money is not the issue. Venturesome capital has an insatiable and nearly unreasoning appetite, with an urge to engulf and devour that, at the time of the Chamber's study, had run from the Four Seasons hotels to Boots pharmacies to Madame Tussaud's wax museums.

And the deals have only grown: If inflation-adjusted, the 1989 buyout of RJR Nabisco for $31 billion would reach about $60 billion and still set the mark, although challenged by the $45 billion price for TXU. The size of these transactions, which would put in play even Deloitte's profession-leading 2016 revenue of $36.8 billion, would be well enough within the grasp of ambitious private equity, but only if sufficiently motivated to believe there was a payoff.

In other words, if those deploying private equity funding had ever seen a compelling case to invest in the accountants' business, they would already be there.

Pumping outsiders' funds into the accounting firms is a solution nobody wants, for a problem that their money cannot solve.

Forensic Audits to Detect Fraud

Of the succession of SEC chairmen in this century, some sympathy for the limitations on his impact in office should be extended to Harvey Pitt — whose 18-month tenure was doubly handicapped by his political overreaching for cabinet status, and the critics' interpretation of his announced promise of a "kinder and gentler" agency as a dog-whistle signal of accommodationism to his friends on Wall Street.

In November 2002, as Pitt headed toward the exit door through which he was to revolve in February, he did unleash one last idea: that the agency should require public companies to submit to a "forensic audit" — that is, an audit specifically designed to detect fraud, to be done by a second auditing firm.

Although Pitt had shown himself politically tone-deaf, that did not mean that all his ideas were automatically unworthy of examination.

After all, the auditors had long before set themselves up for criticism, with the limitations on their work directly and explicitly conceded in their literature. *The Auditor's Responsibilities Relating to Fraud in an Audit of Financial Statements*, ¶ 5 of International Standard on Auditing 240, states that "owing to the inherent limitations of an audit, there is an unavoidable risk that some material misstatements of the financial statements may not be detected, even though the audit is properly planned and performed in accordance with [those standards]."

That is — as conceded, and as stated in the profession's standards and communicated to users via the auditor's report, but broadly unaccepted by nonprofessional readers whose expectations are of "zero defects" — even a properly designed and executed audit may not detect management fraud or other manipulations — whether because of intentional acts of company personnel or collusion with outside parties.

And this limitation is layered with two more. The first is the issue of elastic accounting principles. The second is the inherently limited nature of the audit process.

So, was Pitt on to something? A number of questions require attention — the central one is whether so-called forensic auditors would bring anything new or valuable to the party.

There is, regrettably, no clear path through the fuzzy definitions and self-promotion. "Forensic" means — briefly but not too helpfully — "for use in legal proceedings," or more generally, in argumentation or disputes. Those engaged in and promoting the business itself employ a more elastic concept: the investigation and pursuit of indicators of fraud, accounting irregularities or diversions of company resources.

As defined by its practitioners, then, forensic auditing is a perfectly legitimate area of endeavor. But its role and scope should not be exaggerated. Fraud squads are not set loose until someone else has squealed. Most often, an innocent employee has stumbled onto a problem too large or bizarre to explain away. Occasionally there is a conscience-stricken insider or whistle-blower; sometimes it is a short-seller or disaffected analyst. Only too rarely is it the regular statutory auditor.

In medieval military terms, forensic auditors are not front-line soldiers on the field of battle. They rather resemble the post-bloodshed scavengers, who creep onto the battle scene the morning after, to bayonet the enemy wounded and loot the corpses.

For example: confronted with the dizzying array of entities and transactions at Enron, all at the cutting edge of industry specialization, exotic financial product design and dazzling accounting complexity, a "forensic" team — with a background in expense account fiddling or diversion of petty cash — would have been at least as subject to the snow job from Enron's glib and facile Andrew Fastow and Jeffrey Skilling as were the members of Andersen's regular engagement team.

To generalize, forensic auditors would have no good effect on management's aggressive application of accounting principles that offer the flexibility and opportunism demanded by today's corporate issuers.

Elsewhere, they might have an effect in the detection — and, remotely, perhaps even the prevention — of corporate frauds of the small-change variety: the trusted executive secretary who skims a couple of million off the credulous boss's expense account; the assistant treasurer who diverts a few thousand a month to fund a girlfriend in the Bahamas.

But what might they have made, for example, of the activities of Frank Walsh, the former director of Tyco International Ltd., who in 2001 elected not to disclose his $20 million finder's fee for broking the deal to acquire his former company, CIT Group. Caught out, Walsh later cut himself another great deal, coordinating with both the SEC and state prosecutors in New York: In return for giving back that fee and paying a fine of just $2.5 million, he settled all his problems and received a "Get Out of Jail Free" card.

The SEC's announcement of December 17, 2002, referred to Walsh's "clandestine payments and hidden deals." But what reason is there to believe that an auditor bearing the label "forensic" — who would lack formal investigative or subpoena power — would have elicited from Walsh any more complete or truthful disclosure than the normal process would, or should, have done?

In short, it is one thing to be led to the smoke and flames emanating from a multibillion dollar manipulation of a financial statement, and to be asked to backtrack the entries that stoked the blaze. It is quite another to look at an ostensibly clean situation and successfully ask, "If there is anything seriously wrong here, where would it be, and how might we find it?"

Pitt's forensic audit idea confronted other relevant questions, treated elsewhere in the context of the limited range of choices available in a market of constrained auditor choice, and the paralysis that prevents the development and deployment of truly useful assurance products:

- In a market in which large companies already face few if any real options in the selection of auditors, who would be available to do such work if asked?

- And given the devastating exposure confronting a Big Four auditor trapped in the litigation consequences of a large-scale fraud, if effective fraud-oriented "forensic audits" truly existed as a realistic tool for the identification and management of financial statement risk, would they not already be deployed on a routine basis?

The forensic auditors have not demonstrated an ability to predict where corporate fraud will next rear its head. So it must be for managements and the audit committees of their boards, not legislators or regulators, to decide how much a company should invest in the scrutiny of its people and its processes — in its auditors and its own governance and system of controls. And ultimately, the capital markets will have the last word on a company's reputation and record.

Joint Audits — Nobody's Answer

Joint audit — that is, the shared responsibility of two or more firms for the issuance of audit reports that together provide complete assurance coverage of a set of financial statements — is occasionally floated as a source of support for the emergence of large-company competence on the part of smaller audit firms or networks, and as a measure of quality control on the performance of an audit engagement.

Neither argument withstands scrutiny — as shown mainly by the nearly complete absence of adoption of joint audits in any developed economy, other than those where the lobbying force of the small firms with their country regulators has enabled them to keep their seats, down at the foot of the table.

Scandinavian countries, for example, have evolved steadily away from the use of joint audits, under regimes that have gradually eliminated joint-audit requirements.

The country where the system survives — France — does so only with the presence of a number of smaller players. There, it is notable that, of the large companies comprising the country's main securities index, the CAC 40, all of them have a Big Four firm as their principal auditor, and 27 have a second Big Four firm in the joint auditor's role.

Put another way, if improved market-driven satisfaction with large-company audit competence were achievable through the engagement participation of a smaller network, the French experience would have evolved to the point where a smaller firm would be engaged on lead — and perhaps with at least one large French company jointly audited by two of the smaller firms.

Instead, the history of large-scale audit failures illustrates the dangers inherent in the division of responsibilities between two firms.

The notorious example from the early days of significant auditor liability was that of Equity Funding, the insurance and mutual fund complex, based in Los Angeles, that flamed out in a spectacular collapse in 1973, with criminal proceedings against both its own senior management and members of one of the audit teams involved.

There, division of audit responsibility between two firms — the larger Haskins & Sells, as it then was, and the Wolfson Weiner firm as recently merged into Seidman & Seidman — enabled the perpetrators to run a Ponzi scheme based on the creation of bogus customers and the use of reinsurance to lay off liability to pay death benefits on these fictitious individuals thereby generating real cash.

A generation later, Parmalat in Italy perpetuated a €20 billion scheme, again through the use of bogus accounts — principally and tellingly enough, the notorious *buco nero* ("black hole") — a name crying out to be flagged as a warning — and the division of audit responsibility forced on the engagement by the Italian requirement for periodic auditor rotation — thus splitting responsibility between Deloittes and Grants.

Finally, underappreciated in the faint and limited advocacy in favor of joint audits is the problem of cross-border liability. The auditing standards themselves effectively require a lead audit firm to assume 100% responsibility for an entire engagement, since to do otherwise requires report wording that carves out those areas for which the lead firm disavows such responsibility[4] — a form of auditor's report that is unacceptable to the major securities exchanges and regulators.

Coupled with this self-inflicted limitation, auditors in an international environment would confront the typical applicability of a "joint and several" liability regime — meaning that whatever limited scope of liability they might enjoy in their home country — again taking the historically lower level of litigation in France as an example — their exposure in an Anglo court system would be complete and total, despite the limited nature of their participation in an engagement.

In short — as may be briefly put — the notion of joint audit as a useful tool by which to address any aspect of the structural challenges to the present global regime is far-fetched and lacking in persuasiveness.

Naming the Audit Partners — Will a "Red A" Really Matter?

In a second revival of a project going back to 2009, the PCAOB on December 4, 2013, reproposed, in its Release 2013-009, Docket Matter No. 029, a requirement that audit firms disclose the names of their responsible engagement partners.

In the search for magic bullets aimed at the structural weaknesses perceived in Big Audit, "partner naming" may have been an idea whose time had become politically irresistible, but it was and remains a distinctly small-bore and ineffective weapon.

With persistence, the PCAOB pressed for information:

- Of no consequence to financial statement users sophisticated and informed enough to appreciate both the complexity and the value limits of the audit. (*See* the discussion above on the negligible effect of the partner-based independence issues on the stock prices of Ventas and Herbalife.)

- Of indifference to the bulk of the investor population — already hard pressed even to identify, much less to differentiate, the Big Four firms that audit their portfolio companies.

- Of interest mainly to the critics of the profession, for whom access to individual names would only fuel their continued antagonism.

After 18 months of inactivity, other than frequent promises of further action, Chairman Doty announced on June 22, 2015, and released on June 30, a supplemental request for public comment to consider a rule requiring a new approach by which audit firms would name their lead engagement partners — ultimately emerging in May 2016 for effect January 31, 2017, as a new Form AP.

The triviality of the approach was visible: rather than solve the substance of the American profession's concern with enhanced individual partner exposure, the form would, in Doty's words, "reduce auditors' *perception* of litigation risk" (*emphasis added*).[5]

The naming of partners had been steadily and intensely opposed by the American accounting profession, although long in place in much of the world without measurable adverse effects.

Those charged with auditor selection already knew the details of the firms' personnel and their qualifications. Client managements and audit committees in the United States have never lacked access to the decision-qualifying information necessary about the engagement leaders at their audit firms.

On the other hand, over on the side of public "transparency," branding individual auditors with the scarlet letter "A" might give satisfaction akin to that of the censorious townsfolk around Nathaniel Hawthorne's Hester Prynne.

But to what end? As recognized by PCAOB member Lewis Ferguson, in his remarks on October 11, 2011, when the project was in its first revival, any engagement partner whose work is caught up in multiyear civil litigation and regulatory enforcement effectively suffers the end of his productive career. Even if the partner is judgment-proof and indemnified, the overwhelmingly distracting time demands and the emotional toll of defending even high-quality performance are ruinous to the capacity to exercise complex professional judgment.

Which did not, to take the other side, mean that the US profession's resistance to partner identification was a "hill worth dying on." Partner signature is the practice around Europe, and some European filers so disclose in their filings in America. So the passionate arguments of the US profession against partner naming were undercut by the absence of serious difficulties under the practice in Europe.

Because the world had not come to an end due to partners' report-signing in Europe, however, a proof-seeking skeptic might well ask this: Are European shareholders really so "favored" over their American counterparts, or is it rather that the markets have compared the availability of partner names, and yawned with boredom?

Again, this is a matter on which investors have shown indifference — it being impossible to imagine that they are really engrossed on the subject, when they must suppose that local-country rules on professional qualifications and rights to practice would be no less applicable for auditors than, for example, for lawyers or doctors.

The case that individual partner performance quality would be positively affected by name disclosure was not supported. In Europe, a vacuum of evidence in favor of partner naming combines with an absence of elevated professional virtue. And in the United States, a "name-that-partner" exercise still leaves gaping holes in the base of information. That is:

First, of course, the discovery of rogue partners such as those pleading guilty to the use of inside information[6] involved post-exposure revelations — as to which any prior personal disclosure would have provided no informational value at all.

Second, to be serious, arguments in favor of the disinfectant effects of disclosure should require publication of entire partner lists. That is because the Big Four routinely move senior-level partners among roles involving consultation, concurrence, job review or standard-setting — which under the guidance of Form AP will not require either individual rotation or disclosure.

The many examples are to one effect:[7]

- The question of naming PwC's lead partner on its engagement for Jon Corzine's failed MF Global makes the point: that particular partner seems to have had broad industry-based involvement across the firm's financial services clients, but not in the putatively disclosable capacity as a lead audit partner.

- The partner heading EY's national office was criticized by the SEC in 2009, over its client Bally Total Fitness, not in an engagement capacity at all, but on the basis of one problem-oriented telephone call in 2003.

- KPMG's engagement partner on Xerox, for only one of the four years for which it was charged by the SEC, went on to a senior-level role from which he eventually retired.

- And the Andersen partner who figured in the government's criticism of the application of the firm's document retention policy in Enron, had been the subject of a prior SEC proceeding in 2001 related to Waste Management, not as engagement partner but as an audit practice director in 1995.

Finally, the firms themselves are powerfully incentivized to evaluate and manage any exposure created by the activities of their personnel under legal or regulatory scrutiny.

Early in my courtroom career, my law firm defended one of the then-Big Eight in an entire portfolio of lawsuits involving the clients of a single audit partner — who, as his genial ineptitude became apparent to the world, was a virtual Typhoid Mary of litigation exposure.

Briefly put, that firm quite rightly deserved the expanded civil litigation exposure it attracted, for failure to identify and firewall this at-risk partner as soon as it became known — as a viral exception to its usually high-quality standards — that every job he touched was infected.

With that, a large-firm partner ensnared in a major lawsuit, investigation or enforcement proceeding is, to use the euphemism, already "career impaired." The protracted and unpredictable timetable of judicial proceedings is personally deadening to the soul and the spirit, as well as the capacity to function. No useful purpose is served by publicly drenching such a partner under an opprobrious black cloud.

Leadership Replacement to Save a Collapsing Firm — A Nonstarter

Over the brief years of its existence, the performance of the body announced in May 2007 at the behest of the younger President Bush by Treasury Secretary Henry Paulson — denominated the "Advisory Committee on the Auditing Profession" — amply justified the skepticism of its critics.

The Committee was touted by the Secretary, "to develop recommendations as to what can best be done to sustain a vibrant auditing profession, a profession whose work is critical to investor confidence in our capital markets."

In action, the Committee's membership and activities were so politically calibrated that they were unable to reach a consensus even on the basic notion that the stability of the Big Four's audit franchise faced serious challenges to its survivability. Their insubstantial outputs have managed to sink without a trace.

The one time they did advance a substantive idea, it was positively breathtaking in its misguided impracticality.

On April Fools' Day of 2008, the Committee put forward, in apparent seriousness, the notion that the partners in the large audit firms, anticipating the possibility of a catastrophic threat — that is, a fatal litigation claim or prosecution-based penalty — should voluntarily modify their organizational agreements to trigger the replacement of their leadership. Or failing such a step, the SEC should be authorized to apply in court for a trustee.[8]

As Oscar Wilde described his reaction to a plot by Charles Dickens, it would require a heart of stone to read this pathetic work without dissolving into tears of hysterical laughter.

Who could possibly decide? In the history of leadership, the concept of anticipatory abdication is a complete nonstarter. Especially under challenge, leaders believe with passion and conviction that they can work through their crises, and will fight to the death to stay in office.

In the political sphere, leaders from Louis XVI to Richard Nixon to Robert Mugabe to Mohammed Morsi have shown the inability or unwillingness to anticipate their own downfall.

Business and professional leaders are no different. Would Jimmy Cayne at Bear Stearns or Dick Fuld at Lehman Brothers or Jon Corzine at MF Global have authorized a script for their own defenestration? Sepp Blatter at the *Fédération Internationale de Football Association* defiantly resisted any thought of either transparency or succession, ahead of the Untouchables-like raids coordinated in May 2015 by American and Swiss law enforcement, based on charges that he had presided for decades over a systemically corrupt autocracy.

Or, would the shareholders or directors of UBS or Northern Rock — or, for that matter, of Enron or WorldCom — have enacted advance terms for the displacement of their executives? Is it any more likely that the managing partners of the Big Four would willingly turn over their careers and their fortunes to an outside stranger?

But if not done by leaders themselves, who would pull the trigger? An external decision-maker would be required to be credible to all constituents, to be at least as informed as management itself, and to be presciently ready to act decisively at a moment's notice.

But the corporate world does not keep world-class crisis managers stocked in reserve. Anyone meeting those job definitions already has his energy and talents fully committed elsewhere.

Nor, paying respects to the gray eminences who populate the advisory committees themselves, is this a function to bolster the resumes of the retired. The learning curve of a real-time audit firm survival crisis would be too steep to climb, by those for whom robust knees and lungs are only the memories of youth.

As for the notion of timely SEC intervention, the Treasury Committee's members themselves grasped at least two among the fatal flaws:

First is the issue of timing. Andersen disintegrated in a matter of weeks in 2002, following the tardy but eventual capitulation of its CEO and an aborted effort to bring in outside leadership. Even the provisions of the American Constitution for the temporary transfer and resumption of presidential powers contemplate a timetable of nearly four weeks[9] — far too long in an emergency context.

Second, who is to recognize the need? The PCAOB, regulator of the profession in the United States, disavows responsibility for audit firm viability as outside its remit, and rightly so. The timing and scope of that body's practice quality sampling program is already all it can handle.

Which leads to the unrecognized crux. The Committee's supposed rationale for a rehabilitation process was that new leadership might preserve a firm by dealing more successfully with its litigation adversaries or prosecuting authorities than those on the scene of the wreck.

But such a view, while real, entirely missed the broader point.

Namely, as should have been learned from the Andersen experience — or more recently in and after the era of financial crisis — the franchise value for those selling commodity products rests entirely on the preservation of trust, and not just on fresh negotiating positions or the appearance of new faces. Once the fuse is lit and a credible challenge to that trust has started to run — whether doubts about the "safety and soundness" of an investment bank or eroded "client confidence" for an audit firm — it is already too late, and an explosive disintegration is inevitable.

Finally, it is argued that the SEC's power to apply for a trustee — even if "in the pocket" and never expected to be used — would be an incentive to the firms to improve.

But again, that naïve view defies reality. Big Four leaders already know that they face death-threat exposures today. So if at the brink they would not be saved by SEC intervention — and when existing leadership will have been cashiered in any event — a regulatory tool that is both inutile and ineffective would, if anything, create a disincentive to constructive change.

There is value to wild and unworkable schemes: they can focus attention on what really can and needs to be done. The Treasury Committee's proposal for anticipatory management replacement served its purpose, as a source of humor and ridicule. It can now rest in peace, in the graveyard of bad ideas — as it deserved from the outset.

A Useful New Auditor's Report? The Current Initiatives Lack Real Promise

It has been clear for years, as already discussed, that the familiar language of the standard auditor's report is no longer deemed satisfactory by its intended users.

It has, indeed, been downhill for auditors' reporting ever since Mr. Deloitte's terse report — "Audited and approved" — of February 8, 1850.

This section will explore some of the activities now underway.

The PCAOB's Eventual "Game Change" Proposal — Only Small Change

A realistic assessment of the PCAOB's *Concept Release* of June 21, 2011, which tabled a buffet of possible revisions to the long-standing commodity language, was that it at least put the US regulator's stamp on the vital question, posed by Chairman James Doty during the public meeting, "how audit reports can be more useful to society?"

But optimism was to be carefully tempered. Doty's initiative only reflected the latest in the cycles of user dissatisfaction, going back to such barely remembered efforts as the Cohen Commission of 1974 and the Treadway Commission of 1985.

Vision and will have consistently turned to failure, overtaken by the return of bubbly investor enthusiasm.

In an updating on August 13, 2013, Chairman Doty described the proposed report changes to "mark a watershed moment." When the applause died down, a cooler perspective could see this as mere tinkering — not so much a "game change," but rather raising the stakes from a penny to a nickel.

That was because the PCAOB had played it small all the way. The statement by Board member Steven Harris emphasized "the need *not* to change what auditors do, but to change how they report what they do" (*emphasis his*). Board member Lewis Ferguson concurred, noting that "the standard does not require the auditor to do any additional work."

To focus on what auditors currently *do*, however, missed entirely the point of investor concern. The famous and misunderstood "Expectations Gap" has never been about what auditors *do*.

The gap does not even exist, in the minds or the behavior of investors, until it yawns open after a major corporate fraud or failure.

"Where were the auditors?" does not concern transparency or the disclosed detail of audit work, but the dereliction perceived in the inability to detect or prevent a manifest problem — whether the collapse of Enron or the thievery of Bernie Madoff.

Investors are not demanding more nuanced word-smithing in the PCAOB's standards about, for example, the auditors' attention to an issuer's information outside the financial statements themselves — as between the impossibly elusive articulation of a distinction between whether they only "read and consider" or they indeed "read and evaluate."

What users *do* want are answers about events that actually move share prices — although these are questions that neither the auditors' work nor the PCAOB's changes can ever hope to reach. They include questions such as:

- Might a particular pyramid-structured company — Herbalife comes to mind — turn out to be a Ponzi scheme?

- Could a technology company whose customer base is concentrated on a device that is aging and obsolete, or perhaps fire-prone — Blackberry, perhaps, or Samsung — actually survive in a world of fast-paced and constantly evolving competition?

- How far did the corroded culture run at Wells Fargo, that incentivized the pervasive creation of fictitious customer accounts, into other areas of the bank's operations?

- Which financial institution might be most likely to suffer the next rogue trader at its derivatives desk?

Five years after issuance of its *Concept Release*, the PCAOB in May 2016 issued its reproposed standard — directly facing (if not solving) its own concession, that *"the current form of the auditor's report does little to address the information asymmetry between investors and auditors."*

The small-scale scope of the PCAOB's aspirations was shown in its charge to the profession:

- "Limiting the source of potential critical audit matters to matters communicated or required to be communicated to the audit committee."

- "Narrowing the definition to only those matters that involved *especially* challenging, subjective, or complex auditor judgment ..." (*emphasis added*).

Only one thing is definite, as the finalization of this proposal remains pending — with its expected requirement that the auditors identify so-called "critical audit matters," the PCAOB's anxiety about a bull market in boiler-plate language is well founded. Defensive file stuffing will prevail, as the Big Four prepare for second-guessing in their future PCAOB inspections. That is, the process will proceed in two layers: PCAOB interrogators will not only be asking, "Why was this issue *not* deemed a 'critical audit matter' at all?" They will also press, "How did you decide that this 'critical' matter, which you did identify, did *not* also require disclosure?"

It may be safely predicted that — as a means of fending off the PCAOB's ticket-counting inspection process — every Big Four audit in the United States will very quickly be found to have some minimum number of "critical audit matters."

Moreover, similarities across sectors and industries are far greater than individual differences between companies. For some examples: Every bank has issues with provisions for nonperforming loans. The entire technology sector has been challenged by revenue recognition in all the years since IBM pioneered its manipulation. Any enterprise with significant international operations will have potential issues with both currency exchange-rate fluctuations and the risks of local-country political volatility. So the pick-list of those items will quickly become standardized.

On the other hand, on such significant issues as those in the recent great collapses — Bear Stearns and Lehman Brothers and Merrill, MF Global and Knight Capital, SAC and Valeant — it is right to question whether auditors might have contributed positively, by way of targeted scrutiny and assurance, for the benefit of management, boards and investors alike.

But it could not have happened, and will not — not under the small-bore thinking of "no more work — only more words."

And not so long as the assurance model is hostage to today's binary "pass-fail" report — accurately described by PCAOB member Ferguson as something at which "they merely glance … to make sure that the opinion is unqualified …."

Can Value Be Brought Back to the Auditor's Report — A Tale of Two Systems

Is it the best of times, in the struggle to reintroduce value into the traditional auditor's report — or the worst of times? The age of wisdom or the age of foolishness?

The IAASB brought to its 2011 project the essential combination of intelligence and technical skills. Charged with the promulgation of international standards on auditing (ISAs), it is conversant with such abstruse but centrally relevant topics as the auditor's responsibility for published information other than financial statements (ISA 720), and use of "emphasis of matter" and other paragraphs in an auditor's report (ISA 706).

Where the IAASB may suffer a gap is in its lack of muscle to carry out its aspirations. Sponsorship and support of senior regulators are required — which makes essential the role of those in America. That is because there, a legislative reengineering of the liability landscape is essential, since assurance in any innovative area can only be designed and delivered if relieved from

the devastating exposure to the litigation threat of hindsight second-guessing that today shackles the auditors to their obsolete
model.

Fantasize, for a moment, the arrival of an "age of wisdom" in
which the IAASB and the PCAOB could have made common
cause. What might have been accomplished?

The IAASB's initial release looked at possible adjustments to
the current report itself — whether to move the opinion paragraph
to the top, or to push the explanatory language to a footnote. But
cosmetics should be seen as inconsequential; knowledgeable readers would be neither confused nor influenced by this syntactical
rearrangement, and others simply would not care.

The IAASB did press into important new territory, recognizing
"the demand for additional, and more pertinent, information
about entities and the processes that support the quality of their
financial information."

Its delicate suggestion of "perceptions that auditor reporting is
not meeting the needs of financial statement users" was a rhetorical bow to the tensions among competing constituencies and an
understandable retreat into euphemism. But it was possible to
tease out of the IAASB's sensitivity a blunt call for the desired
removal of this barrier to clear thinking and precise articulation:
today's audit report is obsolete and, beyond fulfilling the requirements of statutory compliance, it delivers no real user value.

If it were an old horse, it would be given due respect for its decades of dumb loyalty — then the wornout old nag would be led
off to the knacker's yard and given the humane dispatch its historically good service deserves.

Within the scope of the IAASB's standard-setting, it listed readily identifiable subjects for auditor contribution:

• Corporate governance arrangements.

• Business model, including sustainability.

- Enterprise-wide risk management.

- Internal controls and financial reporting processes.

- Key performance indicators.

The release further tabled the desirability and value of auditor insights in such financial reporting issues as:

- The quality of the entity's internal controls and financial reporting processes.

- Qualitative aspects of the entity's accounting policies, including the relative conservatism or aggressiveness reflected in management's selected policies.

- The auditor's assessment of management's critical accounting judgments and estimates, including where each critical judgment or estimate falls within a range of possible results.

- The quality and effectiveness of the entity's governance structure and risk management, and the quality and effectiveness of its management.

Here lay the real opportunity. The IAASB received comments on its exposure draft through November 2013; its final release of new standards, scheduled for September 2014, was finally made on January 15, 2015.

Now the level of its achievement will abide the extent of global adoption and the development of country-level practice, including reconciliation with the local legislation required in the European Union.

The Future May Be Arriving — At Least in the United Kingdom

> *"So tell me what you want — what you really really want."*
>
> — *Spice Girls, 1996*

"If you try sometimes, you just might find, you get what you need."

— *Rolling Stones, 1969*

The future may be arriving. Rules of the Financial Reporting Council, issued in the fall of 2013, required auditors' reports in the United Kingdom to describe the greatest risks to material misstatements, explain their application of materiality in audit planning and performance, and summarize their audit scope as responsive to the assessed misstatement risks.

Effective for company years ending after September 30, 2013, the rules were adopted early in a handful of cases.

- Deloitte's report dated May 31, 2013, on the fiscal year-end financial statements of Vodaphone Group plc, addressed the magnitude of material uncorrected misstatements, fixed planning materiality at £500 million — approximately 5% of adjusted pre-tax profit and below 1% of equity — and contemplated reporting to the company's Audit and Risk Committee of audit differences above £10 million.

- Similarly, Deloitte's report on the fiscal year statements of British Sky Broadcasting Group plc, dated July 25, 2013, calculated planning materiality of approximately 4% of adjusted pre-tax profit and 5% of equity, or £50 million, with Audit Committee reporting of audit differences in excess of £2.5 million.

Evolved reporting in the United Kingdom was taken to its fullest, however, with the Independent Auditor's Report signed in London on February 12, 2014, by Senior Statutory Auditor Jimmy Daboo on behalf of KPMG, on the financial statements of Rolls-Royce Holdings plc. Running to six full pages, single-spaced and double-columned, Daboo's opinion implemented the FRC's guidance with vigor.[10]

This was not about motorcars. Rolls-Royce ranked 28th on the FTSE 100 list of large UK companies, with £15.5 billion in 2013 revenue from its gas turbine and reciprocating engine sales to the civil and defense aeronautics sectors, along with marine, energy and power systems — all spelled out in the company's 2014 annual report that occupied a handsome 144 pages.

The interesting question, still unresolved, was whether the world was really waiting for auditor essays of 500-word-length on such complicated topics as revenue and profit measurement, measurement of liabilities from sales financing arrangements, or the concept and presentation of nonstandard "underlying" profit on foreign transactions. Or would information users truly have preferred only the traditional, simple and comfortable opinion in the first paragraph, that a "true and fair view" was presented?

Indications, based on the conspicuous silence of the investor community and commentators outside the precincts of those with self-interest, definitely suggest the latter.[11] Throughout a several-year period of company turbulence — punctuated in January 2017 by the company's agreement to pay fines totaling £671 million to authorities in the United Kingdom, United States and Brazil to settle charges of decades of corrupt contract-procurement payments — blame has been placed on the business and its management; neither investors nor the financial press attributed any connection with KPMG's treatise-length report, one way or the other, either then or afterwards.[12]

To go beyond the anecdotal observations of those interested, in March 2015, the FRC released its report, *Extended Auditor's Reports: A Review of Experience in the First Year*, based on 153 extended auditor's reports. Its second report followed in January 2016, expanded to cover 278 reports. Uptake in the world's other large financial markets remains to be seen.

Actual impacts among the user community, to be found both in the views of commentators and in stock price reactions compared with sector benchmarks, may become observable in due course.

What has yet to be brought forward, however, is any evidence-based study of investor behavior, addressing the question whether any of this expanded report language has an effect, one way or the other.

It also remains to consider, over the next reporting cycles for UK companies and their own broad adoption of the FRC's requirements, whether the investor community's "ho-hum" would implicate the long-running efforts to reengineer the standard auditors' report — by either the PCAOB in the United States or the IAASB globally.

Not, as was observed, that either of these bodies was proposing changes on the scale of the KPMG treatise on Rolls-Royce — they having confined themselves to the identification of the kind of "critical" or "key" audit matters that might predictably elicit generic box ticking and boiler-plate, rather than the sophisticated mini-seminars delivered by KPMG.

Which could be seen as a missed opportunity, especially in the litigation-prone United States — that being the jurisdiction most likely among the world's major large economies to inflict a death-blow jury verdict for an auditor's "getting it wrong." There, under the disclosure-based policies of the American securities laws, adoption of the emerging UK protocols for actually quantifying audit and reporting materiality, and for explicating the range and uncertainty of complex company decisions and judgments, would have potential to go far in drawing the teeth of the litigation beast lurking in the courthouse.

Those arguing for a sustainable model for privately provided assurance could be grateful to Jimmy Daboo. As for further leadership or initiative in that direction, grounds for optimism remain hard to come by.

Limitations of Liability

Pervasive Hostility — The Futility of the Entire Effort
There are reasons for the failed efforts to obtain relief in the statehouses for the large accounting firms' exposures in the

courthouses. They go beyond the generally ineffective efforts at legislative lobbying by the firms themselves.

In one sentence — in the countries large enough to be threatening, the interlocking systems of jurisprudence and politics are stacked against them.

> *Note to readers, who are entitled to ask, "How much 'law' can this story safely convey?"*
>
> *A popular writer on mathematics estimates that he loses fifty percent of his readers for each algebraic equation illustrating his text. Here, the risk is that eyes may glaze over, or lids drop closed in frustration, under the alternate prospects of venturing into "who cares" legal territory, or of treating complex topics too summarily.*
>
> *But in a world of attention deficits, news sources built out of sound-bites, and appetizers served in tapas bars, a short menu of legal snacks may be offered up as worth the risk. Those uninterested for any reason are invited to flip ahead a few pages and return to the main banquet.*

The Political Dynamics — Summarized

Although the post-indictment disintegration of Andersen in 2002 brought to the fore the systemic hazard of the impact of another large-firm failure, and figured in the large but nonfatal punishment imposed on KPMG in 2005 over its role in promoting programs of toxic tax shelters, the ability of prosecutors to exercise forbearance against perceived criminal wrongdoing is limited.

There are competing mantras: law enforcement agencies must resist the creation of a public perception that an institution can be seen as either "too big to fail" or — on the other side — "too big to convict."

Those tensions go both ways, as seen in corporate examples:

- Stephen Cohen's SAC Capital was put out of the business of dealing in customer funds, as part of its insider-trading plea bargain in 2013, while Cohen himself was subjected to a civil SEC proceeding and a bar from managing outside funds, but not criminal prosecution, and at this writing is positioning himself to return to public action at the beginning of 2018.

- The guilty plea extracted from Credit Suisse in 2014 for its facilitation of client tax evasion in the United States was carefully engineered to preserve the licenses and permits that the Swiss bank required to stay in business in America.

- BNP Paribas attempted in the spring of 2014 to inject the well-intentioned but misguided influence of the French government into its fractious negotiations with the US Justice Department — an effort readily seen as ill-advised in the American context because of its encroachment on the prosecutors' exclusive turf, and contributing to the result of fines of a record-setting $8.9 billion plus significant constraints on its US business.

- In mid-June 2014, Bank of America found itself on the spear point between its $12 billion settlement offer and the government's $17 billion demand — a difference only resolved by the bank's caving to a $16.9 billion agreement.

- The May 2015 imposition of fines exceeding $5 billion and guilty pleas for rate and index fixing, already noted as agreed between American prosecutors and a quintet of large banks, were only achieved because of waivers agreed in advance by the SEC and state regulators, under which the banks were allowed to retain their various licenses and permits despite their labels as felonious lawbreakers.

Unfortunately, as the Andersen experience demonstrated, there is a huge qualitative difference between the structures of the corporate financial institutions and those of the Big Four. While the banks have balance sheets robust enough to withstand multi-billion dollar penalties, the mere uncertainty threatened by such large and destabilizing sanctions was fatal to Andersen's global network of private accounting partnerships.

At the same time, the reduction of the large firms to the irreducible minimum of the Big Four makes inappropriate any comparison to sector-wide effects in the areas of banking, securities trading or funds management. The world of large investors does not miss Stephen Cohen, nor would law firm clients have missed the Dewey & LeBoeuf law firm after its collapse in 2012. Nor would the customers of Credit Suisse have taken time to mourn its loss as they promptly moved their banking needs. There is no lack of alternative sources for investment management or legal services, whereas, the loss of another Big Four network would be fatal to the entire four-firm franchise.

Nor, no less unfortunately, can prosecutorial tolerance or forbearance be confirmed in advance. Neither the gravity, the harm to investors and the markets nor the politically disrupted environment surrounding a future outbreak of financial malfeasance can be predicted.

In the second place, there is no available constituency ready to take up the accountants' cause — nor should any be expected. On the right wing of the political spectrum, there is no appetite for further costly programs of government rescue or bailout. While on the left, there would be a distinct lack of sympathy to secure the fortunes of Big Four partners whose average annual incomes exceed a million dollars each.

As for the Legal Environment — Legal Systems Compared

As already noted, the pressures on the large firms to settle their largest litigations are irresistible. Application of the legal standards by which to establish fault — in the United States, typically, proof of recklessness rising to the level of a "fraud" — is decided by a lay jury of citizen "peers" — having uncertain levels of education and doubtful substantive qualifications. Their deliberations are based on competing lawyers' presentations of hindsight versions of facts and expert testimony, in a setting where the very existence of the lawsuit means that enormous economic losses are essentially taken as given.

Very briefly, some of the other factors combining to create a toxic legal exposure environment include the following.

Class Actions, Costs and Contingent Fees. The American legal system has three elements not generally found in those of the other major world economies. These, separately and together, raise the level of exposure of the accounting firms to lawsuits by investors alleging damages when the market price of securities suffers a significant shock caused by financial misstatements issued by the company and reported on by the auditors.

The first is the ability of investors to be aggregated together as a "class" — persons similarly situated with claims sufficiently related that they should be efficiently treated by the legal system in a single action.

The proposition is that no single investor would be prepared or able to assume the cost of pursuing such an individual lawsuit, whereas in the aggregate, the size and interest of an investor class — just as a class of consumers harmed by a defective product or victims of an environmental catastrophe — justify the collective effort.

Secondly, in many other systems, the losing party to a lawsuit may be obliged to pay the costs and legal fees of the other side. This creates a significant disincentive to start into a litigation unless the prospects of recovery are high — where by contrast, the typical American rule is not "loser pays," but that each side bears its own costs and fees.

And finally, unlike most other systems, the American legal system permits lawyers to represent their litigation clients on a "contingent fee" basis — that is, taking no fee at all in the event of a loss, but collecting a portion or percentage of any recovery obtained either through a success at trial or by way of settlement.

In the investor class action context, where damages and recoveries may be measured in modest amounts per share but where the volume of share trading is enormous, total class settlements have ranged into the billions of dollars. The results generate huge funds from which legal fee payments approved by the courts have incentivized the growth of a specialty field of lawyers able to bear the front-end costs and take the risks of possible losses in representing investor classes, in exchange for the prospects that a successful settlement will bring handsome fee rewards.

Privity. As the law of auditor liability developed in its early stages, and is still the case in the United Kingdom, claims against an auditor for negligence could be brought only by those in "privity of contract" — that is, those such as lending banks or customers who had made loans or extended financing, who would have been known to and agreed by the auditors as intended recipients and users of their reports.

Specifically excluded from the circle of intended users, in simpler days, were those described by Chief Judge Cardozo of the Court of Appeals, New York State's highest court, in *Ultramares Corp. v. Touche* (1932) as so removed that their claims would create "a liability in an indeterminate amount for an indeterminate time to an indeterminate class." The law in the United Kingdom is to the same effect — *see Caparo v. Dickman* (1990).

But, although the *Ultramares/Caparo* rule on liability for negligence survives, it was overtaken in America by the securities laws of the 1930s, with their orientation and focus on the interests of investors, and a basic philosophy of public disclosure of relevant corporate information — creating requirements for filing and widespread availability of corporate reports including the opinions of the auditors.

From which, it was a short step for the Supreme Court of the United States to find implicit in that statutory framework, and to make explicit, a legal remedy based upon the SEC's Rule 10(b)(5) under Section 10(b) of the Securities Exchange Act, in favor of an investor plaintiff alleging manipulative or deceptive conduct "in connection with" the purchase or sale of a security (*Ernst & Ernst v. Hochfelder* (1976)).

Limitations of Liability. Any consumer who has ever bought an airline ticket, shopped the Internet or installed a software program would be at least vaguely aware of the "terms and conditions" that are deemed to govern the transaction through tearing open the wrapper or ticking the "I agree" box.

With varying degrees of success, modern businesses do all they can to reduce or limit their liability to customers, restrict their warranties and guaranties and substitute arbitration or other processes for consumers' rights to sue.

Not so, however, with auditor liability under the American securities laws. Although the accounting firms use contract clauses in engagements directly with their clients to limit their liabilities, the SEC has a long and passionately held history of hostility to such clauses, and deems them unacceptable and unenforceable in any context in which investor rights are involved.

Simply put, in their major area of exposure, the auditors are denied access to the tools of liability management that are broadly available elsewhere.

Joint and Several Liability. The typical claim of a class of disappointed investors in a large American public company seeks redress from all available sources of recovery. Their targets — defendants in class actions brought under the US securities laws for the dissemination of false financial information — include the company itself, its officers and directors and their D&O insurers, the investment banks if acting as underwriters of the securities, and the auditors whose opinions accompany the company's financial statements on which the investors allege their reliance.

Each defendant is exposed along with all the others — that is, "jointly" — for the damages — which affords the auditors the comfort that the company's resources along with the insurance protecting the individuals will be brought to the table.

But — as a matter of law, liability is also deemed to be "several" — that is, each defendant can be wholly liable, for the entirety of the damages — an imposition with dire consequences for the auditors, who often may be the last targets standing when a company has failed or where insurance for directors and officers is disputed or not available.

Contribution, Fault Allocation and Proportionate Liability. In theory, the harshness of "several" liability is mitigated by legal theories under which a single defendant, held liable for the entire 100% of all damages, seeks a judgment of contribution from the other defendants, or seeks from the court a judgment of allocation or apportionment — that is, a right to recover from those responsible parties the portions of the total damages that a judge or jury would attribute to their equal or greater fault.

Superficially appealing, either of these approaches would beneficially save an auditor from a devastating litigation impact. It might seem only fair that the greater share of exposure should fall on the primary wrongdoers, where liability is based on false or misleading financial statements issued under the responsibility of the company and its leadership, with the auditor's only connection through its opinion.

Fine in theory, less good in practice — because a claim of contribution is only as good as the availability of a wrongdoer's resources that can be reached through the legal process — while fault allocation percentages are typically overridden by the rule of several liability, noted above, in cases where codefendants are judgment-proof.

Or, put another way, in a hypothetical case where corporate or management defendants might be found liable for 90% of a judgment and the auditor 10%, the auditor may likely still be obliged for all 100%, to the extent the other defendants cannot make good their share — courts being unwilling to leave a shortfall in recovery to the detriment of the injured investor plaintiffs.

With all the above working against them, the possible good news for auditors is that not all the news is bad. Indeed, the United States Supreme Court has made the landscape rather less ominous through a series of decisions in recent years:

- Claims for "aiding and abetting" the bread-and-butter charges of 10(b) violations are no longer allowed — "primary" liability being required instead — *Central Bank of Denver v. First Interstate Bank of Denver* (1994) — although that decision actually delivered far less for the auditors than might appear, since they — unlike lawyers or bankers involved in securities transactions — would routinely have launched their audit reports into the public sphere.

- In *Morrison v. National Australia Bank Ltd.* (2010), the Court held that these antifraud provisions apply only with respect to the purchase or sale of a security either listed on a US stock exchange or otherwise done in the United States, precluding federal securities fraud claims with respect to the purchase or sale of securities on foreign exchanges or otherwise outside the United States.

- And in *Halliburton Co. v. Erin P. John Fund* (2014), the Court left in place the presumption of investor plaintiffs' reliance, based on the "fraud on the market theory," that allegedly false statements affected the company's share price, although the Court did open up the opportunity for defendants to rebut that presumption, at the early and vital stage of class certification, with evidence of an absence of a price impact.

Better-armed with these decisions as the lawyers defending the
auditors may be, the practical reality in the courthouses is that —
for cases that they are unable to have tossed out during preliminary proceedings — the inevitable result is the negotiation of an
exit settlement, on the best terms available from the investors'
own lawyers.

Which must be brought about within the large firm's limited
breakup thresholds — as noted above, presently in a range
between one and three billion dollars — because to go to trial for
any larger amount puts the very viability of a firm at the risk of
an adverse jury outcome.

Yet again, a survivable settlement or verdict limit cannot be
more than a fraction of the size of, say, the $67 billion bankruptcy
at Enron, for which on a joint-and-several basis, Andersen could
have been fully exposed. But no such limits can be assured or
delivered — by the legal systems themselves, the legislatures
unwilling to afford the auditors such protection, or the investors'
lawyers who have an ethical duty to their clients to obtain the best
possible result.

To conclude on this ominous subject, then, nothing less would
be needed, although politically and practically unachievable, than
a dramatic rewriting of the entire body of rules by which the
liability of the accountants is determined and measured.

Europe's Unsuccessful Attempts to Take the Lead. In the otherwise
sterile dialog on the survivability of the large audit firms, there
were two developments of interest in Europe in June 2008:

- The June 5 recommendation from Internal Market
  Commissioner Charlie McCreevy, that EU member states
  should take measures to limit auditor liability.

- The June 30 guidance from Britain's Financial Reporting
  Council on liability-limiting agreements between companies and
  their auditors.

Important — both of them. But not so earth-shaking as to support the sentiment heard on the American street, that the visionary Europeans had come to the rescue, ready to lead them to a promised land of real reform of auditor liability.

Expectations were to be tempered. It did mark a welcome and major shift in the regulators' rhetoric, to have the stark picture of survivability put by Commissioner McCreevy's invocation of higher liability risks, limited insurance coverage and little prospects for new entrants, or the FRC's recognition under the leadership of its chief executive, that another large firm's exit "would seriously threaten the effective functioning of the UK capital markets."

But splashes of cold water were called for:

First, on the Continent. Piecemeal country-level liability reform would have been a doubtful proposition there at best, until the various legislatures were actually seen to act. To this date, they have not. Instead, the Brussels pronouncement offered only a menu of general possibilities, rather than specifics: monetary limits by cap or formula, proportionate contribution rather than the typical "joint and several" exposure to 100% of a loss, or limits by contract with a client. All of these were to be subject to judicial review, and the explicit — and probably overriding — principle that limitations should not inhibit any injured parties from being "fairly compensated."

But even assuming the passage of new local laws — which, all the years on from McCreevy's suggestion has not happened anywhere in the region — no European country's legal system has a fully articulated and predictable jurisprudence of auditor liability, of the type worked out over many decades of litigation experience in the Anglophonic countries. The absence in Europe of a mature history of orderly, predictable government reaction to large-scale financial scandal means that politicized and not judicial or reasonably legislated responses can be expected to newly emerging corporate malfeasance.

Two examples showed the likelihood of ongoing governmental interference rather than good process:

- The licensing harassment of PwC in Russia, over its withdrawn reports on energy giant Yukos.

- The post-events rewriting of the Italian bankruptcy laws to enable the appointment of the special administrator of Parmalat.

Unless governments in non-Anglo countries were to take a real-world lead by putting auditor liability regimes in place that would allow the Big Four to take cases to trial — where today they settle far above any statutory liability limits out of anxiety that a media-sensitive judiciary cannot be relied on to enforce limitations on the books but never tested under stress — auditor survivability will still remain hostage to official caprice and vindictive scapegoating.

Second, as for the British — auditors there were newly empowered in 2008 to negotiate with their clients for proportionate or monetary liability caps, subject to shareholder approval, disclosure and judicial assessment whether terms are fair and reasonable.

Reversing earlier prohibitions on such agreements, this authority was more than the auditors had before, but far less than the mandated limits that would have done their work for them.

Wherein lies the first rub: the track record of the British profession in such negotiations is meek. Faced with resistance from both clients and users, the auditors crumbled. UK investor groups promptly arrayed in opposition, with stakes driven in the ground against monetary exposure limits.

Much more to the point, there were at least three ways in which the Financial Reporting Council's role in broking workable limits in the United Kingdom — assuming success, which in fact has not occurred — left open and unaffected the far larger risks for the UK auditors, over in the ever-dangerous American environment:

Optimists about the efficacy of the new British legislation crucially depended on the legal prohibition in the United Kingdom, under the court case known as *Caparo*, against investors and other third-party financial statement users bringing negligence-based claims against company auditors. Nor is there any British equivalent to the rights of American shareholders under the SEC's law and rules. But both of these undergird the vast structure of US shareholder class action litigation, which was unshaken by any change across the Atlantic.

Liability-limiting agreements between British auditors and their clients would, it was expected, be binding against liquidators or trustees of a failed company. But this constraint was never likely in other countries, including the United States, where such successors can avoid or disavow such limits, in order to bring suits in their own right — four examples include the claims against the Deloitte firm by successors to the company in Adelphia, Parmalat, the funds managed by Bear Stearns and, most lately, Taylor Bean & Whitaker.

Finally, cross-border enforcement of British limits was immediately hostage to both the hostility of the SEC to any attempts to reduce unlimited auditor liability exposure, as well as the uncertain application by US judges of limits contracted under foreign laws.

As reported in the *Financial Times* for March 10, 2009, the SEC wasted no time in declaring that financial statements were unacceptable for purposes of compliance with the US securities laws, in the event UK companies were to follow that country's newly legislated rules permitting negotiated agreements for the proportionate liability of their auditors.

There was no surprise about the SEC's passionate history of opposition to auditor liability limits. The fallback proposal was then to seek the same package via British legislation, but although the law was duly changed, the SEC's attitude was not. The SEC was simply not about to accept limitation agreements. Even as the enabling law limped through Parliament, it was essentially dead on arrival in America — effectively slamming the door on the only remotely influential action affecting the large auditors' deadly litigation exposure.

In the end, even on its own terms the UK "success" was hollow. Not only are proportionate auditor liability — along with its companion, monetary liability caps — politically unachievable in the United States. They are, in any event, ineffectual to solve the fundamental problem — the inability of the auditors' financial capacity to answer litigation claims of death-blow magnitude (as discussed above in Part I).

With those numbers overhanging, no reasonable Big Four leader could with confidence send a team of trial lawyers into court, with the life of his firm in their hands, but depending for survival on achieving a jury's fault allocation at a percentage in the low single digits.

So, the SEC's entrenched if churlish animosity should inspire the large audit firms to redeploy. "Liability caps" has always been a losing position — whether as skirmish, battle or campaign.

Mandatory Auditor Replacement — Rotation or Tender

With all the widespread dissatisfaction with Big Audit, none of the various "solutions" has attracted more attention than the imposition of a maximum engagement tenure for firms of statutory auditors — generally expressed, in shorthand, as a requirement of "mandatory rotation."

Nor do any of the others combine such a level of impassioned if unsubstantiated rhetoric with less evidence-based factual support.

A quick summary of the present state of affairs is in order, before following down a map of the several rocky roads to their current intersection:

- At a public meeting of the SEC on February 5, 2014, the annual
  ritual by which that agency approves the PCAOB's budget, the
  latter's Chairman, James Doty, dropped the comment, as if by a
  through-away line, that "We don't have an active project or
  work going on within the board to move forward on a term
  limit for auditors."

  Doty's climbdown on rotation marked an end to his
  extended advocacy of a policy that was neither new nor attractive, even when launched by the PCAOB's *Concept Release* on
  the subject, Docket 037, on August 16, 2011.[13]

  Reality had prevailed. Mandatory rotation in the United
  States lacked the support of Doty's colleagues, legislative back-
  ing, or a sound intellectual or empirical basis.

- Separate proceedings in the United Kingdom by the Financial
  Reporting Council and the Competition Commission resulted in
  2013 in rules requiring UK-listed companies to put their audits
  out for tender under a ten-year limit. Reengagement of incumbent
  auditors was permissible, but only with an explanation by the
  audit committee that the decision was considered and preferred.

- In the spring of 2014, the European Parliament adopted
  requirements by directive and regulation to limit auditor tenure
  to ten years, although subject to certain extensions — rules that
  started to have effect in the spring of 2016.

The last of these three means that, depending on actions taken
at the country level in Europe, mandatory audit firm replacement
is to be inflicted on the entire global model of Big Audit. The
effects will be disruptive in the United States, and in conflict with
the UK approach. And it will occur on the *ipse dixit* of regulators
lacking any empirical basis on which to conclude that there is a
relationship of any kind — causal or otherwise — between the
quality of an audit and the length of the audit firm's tenure —
whether long or short.

What is known today is that massive expenditures of time, money and effort have been and will continue to be incurred, along with the enforced rupture of long-successful professional advisory relationships. The likelihood of highly disruptive unintended consequences, on no evidence of tenure-based auditor inadequacy, is for the sake of a goal that has not been adequately described, much less measured.

Together with recently enacted, untested and mutually inconsistent rules for mandatory rotation in a handful of smaller economies, along with pending proposals that threaten to spread, an international patchwork foretells that the process for large-company auditor selection, retention and replacement, as well as international audit engagement coordination and performance, will be increasingly fraught for years to come.

The Usual Themes and the Unexamined Theories[14]

In 2002, as American politicians scrambled as if legislative action would prevent future Enrons, there was renewed attention to an old idea: requiring public companies to periodically rotate their audit firms. Provisions in Sarbanes-Oxley put the question to the General Accounting Office in Washington for a one-year study.

Under its charge, the GAO duly reported on November 21, 2003, that, in summary, the case for mandatory rotation was not made. The GAO did a major service. What it could not do, unfortunately, was drive a spike through the heart of the idea.

Proponents of mandatory rotation had argued that auditors — if they knew that their work was for a limited period and would eventually be scrutinized by a successor — would have an incentive to be more thorough and demanding with their clients. Said the rotation advocates, the temptation to sacrifice professional rigor for the sake of a friendly relationship with a client would be diminished.

Seemingly behind the recurring advocacy for rotation is that it would favor an improved mind-set of auditor skepticism — a view sometimes couched in terms of the claim for virtue of a "fresh eyes" approach.

History has consistently been to the contrary. The assurance function had never reflected the kind of innocent, pre-lapsarian virtue ascribed by the proponents of "freshness" or "independence."

Instead, since its invention in the Victorian 1850s by Mr. Deloitte and his pioneering contemporaries, professional assurance has been under the direct engagement and payment by the investor-owners, who until then had selected "auditors" from among their own, surely interested ranks.

The nascent profession, together with its clients, successfully saw off the English parliament's threat to nationalize audits of railroads in the 1860s, and it did so again in the United States with the passage of the securities laws in the 1930s. The choice between government and private audit was firmly resolved in favor of the accounting firms.

Over the entire unmodified history of "client pays," the full-service firms' economic incentives to satisfy those paying clients' audit needs should have been at least arguably no more than for a firm dependent solely on its audit practice and deriving no revenue at all from ancillary services.

In brief, the intellectual stability of the entire structure of independence restrictions and limitations on the scope of permissible services, based on "appearances," has been an elaborate edifice built on a platform of shifting fragility.

Could it really be, that a corporate oversight function, paid for by an enterprise but charged with legal duties and public responsibilities, was to be made better by requiring that those entrusted with the task be fired?

The presumption might have been thought deeply troubling, that in a set of relationships characterized by public trust, personal confidence and professional responsibility, problems of performance could be so pervasive that the only solution was to be comprehensive and compulsory replacement. No such dialog has ever surfaced elsewhere, and examples to the contrary abound.

Look at sport. Every college football or basketball coach is expected to build a winning program — all the while juggling such varying goals as competitive recruiting, some respect at least for academics, and meeting the expectations of alumni. There are occasional abuses — slush funds and recruiting malfeasance, drug use and academic cheating, even the rare but egregious cases of misconduct rising to the level of criminality at the core of university governance. But would overall performance be made better if, *regardless* of their teams' records, all coaches were automatically sacked after five or ten years?

Or consider undercover law enforcement programs. Infiltration of criminal groups requires skills honed to a fine edge, and daily life exposed to peril. Bribes and payoffs are readily available. But as a deterrent to the occasional rogue cop, should police departments force their experienced undercover sources to rotate, say, among a city's various neighborhoods? A high-performing Harlem veteran is forced out of his experienced turf, to start again in a new post in Chinatown? Relocate an effective Hispanic detective to unfamiliar Hasidic precincts in Brooklyn? Would city streets really feel safer that way?

What about elected officials? In response to calls for term limits, many incumbent legislators — immunized from real opposition by the protection of the gerrymander and the power of political donations — argue that constituents are better served by extended retention of their experience. If that argument is valid, the argument in favor of long-term auditor retention is at least as much so.

And at the very most personal level — consider the ludicrous and illogical behavior of a loving and faithful spouse, arriving home bearing flowers and an anniversary gift to celebrate 25 years of a successful marriage:

> "*Congratulations my darling. We have trusted and supported each other through thick and thin, raised and educated and launched our children into the world, and provided a model for marital success across our community.*
>
> "*Because we have been so successful, and for so long, it's now time for a 'fresh look'. You'll be hearing from my divorce lawyer in the morning.*"

Preposterous. Against all the arguments, and in the entire post-Enron period, there is not so much as a study, much yet any evidence-based showing, that length of audit firm tenure at large public companies is *at all* related to issues of audit quality — even coincidentally — much less that there is any causal relationship of any kind between the two. Instead, the debate on mandatory rotation has been conducted in a vacuum of research, evidence or intelligence.

Such a research project should be so straightforward as to embarrass all participants that it has not already been performed. It would look as simple and elegant as this:

Using some satisfactory proxy for "financial statement failure" — possibly the withdrawal or restatement of previously issued figures, or the commencement of litigation or law enforcement proceedings including credible allegations of violations of law or regulations — a suitable population of large-company issuers would be compared over a relevant time period — say, the S&P 500 or the FTSE 350 for the five years surrounding the spate of problematic situations in the "Enron era."

Lengths of audit firm tenure would be obtained and compared. Vitally, data sets would include both those defined as "failures" and those not. Relative "failure rates" among subsets of the populations would illuminate both the anecdotal assertion that audit quality problems are more common in the *early* years of auditor-client relationships, and also the so-far unsupported proposition that lengthened tenure has a degrading effect on audit quality.

The charge to fill that research vacuum remains unanswered.

When the PCAOB Chairman Revived an Old Idea

In August 2011, when as noted, James Doty was fresh on his new job as chairman of the PCAOB, he promptly flagged the prospect of a revisited approach to the standard auditor's report. He promised "a holistic approach to addressing the cultural challenges inherent in auditing" — a cosmically lofty notion of "addressing relevance, credibility and transparency of the audit by *all* available and effective means" (*emphasis his*).

His one specific was to revive the question, "whether mandatory audit firm rotation would help address the inherent conflict created because the auditor is paid by the client."

Doty did have the candor to concede that "the idea of a regulatory limit on auditor tenure is not new," going back to 1977 — back when audit choices included the Big Eight as the largest firms as well as a real middle tier. But — unlike fine wines or monumental architecture, which mellow and improve with age — the idea of rotation had not acquired respectability with the passage of time.

The feasibility of rotation clashed with the practical reality of global concentration. Since the days when they were the Big Eight, the large firms had steadily increased their hold on large-company assurance. As the risk management leaders of the surviving mid-tier firms will admit (if only off the record, and despite the public positions taken by their leaders), the smaller firms could not take over the audit of a global-scale bank or airline or manufacturer or service enterprise, if offered the job on a platter.

The consequence — again with focus on the world's largest companies where both the risks and the concentration are greatest — is the absence of auditor choice imposed by the constraints of service delivery under the shibboleth of independence.

That is, a large company, engaging one Big Four firm for its audit, will disqualify another that is used for consulting services, one that provides financial and transactional advice and yet another engaged for tax-related advocacy.

Furthermore, mandatory replacement raises the fundamental problem of practical choice. A large global company setting out to replace its Big Four auditor today has a practical maximum of three candidates. But it quickly gets more complex. Even before passage of the new oversight laws, the Big Four had been forced by political pressure to discontinue nonaudit consulting for their audit clients. In the era post-Sarbanes-Oxley, however, they have all been expanding their nonaudit practices with enthusiasm verging on aggression.

Under a mandatory replacement regime, firms are already showing an appetite to prefer the retention of ongoing advisory work, rather than to pursue a new audit engagement that, by legislative fiat, would be short term.

A marker for the vigor of the large firms' re-expansion into nonaudit services is that it has managed to attract the attention of regulators. In a Washington speech on December 9, 2013, PCAOB Chairman Doty observed that:

> "We have, in recent weeks, seen publicly reported examples of a resurgence of audit firms into consulting to bolster revenue. Of what consequence are these developments for the audit function? What are the implications for independence of the audit function? ... What are the risks of other business lines and how do they affect resource allocation and investment in audit? The PCAOB should focus the best minds on these types of issues. We need roundtables and task force attention on the implications of the regeneration of non-audit consulting at the global firms."

In such an environment, it may be unattractive for the accounting firms to invest in the specialized, industry-specific expertise necessary for an audit opportunity known to be short term. In smaller or less-developed economies, a long-standing global audit relationship for a locally dominant industry encourages auditors to develop local expertise. But with mandatory rotation, an experienced local team would be stranded with no further application for its talent.

On the other hand, barriers including language, culture and relocation costs would prevent the easy relocation or mobility of audit teams made up of industry experts, and firms could hardly be expected to train and place new teams in remote locations every few years. Add in the cases of hurt feelings or distrust left when client and auditor had previously parted on unfriendly terms, and the scope of replacement choice becomes truly limited.

Then comes into play a factor usually omitted from discussion, namely the uneven distribution of expertise around the large world economies. There is significance in the diversity of market leadership: KPMG in Germany, EY in France, Deloitte in Spain, or PwC in the United Kingdom or Switzerland. A global-scale company requires audit services in all of those countries, yet mandatory rotation requirements will become viral in application, whether originating from the European Union, the United Kingdom or any other single country. Yet, as already observed in the cases of BT Group and Toshiba, shortcomings in available industry competence and geographic coverage constrain alternative choices. Enforced rotation would confront severe dislocations, amounting in effect to unachievable demands.

The Arguments in Favor of Mandatory Rotation

The context for rotation — especially the long tenure and duration of auditor relationships among large companies — calls to mind the competing brand loyalties in the farming community of my youth.

There, partisans of the trucks made by Ford or Chevy passed their abiding devotion along from fathers to sons. On each farmstead along the rural roads, the tractors and harvesters glowed exclusively in bright Farmall red or the deep green of John Deere.

These intense brand affinities were debated nonstop in the village café and the adjoining pool hall, by sunburned advocates wearing baseball caps that proclaimed the fidelity of their choice of machinery. The system was stable — client service was dependable if unimaginative, and the cartel of dealers prospered. It would have been thought foolish to sacrifice decades of accumulated knowledge and relationships, or bins of technology and spare parts, for no identifiable advantage.

Out in the fields of corn, oats and soybeans, there was no rational performance differentiation between the competing commodity brands. Cosmetic differences were immediately obscured under the prairie dust, and a dirty red tractor worked not any better or worse than a green one.

In today's Big Audit market, to which the metaphoric characteristics of farmyard equipment extend, the endorsement of mandatory rotation omits a number of considerations.

To start, there is the stumbling block of international impossibility. The consequences that mandatory rotation will impose on such global-scale but US-listed companies as Deutsche Bank, Total, Banco Santander or Nokia will oblige the regulators in Germany, Switzerland, Spain or Finland to enforce the obligatory sacking of, in these cases, KPMG, EY, Deloitte and PwC, with the consequences running directly to their US affiliates doing their US-obligated statutory engagements.

Where then does the wheel of rotation turn for these companies? The effects of independence and scope-of-service restrictions, and the uneven distribution of Big Four resources in the large economies, have squeezed or eliminated the viable rotation opportunities. A study by the Oxera consultancy firm, done in April 2006 for the Department of Trade and Industry and the Financial Reporting Council, *Competition and Choice in the UK Audit Market*, remains vital, with its citation of instances in the United Kingdom where "companies may have *no* effective choice of auditor in the short term"(*emphasis added*).

Third, there is the lack of evidence that audit firm rotation would work to good effect. The truth is, there is none. The only experience of a major economy having lengthy experience with mandatory auditor rotation is Italy. There, rotation has contributed to greater Big Four concentration, and figured not least in the divided-audit environment at Parmalat.[15]

Finally, it is asserted that the overhanging prospect of rotation would improve performance. In the typical hypothetical, it is claimed that in the last two years of a relationship of a maximum five or seven or even ten years, a not-yet-disclosed successor auditor would have every incentive to examine the prior work with a fine tooth comb.

This gets it backwards — the incentives go the other way. As provided by professional auditing standards,[16] a successor auditor's only mandate is narrow — to inquire of a predecessor and, for a limited purpose only, to access and examine prior-years' work. The new firm is required only to lay a foundation for its current year's engagement. Recalling that a successor is not an agent of law enforcement or regulatory oversight, it would have neither motive, incentive, nor tools by which to pry for skeletons in old closets on a gratuitous basis.

Consider the hindsight judgment that a prior error might require correction. The company would be in no position to force the now-dismissed prior auditor back onto the job to do further new work and reissue a prior report. Yet the successor can only be in a position to reperform old and stale work with the infliction of massive additional time and cost on the current job.

Auditor Replacement as a Sanction Could Better Be "Case-By-Case"
As Gilbert & Sullivan's *Mikado* nearly put it in 1885:

> *"An object all sublime*
>
> *"They shall achieve in time*
>
> *"To let the punishment fit the crime."*

There is a practical way that auditor replacement could be tried and tested, without the cost, disruption and doubtful achievability of a mandatory wide-scale requirement.

Which is that in a specific case, if a regulator such as the PCAOB could sustain its proof that long audit tenure was indeed causally related to its definition of "audit failure," it could include enforced rotation in its toolkit of sanctions.

Since the PCAOB looks annually at a sampling of engagements for each of the large audit firms, and claims to target its inspections on the basis of perceived engagement risk and exposure, the agency's experience base should bring to light cases — *if any* — where audit quality might demonstrably be affected by length of tenure.

In which case, rotation could be proposed, and if necessary, imposed.

The sanction would not be an enforcement reach, *if* a credible case were made. The agency could act on its own statutory authority or in coordination with the powers of the SEC — guiding equivalents being, for example, the SEC's imposition of a government-appointed monitor on KPMG as part of the resolution of the criminal investigation of its tax-shelter practice, announced by the Internal Revenue Service on August 29, 2005, or the six-month bar on new SEC clients imposed on EY by the SEC's decision of April 16, 2004, for its impaired independence arising out of business relationships with its audit client PeopleSoft.

Due process and negotiations would sort out the appropriate cases to require rotation. Many cases would not. For one reason,

cases of financial statement failure often result in termination of
the auditor/client engagement in any event, and so would fall out
of the long-tenure population.[17]

Other inspection cases could involve causal facts unrelated
to tenure — such as individual personnel competence or supervision — where rotation would be a doubtful remedy. And since
real sanctions would presumably only be applied in a publicly
transparent environment, the PCAOB would achieve the disclosure it professes to desire — along with the obligation to establish
the credibility of its findings.

Rotation if proposed as a sanction would allow the incumbent
auditor to be heard and argue its case — or perhaps even to reach
an agreement to stand down. It would also open the record to
commentary or even possible resistance by a foreign regulator, in
the especially challenging cross-border cases involving global companies — as well as to a fact-based airing of issues of impracticality or constrained choices of successors.

The principle of "first, do no harm" was cited by PCAOB member Lewis Ferguson in his statement of August 16, 2011, on the
Concept Release. Case-by-case use of mandated rotation as a
sanction would satisfy the corollary: anticipate unintended consequences whenever possible, and do minimal harm in any event.

Mandated rotation in those rare cases where tenure length
might demonstrably be an issue would present such an environment. Properly defined "audit failures" being real, but also rare,
across the entire timeline of auditor tenure, enforcement sanctions,
including rotation, should be conserved and only deployed
accordingly.

*Auditor Rotation Prohibition — HR 1564's Bump in the Road to
Nowhere*

"Ancient Rome declined because it had a Senate," the
American cowboy philosopher Will Rogers querulously

observed. "So what's going to happen to us, with both a Senate and a House?"

While policies on rotation and re-tender in the United Kingdom were going through the evolution of views among its regulators in mid-2013, addressed below, the House of Representatives in Washington on July 9, 2013, passed HR 1564, the "Audit Integrity and Job Protection Act."

Neither topic in the title of the Act — either audit integrity or job protection — was in fact addressed. Instead the bill, if fully enacted, would have prohibited the PCAOB from acting to mandate the rotation of audit firms.

Finding a rationale for this strange piece of legislation was a challenge. The supportive record was bare; the House Financial Services Committee had launched HR 1564 without report, analysis or commentary.

The PCAOB was a critic's easy target, but momentum there in favor of rotation had already flagged. Comment letters had taken 95% unfavorable positions — and, in the event, there were plain signals that Chairman Doty lacked the votes, if indeed he ever had the desire.

The answer to Will Rogers's jaundiced question on the legislative process may have been in Washington's devotion to "motion" masking as "progress." If so, the bill's apparently permanent consignment to legislative limbo appeared well deserved.

How The British Went Their Own Way

While the PCAOB was going nowhere on rotation, on the way to Chairman Doty's 2014 capitulation, the Financial Reporting Council and the Competition Commission in the United Kingdom took a deep finesse, eventually reconciling their rules so as to require large public companies to put their audits out for re-tender every ten years.

The innate good sense of re-tender was, that if potential replacement auditors had the commercial choice of giving up ancillary services for their clients — tax, consulting, valuation — in order to be eligible to take up a new audit engagement, the market itself could determine the range of competition and available choice — solutions preferable to leaving underinformed regulators to attempt the drawing of such bright lines in the wrong places.

The process in the United Kingdom had begun in September 2012, when the FRC slipped this single, subtle sentence into section C.3.7 of its Governance Code:

> *"FTSE 350 companies should put the external audit contract out to tender at least every ten years."*

Called "limited changes" by the FRC, this provision was little remarked at home and virtually ignored in the United States. But the dust is still settling, and the global impact and effects may, if difficult to predict, eventually be profound.

Consider first the global market impact. The largest 100 and second 250 British companies span the globe in their size and reach — from the agency giant WPP to Royal Dutch Shell and BP in the energy sector to consumer leaders Diageo and Unilever to global bankers HSBC and Barclays. They have dominant business operations, multiple securities listings and deep capital market participation across the world's developed economies.

As already noted, audits of the large British companies are, with a handful of exceptions, the province of the Big Four. For reasons of cost and efficiency in any process of re-tender, audit committees and senior financial officers of those companies will invariably seek either the retention of the incumbent auditor, or the ability to transfer to another single provider. Choices made in London will be reflected in the structure of the Big Audit market across the globe.

But, given the unequal worldwide distribution of audit competence and technical expertise, it is predictable that auditor shifts resulting from the tender process will, if anything, further tighten concentration at the top of the market.

What real changes might emerge? Two competing assessments were offered.

One was that there could be a reluctance to tender. The audit firms — Big Four and smaller firms alike — would be unwilling to invest the considerable time and expense to build sufficient size, expertise and geographic presence to pursue an uncertain tender process, especially when obliged to forego the certain revenue streams now generated by their nonaudit work for these global giants.

In that case, nonincumbents might well take a pass. The result of re-tendering would only be the rationalized reengagement of incumbents — a public relations exercise in "comply or explain" that might buy a decade or two of rhetorical peace but little else.

A second scenario rested on the hypothesis that large global companies now concentrate their nonaudit services mainly in a single alternate Big Four provider. That firm might be a rotation candidate, assuming a "shadow cabinet" of existing skills that would enable it to switch over to the audit with intrusive if manageable disruption — and likely resumption of the nonaudit *status quo ante* when it would yield back the audit brief a decade hence.

A skeptic would be entitled to question whether professional skills are so fungible and transferable, much less available; or that the large firms' current client relationships organize into such neat duopolies; or that, indeed, such a file-passing exercise among the Big Four was what the proponents of mandated replacement had in mind.

Following the FRC's rule change, the UK Competition Commission issued an initial proposal in 2013, that public company audits should be put out for mandatory re-tender every five years — which would have halved the FRC's more permissive ten-year "re-tender or at least explain."

The large firms complained that the five-year period was too short, while others argued that the provision was still too soft.

The statement of the chairman of the Competition Commission's Investigative Group, that "the audit function is too important to be left undisturbed for longer than five years," clashed with the wide and credible belief and research that the early years of an auditor-client relationship, on the steep slope of the learning curve, are the times of *heightened* audit risk.

The Competition Commission's proposed reduction to five years promised perverse results. Taking account of the huge costs for too-frequent proposals, engagement transitions and first-time learning curves, they would have included:

- Round-robin exchanges of engagements among the Big Four.

- Further Big Four concentration as smaller firms would be squeezed out by the costs involved.

- Replacement firms issuing otherwise identical auditor reports, with no observable difference in innovation, performance or quality.

Eventually, the Competition Commission did come to ground, in October 2013, extending its period for mandatory audit tender to ten years, while also eliminating the option offered by the FRC of a company explanation for not doing so.

London had already been a-flutter after the FRC's own rule change. Rumblings in the City of London were that tender opportunities might become numerous. The anticipation was that individual client gains and losses among the Big Four would be offset, in a balance that would largely preserve the equilibrium and — after deducting from their profits the sizable if unproductive costs of the entire process — would leave the entire Big Audit franchise largely in its present state.

Three years on, the principle is already clear — that *plus ça change, plus c'est la même chose.*

The range and variety of outcomes could be seen in the experiences of PwC, which as the dominant player in the FTSE 100 market would inevitably see the most activity. In addition to its scandal-driven loss of Tesco to Deloitte, PwC was replaced at Sainsbury by EY. PwC lost Royal Dutch Shell to EY and Wolseley to Deloitte. It picked up from KPMG the audit of HSBC, the county's largest engagement by fees, and gained Vodafone from Deloitte. It was explicitly excluded from the tender process announced by Barclays Bank, which in June 2015 announced its switch to KPMG. After half a century auditing Schroders, it was tipped for replacement by KPMG, which were however obliged to stand down with the discovery of an unmanageable independence issue, eventually giving way to EY.

What has not changed, at least to date, is the penetration, role or influence of the smaller firms. After thousands of man-hours and millions of pounds, dollars and euros expended in the tender-proposal-succession process, instead, the concentration *status quo* held by the Big Four appears steadily maintained.[18]

The Rotation Environment in Europe

Briefly noted above, dramatically impactful rules on rotation in the European Union were among the subjects of wide-ranging legislation adopted by the European Parliament as summarized in its press release of April 3, 2014.

The breadth of the other topics, discussed here at greater length later, had been the subject of extensive discussion and reporting, going back to 2010, under the tenures of the commissioners holding the Internal Market and Services portfolio.

On mandatory rotation, as the EU press release put it:

> *"Public-interest entities will be required to change their statutory auditors after a maximum engagement period of 10 years. Member States can choose to extend the 10-year period up to 10 additional years if tenders are carried out, and by up to 14 additional years in case of joint audit, i.e. if the audited company appoints more than one audit firm*

*to carry out its audit. Calibrated transitional periods taking
into account the duration of the audit engagement are also
foreseen to avoid a cliff effect once the new rules apply."*

The Regulation gave June 2014 as its date of "entry into force,"
meaning that Member States were given two years to pass
implementing legislation, projecting the rules to be in effect from
June 17, 2016.

That date loomed large, for several reasons:

First, there were significant ambiguities in the application of the
transitional provisions, depending on an incumbent auditor's
length of tenure as of the 2014 date. Unless resolved, the possibility existed that those with longer tenure would have until 2020 or
2023 to be replaced, while some with shorter tenure would face
rotation by June 2016 — a deadline date for the required country-
level legislation, but missed by many.[19]

Second, the EU timetable was at odds in important ways with the
UK mechanism for ten-year tender, including possible incumbent
retention, discussed above.

Third, the consequences and global impact of the EU structure
remain and are still to be developed — for example, in respect of the
entire banquet of countries where EU-based public companies
require audits of their local subsidiaries and operations. These would
range from the United States — where as discussed, the PCAOB's
rotation initiative finally died — to the panoply of requirements
being brought forward in smaller countries around the world.[20]

The impact of such a disparate set of rules and requirements for
rotation threatens to be severe, and disproportionate to the size of
the economies involved, individually or in the aggregate.

That is because large players in whole industries would have
operations in all the affected countries — examples would include
the petroleum majors, the large auto and truck manufacturers, the
global airlines and the big banks.

Fourth, even the mature regulators are bringing forth questions as to the possible adverse consequences of mandated rotation. As reported in *Accounting Today*, PCAOB member Lewis Ferguson, speaking on December 5, 2014, at the Financial Executives International's Current Financial Reporting Issues Conference in New York, expressed his agency's concerns about the effects wrought in Europe:

> *"The Public Company Accounting Oversight Board is finding that the push toward mandatory audit firm retendering and rotation is leading to lower audit fees in Europe, sparking audit quality concerns."*

Quoting Ferguson on what the report called "disturbing trends":

> *"One of the things we are looking at is the consequences of the requirements of the European community with its new audit directive that requires rotation by auditors between 10 and 20 years.*
>
> *It seems to be an exception in the United Kingdom, but in the rest of Europe, [audit fees] seem to have dropped between 20 and 40 percent," said Ferguson. "As regulators, we are obviously very concerned about whether you can have a high-quality audit if the fees go down by 20 percent, or is the work going to get squeezed?"*

A decade of rotation-driven challenges faces the auditors themselves, but also audit committees and chief financial officers — obliged to engage new firms of auditors, from outside the network of their main firm, for significant country-level audits on any number of different and irreconcilable cycles and deadlines.

Administration of the very basics of engagement performance will be horrifically complex: deployment of replacement firms in some uncertain number of countries perhaps every year — each with its own culture, personnel and methodology — the upstreaming of country-level results for global consolidation, and the difficulty of achieving uniform standards of quality and execution.

William Welch Deloitte (1818–1898) — pioneering English accountant, founder of the Big Four firm that bears his name. *Source*: Public Domain.

The Great Western Railway: Lithograph of the railway's "Acheron" 2-2-2 steam locomotive, 1846. *Source*: The National Railway Museum/Science & Society Picture Library.

Arthur Edward Andersen (1885–1947) — Alumnus of Pricewaterhouse, professor of accounting at Northwestern University in Chicago, founder of the firm that bore his name (1913–2002). Abstemious, punctilious — practiced and worked hard under the maxim, "Think straight, talk straight." Imposed a work ethos of bare desks, half-day work on Saturdays and mandatory hats as part of the "Arthur Andersen" appearance.

Source: The Accounting Hall of Fame.

Warren E. Burger (1907–1995) — 15th Chief Justice of the Supreme Court of the United States (served 1969–1986), author of the opinion in *United States v. Arthur Young* (1984), involving IRS access to the firm's tax working papers, and gratuitously ascribing "public watchdog" status to the accountants. *Source*: Collection of the Supreme Court of the United States.

Kenneth Lay — chairman and chief executive officer of Enron Corp. — convicted of securities fraud and related charges in 2006, died of a heart attack before sentencing. *Source:* United States Marshal's Service.

Paul Sarbanes — United States Senator, 1997–2007 (D-Md.) — together with Representative Michael Oxley, principal legislative sponsor of the Public Company Accounting Reform and Investor Protection Act of 2002, popularly known as Sarbanes-Oxley. *Source:* The U.S. Senate Historical Office.

Michael Oxley (1944–2016) — Member of the House of Representatives, 1981–2007 (R-Ohio) — along with Senator Paul Sarbanes, principal sponsor of the Sarbanes-Oxley law of 2002. *Source:* Laurel Stern Boeck, 2006, Collection of the U.S. House of Representatives.

Sir David Tweedie — chartered accountant in Scotland, KPMG alumnus, chairman of the International Accounting Standards Board (2001–2011), chairman of the Board of Trustees, the International Valuation Standards Council (2012). *Source:* The International Valuation Standards Council.

Robert H. Herz CPA, PricewaterhouseCoopers alumnus, chairman of the Financial Accounting Standards Board (2002–2010). *Source*: Robert H. Herz.

James Doty — American lawyer, general counsel of the SEC (1990–1992), longest-serving chairman of the Public Company Accounting Oversight Board (2011–). *Source*: The Public Company Accounting Oversight Board.

Charles McCreevy — Irish politician, European Commissioner for Internal Market and Services (2004–2010). *Source*: The International Monetary Fund.

Michele Barnier — French politician, European Commissioner for Internal Market and Services (2010–2014). *Source*: The European Parliament.

NOTES

1. Adapted from the original in the *International Herald Tribune*, March 10, 2006.

2. Publicly unaddressed, in what was billed as a "client driven" strategy, was the extent or degree of mutuality by which the local Deloitte partners or their surviving locally regulated entities would provide financial support to each other — either in respect of the capital needs of their growth ambitions or — perhaps more ominously in light of the history of Andersen's network fragility — in the event of a litigation shock having local impact but with regional or global ramifications.

3. Adapted from the original in the *International Herald Tribune*, April 6, 2007.

4. See International Standard on Auditing 600, *Audits of Group Financial Statements*, ¶ 11 and Appendix A 8–9.

5. The PCAOB approach was instead all about the optics — diminishing the stature of the agency and distracting its energy from serious issues:

- The user community is indifferent to partner naming, as shown by the absence of distinction between practices that vary among countries.

- At the same time, audit quality differentiation based on partner naming is elusive. There is no study at the large-company level of share price effects or financial statement quality differentiation between US-based companies that do not provide partner names and European ones, including those listed in America, that do.

- Exposure of engagement partners to real litigation will not be reduced, because their identity is readily knowable and lawsuits could, if strategic for plaintiffs, be readily amended to add them as defendants.

- In any event, that exposure is largely illusory. Plaintiffs' attorneys do not make a practice of naming individual partners, because their evidence for use against their firms is always available, and their personal assets are insignificant in context of multimillion dollar damage claims.

- Cutting the other way, lead partner careers are impaired by litigation in any event, whether they are named in the suits or not, by the combination of reputational effect and protracted distraction while dealing with the time and emotional demands of participating in a large pending lawsuit.

6. See the *Chicago Tribune*, August 8, 2012, regarding Tom Flanagan of Deloitte, and the *Los Angeles Times*, July 2, 2103, regarding Scott London of KPMG.

7. Believing as I do that engagement partner identity disclosure is not desirable even contemporaneously, I stay consistent in principle here, omitting these partners' names as gratuitous. For anyone voyeuristic enough to care, the records are public and readily searchable.

8. The text of the recommendation and the webcast of the Treasury Committee's March 13, 2008, discussion meeting are available through the SEC's website.

9. *Amendment XXV, Section 4 (adopted 1967).*

10. At 5,400 words in length, a copy of the KPMG report would exceed practical space limits here. Readers are invited to find it starting at page 130 of Rolls-Royce's 2013 annual report – available at ar.rolls-royce.com/2013/

11. The company's stock price had suffered a 25% pounding, its largest price drop in 13 years, with the profit warning in its February 13, 2014, announcement of the year's results. That price drop was significantly recovered — the share price rebounding from 961 p to 1100 p by the end of March 2014. The following months were not kind — further profit warnings came, and the stock slid below 800 p in the summer; from there it peaked above 1000 p in May 2015, slumped to near 500 p that summer, and currently struggles around 750 p — well below the price when KPMG issued its first expanded report.

12. By contrast, the FRC announced in May 2017 that it would investigate KPMG's actual audit work for the earlier years 2010 through 2013 — the period spanning the bribery and corruption for which the company was fined.

13. Attention to rotation – but no uptake or implementation — is traceable at least to the 1977 study by a US Senate Committee on Government Operations sub-committee chaired by Senator Lee Metcalf

(D-Mont.), and the report the following year by the Commission on Auditors' Responsibilities established by the AICPA.

14. Adapted from the original in the *International Herald Tribune*, August 31, 2002.

15. For research findings that "rotation is costly and earnings quality improves with longer auditor tenure, (and that) the evidence from Italy does not support the case for mandatory rotation," *see* Cameran, M., Francis, J. R., Marra, A., & Pettinicchio, A. (2015), "Are there adverse consequences of mandatory auditor rotation? Evidence from the Italian experience," *Auditing: A Journal of Practice & Theory*, Vol. 34(1), 124.

16. *See*, for example, the PCAOB's AU 3.15.10-.11.

17. Note may be taken here of the May 11, 2015, announcement by Tesco in the United Kingdom, that after a 32-year relationship, it was replacing PwC with Deloitte, through a tender process that did not include the incumbent. The eventual consequences of the far-flung accounting irregularities disclosed at Tesco in September 2014 are still emerging, but the company's own action made moot the possible intrusion of regulatory oversight into the company's choice to change its auditor.

18. Although any attempt to summarize will be quickly out of date, a survey of press reports identifies 23 FTSE 100 auditor changes from 2014 through late 2016, with these gains/losses: Deloitte – 5/5; EY – 6/2; KPMG – 6/3; PwC – 6/13. Firms outside the Big Four did not figure at all.

19. According to information gathered by the organization known until December 2016 as the *Fédération des Expert-comptables Européens*, then re-branded *Accountancy Europe*, along with updating press reports, of the 31 affected countries in Europe, only 15 had full implementation at the *end* of 2016, two (France and Austria) were in partial fulfillment, and 14 had failed the deadline altogether. Later data from the *European Contact Group* indicated full implementation in 20 countries, partial in one, with implementation in ten mostly smaller countries still to come.

20. A shifting country list, concededly subject to updating, shows these varying and mutually inconsistent deadlines and provisions:

- Italy retains its nine-year rotation schedule, despite scholarly criticism and even after the 2003 debacle at Parmalat. Also in the EU, according to data from *Accountancy Europe*, Portugal and Belgium are on nine-year schedules, and Bulgaria on seven.

- The Netherlands enacted an eight-year rotation schedule with effect at January 1, 2016, later proposed for withdrawal to conform to the EU legislation.

- In India, under a new Companies Bill, rotation is to be imposed after five years for individual practitioners and two five-year terms for audit firms.

- Abu Dhabi — four years.

- Argentina had incomprehensibly set out to require firm rotation every three years and audit team rotation every two years, and eventually scrapped the entire exercise.

A partial further listing, in a constantly changing environment, has seen these inconsistent and conflicting requirements as to timetables and sector coverage: Chile, five-year rotation for certain funds; Paraguay, tax auditors to rotate every three years, banks every three, and insurance companies every five; South Korea — required rotation after seven years withdrawn, under rules put in place in 2006, the academic research having concluded that "mandatory auditor rotation increases the cost for audit firms and clients while having no discernible positive effect on audit quality"; Brazil, requirement of rotation after five years withdrawn; Israel, mandatory rotation, but only for banks and insurance companies.

IV

THE ACTS AND ATTITUDES OF THE PLAYERS IN BIG AUDIT

Up to this point, the impracticalities in the array of "solutions" variously advanced to address the fragility of Big Audit have involved the structural impediments in the model itself — limitations that inhere in the size, diversity and uneven distribution of resources of the Big Four; their financial, performance and environmental weaknesses; and their impacted relationships with the other participants.

But — meaningful dialog will be essential among all those involved in the issuance, auditing and use of financial statements, for there to be any chance of evolution toward a newly designed and sustainable Big Audit model. Yet, among the grounds for concern, verging on pessimism, whether shared approaches are possible in aide of a holistic conversation, the behaviors suggest unlikelihood.

It is not necessary to ascribe malign intent or motives — nor do I — but only to recognize that behaviors are shaped by perspectives and interests — the characteristics deeply embedded in all the diverse and varying qualifications and aspirations. For this, some examples to "tell the story" are usefully illustrative, among these:

- The regulators — especially those presumably most experienced — the Americans, the Europeans and the British, but others as well.

- The issuers, in the voice of their lobbyist, the US Chamber of Commerce.

- And the firms themselves.

Start with the regulators, because there is an instinctive public desire to default the responsibility for difficult policy problems over to government. So it is worthwhile to give a sampling of the examples by which elected and appointed gatekeepers have shown the limits of their capacity for constructive contributions — in addition to the earlier examination of their positions on accounting standards convergence and mandatory rotation.

THE SEC SETTLEMENT WITH THE BIG FOUR — A CHINESE PUZZLE THAT MISSED SOME KEY PIECES

Regarding the significant challenges to a regulator in the increasingly globalized world, a central theme of SEC Commissioner Luis Aguilar's speech at the University of Georgia on March 20, 2015, was his agency's need to:

> *"think more globally and recognize that its registrants will increasingly be global players, that fraud perpetuated at home can be initiated by those who have never set foot in the United States, and that a market meltdown can have global origins and ramifications."*

With candor, while he admitted that "the protection of American investors will require that the SEC increase its efforts to communicate, coordinate, and cooperate with its international counterparts," it would be "something that is easier said than done."

The gap between aspiration and reality had only been emphasized the prior month. On February 6, 2015, the SEC announced its order, settling its long-running conflict with the Chinese affiliates of the Big Four. The confrontation had come down to an enforcement order by an Administrative Law Judge dated January 22, 2014 — for which the foundation had been SEC subpoenas demanding working papers of the Chinese auditors, which the Big Four's local firms had refused to produce, based on their claims that Chinese law required those papers to be withheld from a foreign regulator.

A forthright assessment confronts the question whether this "settlement" was real, or another exercise in governmental optics by which bureaucrats act as if they have delivered something substantive, and observers must pretend to believe them.

Reviews from the commentators were mixed. The *Corporate Counsel* blog exclaimed on February 9 that the "Tug-of-War Over Audit Files Finally Ends!" By contrast, blogging from over in China on February 7, Paul Gillis viewed it as the SEC's "near complete capitulation to the Chinese."

The claim in the SEC's staff release that "the settlement is an important milestone in the SEC's ability to obtain documents from China" would no doubt be agreed by both the Big Four and the Chinese regulators. But they would each have their separate, distinct and mutually antagonistic reasons.

The deal included no reference to the perpetually frustrated aspirations of the PCAOB to inspect the operations of China-based auditors. This hostage to fortune had originated with the very launch of the PCAOB itself under Sarbanes-Oxley, when the PCAOB agreed to register non-US audit firms despite their explicit declarations of foreign legal impediments that would prevent their compliance with its inspection regimes.

To update the state of play, Commissioner Aguilar in his speech had observed that "the PCAOB has faced significant regulatory obstacles to its inspections in a number of international jurisdictions." As of June 30, 2014 — then twelve years after its creation — "the PCAOB was unable to conduct inspections of firms located in 14 jurisdictions."[1]

The PCAOB's credibility has been impacted for years by its inability actually to make the "progress," against the entrenched resistance of the Chinese regulators to fall into line with its cross-border ambitions, that had been claimed repeatedly by Chairman Doty[2] and his colleagues[3] Real achievement in that country has instead proved continuingly elusive, with no substantive progress actually in view.[4]

As for the SEC itself, the devil lurking in the details of its deal with the Big Four would have been clutching his Satanic ribs with bemusement. Because under the agreement:

- The firms conceded, as they must have done, that they had refused to comply directly with the SEC's requests — under the arguable justification of the inhibitions of their local Chinese laws.

- But they were permitted not to admit — also not to deny — the SEC's charges that they were lawbreakers.

- Each of the Big Four put up the trivial sum of $500,000 — a sum lost in the rounding errors of their fees and expenses to accomplish a four-year armistice.

- Most important, they were put under no restrictions in any aspect of their ongoing services to their Chinese clients, including those with presence in the American capital markets.

The SEC's press release plumped the "additional remedial measures" it might invoke in the event of future noncompliance with its further requests. But reference to the actual text of the Order confirms these to be no more than the modest weapons the SEC had already deployed to little effect.

That is, the SEC retained the right to commence new enforcement proceedings —which was a tool always at the ready in any event. Or it might restart the existing proceeding — the final legitimacy of which was left untested by the Big Four's pursuit of review or appeals, their rights to which were also explicitly preserved.

What the Big Four affiliates did accomplish was a local accommodation — a process to produce their documents directly to the China Securities Regulatory Commission instead of to the SEC. By that step, they successfully inserted their home agency as a protective shield against future exposure in America.

That is, the Big Four undertook that for future SEC requests, either they would make actual production to the SEC — an unlikely prospect until and unless the recalcitrant CSRC were to change its attitude — or they would produce locally to the CSRC, while sending along separate logs of documents subject to claims of privilege or the constraints of Chinese rules regarding state secrets or information deemed sensitive for political or any other reasons.

In the future, the cost-heavy housekeeping burden of preparation and submission of these elaborate document listings will work primarily to the enrichment of the inevitable teams of lawyers involved. The Big Four firms will, in the process, fulfill the letter of the their obligations — plainly in coordination and dialog with the CSRC, and in compliance with that agency's views on the permissibility of onward production to the American agency.

As to the spirit, the CSRC is not a party to the Big Four's agreement. Instead, it retains unfettered authority over the ultimate release of the documents. So the SEC is left not a step further down the road to real cooperation and enforcement compliance than it was before.

SARBANES-OXLEY ITSELF — ITS FIRST TEN YEARS, THE YEARS SINCE AND COUNTING

The context of my long-held skepticism about Sarbanes-Oxley as a reflexive post-Enron legislative exercise was my July 20, 2002, observation in the *International Herald Tribune* about the

preliminary Senate vote, that "any legislation receiving the biparti-
san margin of 97-0 is bound to be fundamentally defective."

Nor did the following decade *horribilis* give any reason to feel
better. In the summer of the law's tenth anniversary, the law's
sponsors joined an agency webcast on July 30, 2012. Instead of
holding a celebration, some unasked questions might better have
been advanced:

First, regarding the back-patting of those with careers to be
served — the PCAOB's members and staff and the spokesmen for
the Big Four — "Would the self-interested be expected to vote
against it?"

Second, as for those purporting to see some claim of benefit, the
challenge remained conspicuous, that the cyclical nature of market
bubbles made inevitable a post-scandal period of cleansing and
temporary return to virtue —political dynamics notwithstanding.

Put another way, the storm of both scandal and outrage after
Enron and WorldCom was bound to clear, no matter what. So
instead of the wrong question, whether post-Enron corporate
behavior was now improved — under both Sarbanes-Oxley and
the law of unintended consequences — the proper operative question *should* have been:

> *"Would financial reporting and assurance today be better,
> or worse, if Sarbanes-Oxley had not been passed at all?"*

That's because since 1934, it had already been illegal under
American law to make false statements in connection with the
purchase or sale of securities. So — as confirmed by the absence
of prosecutions under the new law's requirements for executive
certifications of financial results — it is arguable that Sarbanes-
Oxley was from the outset never more than a redundant exercise
in optics and cosmetics.

Third, for more than a decade, the rule-setting and inspection programs of the PCAOB have intruded into the relationships between

auditors and clients, engulfing the corporate reporting process in cost, paperwork and degradation of the assurance function. Into the bargain, it has failed either to advance coordinated global-scale assurance regulation and oversight in many of the world's major capital markets or to prevent (among others) the wave of securities malfeasance of offshore origin, notably from China.[5]

Fourth, as to the law's centerpiece obligations on internal controls reporting and assurance, it was always true, even before Sarbanes-Oxley, that most *decently* controlled companies would do *reasonably* well on compliance, *most* of the time. But a parade of horribles since then has made it clear that, for reasons of scope limitation or plain enforcement dysfunction, the law has been ineffectual against the rare but all-too-frequent and truly consequential cases.

A brief sampler illustrates that — as generally true of large-scale challenges to risk identification and management — it has been the cases viewed as "outliers" that really matter:

- The control failures that brought down Bear Stearns and Lehman Brothers.

- The *buco nero* at Parmalat in Italy, and the ghost employees at Satyam in India.

- The in-house looting by the chief financial officers of Koss in Milwaukee and the city of Dixon, Illinois.

- The undetected Ponzi schemes of Bernie Madoff and Allen Stanford, unremarked by gatekeepers, regulators and client advisors and abettors alike.

- The valuation fantasies behind the window-dressing at Fannie Mae and Freddie Mac.

- The incentives-driven deceptions in the mortgage business models of Washington Mutual, Countrywide and New Century.

- The derivatives and trading fiascos at UBS, JP Morgan Chase, MF Global and Knight Capital.

What is the purpose of lawmaking? If Sarbanes-Oxley did not ameliorate the flaws revealed by these events to persist in the corporate reporting and assurance structures, in the United States in particular, much less globally, then of what use or benefit has it been — except as a politically motivated placebo?[6]

THE PCAOB ASKED AUDITORS AN UNANSWERABLE QUESTION — DO COMPANY CONTROLS "WORK"?

"Measure twice — cut once."
— Quality control maxim of carpenters and woodworkers

If there can be a 50-million-euro laughingstock, it must have been Guillaume Pepy, the head of the SNCF, the French national railway system, who was obliged on May 21, 2014, to confess a problem with its €15 billion order for almost two thousand new trains. It had been discovered, only *after* their fabrication, that the upgraded models were a few critical centimeters too wide to pass through many of the country's train platforms.

Owing evidently to unchecked reliance on the width specifications for recently built platforms, rather than actual measurement of some 1300 that were older and narrower, the error required contrite remediation — the nationwide task of grinding down the old platform edges.

That would have been the good news. The bad was that since the nasty and thankless fix doubtless fell to the great cohort of underutilized public workers who so burden the sickly French economy, correction of the SNCF's buffoonish error would have done nothing by way of new job creation to reduce the nation's grating rate of unemployment.

The whole fiasco raised the compelling question for evaluation and control of performance quality, "How can you hope to improve, if you're unable to tell whether you're good or not?"

That very question was being reprised in Washington, where the PCAOB was grilling the auditors of large public companies over their obligations under Sarbanes-Oxley to assess the internal financial reporting controls of their audit clients.

Quoted on May 20, 2014, from a speech at Compliance Week 2014, PCAOB member Jay Hanson — while conceding that the audit firms had made progress in *identifying* and *testing* client controls — insisted on pressing a remaining issue: how well the auditors "assess whether the control *operated* at a level of precision that would detect a material misstatement .... Effectively, the question is 'does the control work?' That's a tough question to answer" (*emphasis added*).

So framed, the question was more than "tough." It was fundamentally unanswerable. It posed a problem that, unless revised, had potential for ongoing regulatory mischief if enforced in those terms by the agency staff.

That was because whether a control actually "works" or not can only be referable to the past, and cannot speak to future conditions that may well be different. No matter how effectively fit for purpose a control may have appeared, over any length of past time, any assertion about its future function must at best be contingent: perhaps owing as much to luck as to design — simply not being designed for evolved future conditions — or perhaps not yet having incurred the systemic stresses that would defeat it.

Examples are both legion and unsettling:

- Back in 1912, the safety measures on *RMS Titanic* were thought to represent both the best of marine engineering and full compliance with all applicable regulations, right up to the ship's encounter with the iceberg.

- A recovering drunkard may appear controlled, under disciplined compliance with the meeting schedule of Alcoholics Anonymous — but the observation is always subject to a possible shock or temptation that would hurl him off the wagon, however long his prior ride.

- The blithe users of the Value-At-Risk models, for the portfolios of collateralized subprime mortgage derivatives that fueled the financial spiral of 2007–2008, scorned the notion of dysfunctional controls.

- Nothing in the intensity of the risk management oversight and reams of box-ticking at Bank of America proved satisfactory to prevent the capital requirement miscalculation disclosed by the bank on April 28, 2014, that inflicted a regulatory capital shortfall of some $4 billion.

Hanson was in a position to continue his record of seeking improved thinking at the PCAOB — having quite rightly called out his own agency, for example, in a speech on March 18, 2014, on the ambiguous and unhelpful nature of its definition of "audit failure."

But an attitudinal challenge for Hanson and his PCAOB colleagues, on the measurement of control effectiveness, would be to resist the misleading temptation to rely on "input" measures to reach a conclusion on effectiveness:

- To the contrary, claimed success in crime fighting is not validated by the number of additional police officers deployed to the streets.

- Nor is air travel safety appropriately measured by the number of passengers screened or pen-knives confiscated.

- Neither will any number of auditor observations of past company performance support a conclusive determination that a given control system will be robust under future conditions.

So while Hanson did credit the audit firms — "They've all made good progress in identifying the problem" — he went too far with the chastisement that "closing the loop on it is something many firms are struggling with."

Well they would struggle — because with their oversight agency taking such an antagonistic view, they are not dealing with a "loop." Instead they face an endless road to an unknown future.

EPIDEMIC LEVELS OF AUDIT DEFICIENCIES — IFIAR AND THE PCAOB OVERPLAY A HAND

A major challenge for any regulator is the gap between rhetoric and accomplishment. That has been the case so far in the modest history of the awkwardly named International Forum of Independent Audit Regulators.

IFIAR came together in 2006, an outgrowth of the American audit regulator — known for short, and no more poetically, as the PCAOB.

Around the world, the agency members of IFIAR were born or redesigned in the post-Enron outburst of legislation that began with Sarbanes-Oxley, the law that marked the end of the accounting profession's exercise of self-inspection and quality oversight. The PCAOB and its children in fifty more countries now gather under the IFIAR banner with the mission of providing a "platform for dialogue and information-sharing regarding audit quality matters and regulatory practices around the world."

That message was from the group's press release of March 3, 2016, issued at a meeting in Amsterdam. Chairman Janice van Diggelen bid for media attention to IFIAR's inspection and oversight programs, done "in response to persistent levels of deficiencies in public company audits reported by members":

> "IFIAR is not yet satisfied that enough has been done by the audit profession to understand and address shortfalls

in audit quality. The outcomes continue to show a lack of consistency in the execution of high quality audits and highlight concerns over the robustness of the firms' internal quality managements systems."

The survey reported deficiencies in fully 43% of the 872 public company audits inspected, and 45% of the inspected audits of 96 financial institutions.

What is an interested public to make of these alarmist messages — a 40-plus percent deficiency rate in what IFIAR had called the year before, "vital areas of public company audits"?

On the one hand, while IFIAR cautioned against extrapolating, it said that the findings of deficiencies:

"imply that the auditor's performance falls below the expected level of diligence to satisfy the public interest role the audit is meant to fulfill, and that the audit failed *to provide the* level of assurance *about the financial statements that it purported to do and that is* required *by the professional standards"* (emphasis added).

The litigation implications of such charges of substandard performance, under the threatening regimes of legal liability in the world's large economies, should be taken as grave. Further, such a failure rate in any other sector would also — if credible — be intolerable.

Some examples serve to test the nature of the measurements. Dangerous activities such as construction sites and chemical plants advertise their accident-free periods over months and years. New car warranties are now in place above and beyond 100,000 miles. Airline casualties are measured per 100 million passenger miles. Food safety and environmental pollution standards are expressed in parts per billion.

Even at the hands of the most casual food-safety agency, a pervasive rate of "deficiencies in vital areas" at the IFIAR level would in a heartbeat cost the operator's license of a neighborhood coffee shop or a curbside taco truck.

And yet — *every* securities trade on *every* stock exchange in *every* IFIAR country is based on financial statements audited by a firm subject to inspection by an IFIAR member. And the very *raison d'être* of those members is, as their press release put it, their "mandate to improve audit quality."

Which calls for a choice: Is the quality of Big Audit so fundamentally degraded that large-firm performance deserves the headline-grabbing assertion of persistent, recurring serious deficiencies?

Or — perhaps — is IFIAR as a global aggregation of audit regulators actually choosing to devise and apply the *proper* standards of measurement and evaluation in the first place? In other words, what counts? Who is doing the counting? And what's the point?

Take the case of Andre Drummond, the 6'11" center for the Pistons, Detroit's professional basketball team. Through the 2016 season, he carried the NBA's worst career free-throw shooting record, at 35.5% — compared to the range of 90% for the league's leaders. Yet he enjoyed his fourth successful year, based on his skills in rebounding and defense.

The same in professional baseball, where a batter failing to hit safely three times out of four could still achieve Hall of Fame status (*see* the career batting averages of Bill Mazeroski — .260, Ozzie Smith — .262, and Harmon Killebrew — .256).

Properly defined measures of performance quality and rates of failure and error are not designed or intended, if legitimate, to be evaded or eroded. So IFIAR's assertion, as van Diggelen put it — that its finding of deficiencies "may not reflect the state of the auditing profession at the current time. The survey is not meant to measure empirically or for statistically significant changes in audit quality ..." — is in tension with its own inability to give affirmative comfort that its findings are indeed consistent with good reliable audit practice.

IFIAR's promotional efforts are challenged by the dubious usefulness of the maxim, "manage what you can measure." So it was left not only unable to find a satisfactory answer to the wrong question — it was so hindered as not even to ask the right one.

There are two lessons in the legend of the shepherd boy who cried "wolf":

First, the publicity-seeking little boy was met with public rejection and lack of respect for his overreaching. And second, when the wolf actually did show up, the villagers really did lose their sheep.

THE EC'S 2010 GREEN PAPER — THE BUREAUCRATS ADD LITTLE

"We've gotta do something. They're serious this time.

"You know what we gotta do. Toga party.

"We're on double secret probation, whatever that is.
We can't afford to have a toga party.

"You guys up for a toga party?"
— *"Animal House"* — 1978

As seen in the discussion of the tortured history of mandatory audit firm rotation, the protracted legislative process in Europe came in the spring of 2014 to a set of compromised positions. As these are coming into force at the national level, they will inevitably conflict with the more sensible approach of re-tender, as taken in the United Kingdom, and threaten perverse and disruptive consequences as companies with global operations wrestle with the unreconcilable conflicts.

Lawmaking in the European Union has long defied analysis, reflecting a hodgepodge of minority political interests, bureaucrats with qualifications in proportion to their small-country economies, and lobbyists passionately committed to the protection of their turf.

Little wonder, then, that attention to the accounting profession has been both spasmodic and unhelpful. Fuller history is left elsewhere, with only brief attention to recent events offered here.

The October 13, 2010, release of the European Commission's Green Paper, *Audit Policy: Lessons from the Crisis*, by Internal Market and Services Commissioner Michel Barnier, then in his first year in office, illustrated the observable behaviors.

A desirable principle for any newly arrived bureaucrat, tempted to launch the machinery of inquiry, should be to demonstrate a real need for further admiration of an already-explored agenda, and the perception and will to do more than replow the same ground.

Instead, on the grave issue of the viability of Big Audit, the naïve tone in which the Green Paper articulated the role of auditors, and the innocence of its "questions," made evident that it was at risk to be another exercise in resource-wasting.

The Green Paper started with the customary observations — for example, that audit "provides assurance on the veracity of the financial health of all companies," and that "continuity in the provision of audit services to large companies is critical to financial stability."

But this exercise in self-congratulation was basically empty. Its adherents had never known a world in which public company financial statements did *not* bear the familiar blessing of a one-page standard auditor's report. The alternative proposition, of life without the legal requirement of an audit — an obligation that survives only by force of law, not by market choice — had never been tested.

A few examples of the Green Paper's recycling of old material (*question numbers are kept; some wordings are streamlined*):

Can smaller firms emerge to become viable participants in the large-company market segment (# 27):

Doing the arithmetic, and assuming the impossible — that the audit practices of all the small firms doing public company audits

were merged into a single practice — that unmanageable aggregation would only approximate the size of the smaller of the Big
Four (*refer* to the *Sidebar* back in Part I).

Just as the case has never been made that smaller firms can
deliver competitively *superior* quality of service, their limitations
of geographic scope, breadth of expertise and capacity for risk tolerance are disabling to the notion that a new global-scale audit
provider can be either grown or built. And their leaders, when
challenged to be both willing and candid, will admit it.

*Should alternative structures be explored to allow audit firms to
raise capital from external sources (# 23):*

As seen, the Big Four capital structures, with their modest partner investments and operations financed by their client receivables,
do not need and could not constructively deploy major outside
capital even if offered. Rather, such funds would only be a honey
pot to attract the further attention of potential litigants.

*Would contingency plans, including "living wills," address the
systemic risk of a large-firm failure (# 31):*

First advanced in 2008 as part of the output of Treasury
Secretary Henry Paulson's Advisory Committee on the Audit
Profession, this trial balloon had deflated without lift-off — for
the obvious reason, as shown by Andersen's rapid disintegration
in 2002, that with the loss of trust, the death spiral of client and
personnel flight, once started, is irreversible.

*Are there benefits to joint audits or consortia including smaller
firms (# 28):*

The French structure of joint audits is argued for, but is profoundly unsatisfactory as a persuasive example — perpetrated as
it is by the lobbying of the smaller firms' appeals to preserve a
local slice of the Big Audit market.

The notion that minor participation in an otherwise global-
scale audit engagement could position a small firm to supplant a

failed Big Four firm is belied by the record: at present, *every* audit of the CAC 40 in France is led by a Big Four firm. If small-firm consortia were credible, unconstrained choice in the marketplace means that there would already be at least one example in practice.

Should audit appointments and remuneration be managed by government (## 16–17):

Consider this long step down the short road to nationalized audit agencies. Nowhere else are markets for commodity products subject to such artificial constraints — whether auto manufacturers, retail bankers or espresso vendors.

Yet if viewed as a legitimate target for government takeover, audits performed by low-grade civil servants — the only ones who would find appeal in such a career post — would descend even further in value and repute.

Should audit mandates be limited in time (# 18), *or should rotation be mandatory* (#29):

To this, the complete one-word answer has always been, "Italy." The only country of significance having experience with mandatory rotation produced the scandal of Parmalat — world-class malfeasance enabled by the rotation-inflicted division of responsibility between two audit firms. That, and the PCAOB's retreat on rotation in America, should have sufficed.

INSTEAD OF EU REFORM — COMMISSIONER BARNIER'S FURTHER EFFORTS[7]

It might have been hoped that Commissioner Barnier, green as his paper in 2010, might with sunlight and fertilizer have ripened quickly into his office.

But a hoped-for maturation was not to be. On November 30, 2012, he released his "final" proposal to reengineer the structure and business model of the large accounting firms.

A neutral observer could have taken some issue with the tendentious tone of Barnier's assertions, of which an abbreviated sample:

- "The lack of regular tendering of audit services and periodic rotation of audit firms has *deprived* audit of its key ethos: professional skepticism."

- "(T)he prohibition of the provision of nonaudit services in general would *effectively* address the need to reinforce independence and professional skepticism."

- "(T)he introduction of mandatory audit firm rotation would *contribute* to higher quality audits."

- "The appointment of more than one statutory auditor ... would ... *contribute* to increasing audit quality" (*all emphasis added*).

A full list here of the serious problems in Barnier's proposed regulatory structure would exceed reasonable length limits. For a partial catalog:

- No single client could sustainably represent more than 15% of a firm's total annual fees (Art. 9) — a limitation with nasty if unanticipated potential consequences for the ability of smaller firms to ramp up their competitive scale at the upper end of the client size range.

- The broad prohibition of Article 10 on nonaudit services to clients — the full range from litigation expert services to valuation, technology consulting and legal and brokerage — would extend to network members *and* to client parents and foreign subsidiaries — thus clashing with permissible scope of services in the entire non-European world.

- The further obligation of the large firms to hive off all their nonaudit capabilities (Art. 10, § 5) would apply to their non-EU networks' operations within the EU, thus forcing any ex-EU company to incur the cost and disruption of dividing its otherwise-permitted nonaudit service engagements between a Big Four firm and another, unrelated niche provider.

- The requirement that statutory auditors provide their own annual financial reports would oblige those reports themselves to be *audited*, at both the firm and network level (Art. 26.2 and 26.3(d)).

- Not only would rotation be mandatory under Article 33 — every six years (extended to nine years for optional joint audits). But invitations-to-tender would be required from at least two nonincumbent choices (Art. 32.2), of which one must be such a small firm that it could derive not more than 15% of its audit fees from large companies, as defined (Art. 32.3(a)).

  Therein lay a recipe for paralysis for large-company audit committees. Audit competence is built on both scale and industry expertise — so the small-firm ceiling would have made it inevitable that an invitee to tender would lack the size and breadth of experience to provide adequate service, while outreach to two other Big Four firms would clash against the global-level disqualifications of networks serving a client's ex-EU needs.

- "Contingency plans" were to be required from the large firms to address life-threatening events (Art. 43) — as if there could be disruption avoidance from the impact of a "black swan" litigation or law enforcement sanction.
  - That is because, unlike a corporation's ability to continue in business during bankruptcy as a supervised debtor-in-possession, the private accounting partnerships have no retention hold on their partners or staff, whose rapid departure — proved in the case of Andersen in 2002 — would make Barnier's "orderly failure" an oxymoron.

- The revised requirements of a redesigned audit report (Art. 21) would include 23 subsections, adding such new information as the length of audit tenure (§ e), the extent of direct balance sheet verification (§ h), the details of materiality (§ j), and the identity of *each member* of the audit team (§ q).
  - Potentially useful and worthy of debate, some of these might have been — yet quoting § 22.4, "the audit report shall not be longer than four pages or 10,000 characters (without spaces)."

This last proposal was in a different league from Barnier's quest to impose mandatory rotation. Because it is routine that a large-company audit team has a headcount above one hundred members, Barnier's four-page limit would have been exceeded by a list of personnel all by itself.

While most of Barnier's suggestions deservedly fell by the wayside, his effort on rotation actually took hold, as discussed above, with the EU legislation foreshadowing mandatory rotation, on a schedule the disruption of which will only be seen as it follows the run-in timetable of between ten and 24 years — by which time all those responsible for its infliction will have long since passed from the scene.

DISINTEGRATION — THE BIG FOUR TELL THE HOUSE OF LORDS, "WE DON'T SEE THAT ON THE HORIZON"

In assessing the performance of the world's lawmakers, there is a good way to increase the chances for satisfaction: start with very low expectations.

As discussed above, a ten-year "re-tender" approach to auditor tenure in the United Kingdom eventually emerged in the interplay between the United Kingdom's Financial Reporting Council and its Competition Commission. That solution — as only time will tell — may prove workable for the audit firms and their global clients — although any beneficial effect has yet to be shown — and it is certainly superior to the mandated rotation legislated in the EU although eventually dropped by the Americans.

So much for the British regulators. As for its legislators, they were on display in the broadcast on Parliament TV of the House of Lords Economic Affairs Committee session of November 23, 2010. That exercise was billed as a look at concentration in the audit market and the role of the auditors in the financial crisis. In practice, the heads of the Big Four in the United Kingdom batted away slow-pitch questions that ranged from the naïve and misinformed to the incomprehensible.

During an amiable 90-minute wandering around the topic of auditor concentration, the House of Lords Committee queried the invited heads of the Big Four, "You do share the general unease about the fact that it could be Four coming down to Three?"

For the quartet's response, the then-senior partner of Deloitte's UK firm, John Connolly, contributed this: "I don't see that on the horizon at all."

Mr. Connolly's invocation of an empty horizon invited military comparison, with real but unfortunate historical resonance. General Custer did not foresee danger from the invisible Indians. The American forces at Pearl Harbor were heedless of the approaching Japanese. To Adolph Hitler and his generals, the beaches of Normandy were both well defended and bare of Allied threat.

As with these examples, the lessons of hindsight about Mr. Connolly's limit on his vision is that a clear view of a blank horizon is of little value, if the surveyed circumference extends no farther than arm's-length.[8]

Consider the Sanskrit folk tale of *koopa mandooka* — the "frog in the well."[9] The frog lives in blinkered comfort, so long as confined within the boundaries of his closed, cool and nourishing little world.

Should he venture forth, the perils of the world outside are unknown. It may indeed be a paradise, full of succulent insects

and comfortable lily pads and luscious companions with which
the frog can disport and sire entire populations of little tadpoles.

Or, it may be a hell of deadly predators — voracious snakes and
hawks and sharp-toothed fish. Or a searing desert beyond the fringes
of the oasis, where a clueless frog will be pan-seared in minutes.

Unless informed and prepared, the frog in the well has no way
to differentiate a prosperous future from one of mortal danger.
And the consequences of his ignorance are just as fatal as those of
being wrong.

Here's what the Big Four leaders might have said, in answer to
the Lords' call:

> *"We not only share your unease. We are terrified for the
> survival of our firms. Not so much for our generation,
> who if fortunate may hope to ease soon into our retire-
> ments, but for the future of a profession that depends for
> its sustainability on the talent and commitment of our
> younger personnel.*
>
> *"Our ability to provide valuable assurance remains impor-
> tant to the capital markets. But it must evolve beyond the
> binary choice, whether or not to pronounce "true and
> fair" — a choice exposed in the banking crisis by our
> delivery of unqualified audit reports on soon-to-fail institu-
> tions as not only unresponsive but affirmatively dangerous.*
>
> *"Yet regulatory requirements confine us to an unhelpful
> commodity product. Here is what we could do, but only
> with your help:*
>
> - *"Supplant the current report form which no longer serves
>   a useful purpose, tailoring our reports to the real needs of
>   particular users.*
>
> - *"Deploy a full range of services that would include
>   access to the expertise of nonaudit personnel to achieve
>   more sophisticated performance and improved quality.*

- *"Support the interests of investors under government oversight, enforcement and protection such that our reporting would not create liability exposure of a magnitude that would destroy us."*

They *might* have said that. But they didn't. For want of a vision extending to that far but visible horizon, an opportunity was allowed to pass.

And Then Everyone Went for Tea

The House of Lords Committee hearing showed that the challenges to the viability of Big Audit were not about to be solved at the hands of the British legislators. Examples of their limited scope:

- "Are you happy," they asked, with the degree of market concentration? In answer, the Big Four could hardly admit displeasure, when they control the entire large-company audit market with no prospect of emergent competition.

- What about a threat to withdraw from the audit market? "Oh, not us — audit is at the very core of what we do!"

- If that's so, "are you uneasy" that the large firms would go from four to three?

- Amplifying the straight-faced answer on disintegration, that "we don't see that on the horizon" — the speakers at the same time conceded that although the events of the credit crisis were "unprecedented," there were "lessons to be learnt" for everyone.

Sometimes the unthinkable does happen — as the events since the very real disintegration of Andersen had made clear. As to "lessons," however, this logical follow-up question went unasked:

- "What would you do — what would any of us do — if despite your intentions, one of the firms incurred what was described with British euphemism as an 'Andersen moment'?"

For this, there was no suggestion of an answer from either side of the tables.

In the middle third of the proceedings, the Committee were able to become better informed, if not wiser, as their invited guests did give a concise rundown of a list of the unachievable ideas — namely:

- Breakup of the Big Four would add nothing to global-scale competition, since — with the geographic breadth required because most of the revenue of FTSE 100 companies is actually generated outside the United Kingdom — the resulting fragments would lack scale, coverage and investment capability.

- The current restriction on scope of services to audit clients — where in the year leading up to the hearing, no FTSE 100 company paid consulting fees to its auditor — was claimed to be working well: an assertion which, considering the unsolved nature of the survivability threat, meant that if the current environment represented success, what would failure look like?

- The arguments for joint audits or mandatory rotation founder on the examples of degraded quality — the likes of Parmalat in Italy and BCCI in the United Kingdom itself.

- And the day's topper: if audit is "implicitly a form of insurance," why had that industry not ridden to the rescue? — a proposition so discredited that even the committee chair hastened onward.

The hearing wound down to a well-choreographed break at 5 p.m. for afternoon tea, but not without an "Alice in Wonderland" moment on the question of the auditors' issuance of unqualified opinions in the months before the failures of such British institutions as Royal Bank of Scotland, HBOS and Northern Rock.

At the assertion that the auditors actually "performed well" in light of the complex events of 2007 and 2008, adjectives such as "astonishing" and "misleading" were tossed around.

But the pointed observation by one of the Big Four that an auditor does not assess the risk of a business, only rendering a "pass-fail" report — always in identical language, whether the leverage of the enterprise is one hundred times or none at all — starkly contrasted with a plea from the questioners that an assessment of the "dangers" in a business was precisely, if simplistically, the assurance sought by a wishful user community.

In that context, the fact that technical reporting requirements had been satisfied, to avoid a going-concern qualification — if only through closed-door communications with the Bank of England and the Financial Services Authority — definitively exposed the raw insufficiency of the current audit model.

As was equally the case in the 1980s when the American auditors trailed the emerging catastrophe among the savings and loan associations, the profession lacks satisfactory tools when the regulatory regimes put them to the choice — whether to qualify their opinions and generate a self-fulfilling prophecy of disaster, or to rationalize a demonstration of the emptiness of the report that constitutes their core product.

If that much could have been taken as established, before everyone went off for tea, then the day would have shown some real accomplishment.

DELOITTE'S AUDIT BAN IN SAUDI ARABIA — THE POTENTIAL FOR GLOBAL EFFECTS

For all the existential risks to the Big Four originating in any one of the largest and most threatening of the world's most developed economies, the hazard cannot be discounted of a disruptive event arising in a location mistakenly assumed to be peripheral.

As first reported by *Accountancy Age* on December 2, 2014, the Capital Market Regulator in Saudi Arabia acted to ban Deloitte's firm from auditing public companies in that country, provisionally from June 1, 2015, extended in June 2016 for a further two years, on account of its work for the loss-making company MMG. In addition to the local impact, the potential knock-on consequences did not bode well across Deloitte's global network, the largest by revenue of the Big Four.

Further and even more ominously, a collateral outcome of a Saudi black-ball might be the long-feared destabilizing of the Big Four's trust-based franchise to audit the world's largest companies.

It has been well recognized, since 2002 when Andersen's leaders fatally failed to placate the US Department of Justice over its conduct related to Enron, that it hurts to be on the wrong side of the life-or-death power of an angry prosecutor.

Conversely, there are ample examples of the Big Four's escape from scrutiny in settings that are too far down the global scale to be consequential.

It is the combination that is dangerous: an enforcement authority without a mature history of regulatory predictability, but with enough influence to unsettle the Big Audit model.

For some illustrations:

- In 2000, the Italian antitrust authority had the then-Big Six firms dead in its sights, with charges of price-fixing and other coordinated anti-competitive conduct. Lacking either the will or the motivation to push for practice prohibitions or other structural change, however, the agency's application of the nuances of "Italian justice" was to tap the large firms gently on the wrist.

- PwC's firm in Russia spent several years in litigation over its 2002–2004 audits of Yukos, under potential threat to its license to practice. But as was reported,[10] PwC having remitted its fees to the government in settlement, it was able to be retained as *persona grata*, as shown by its long-running engagement for Gazprom.[11]

- PwC also suffered the protracted pretrial incarceration of two
  of its Indian partners, their lengthy criminal trial and the imposition of seven-year prison sentences upon their conviction, over
  the billion-dollar "ghost employees" scheme confessed in 2009
  by Ramalinga Raju, founder and CEO of Satyam Computer
  Services. But PwC global chief Dennis Nally's travel to Delhi in
  November 2014 to head up his firm's vigorous support for the
  country's economy under Prime Minister Modi[12] indicated his
  comfort and confidence that the firm's presence and franchise
  there were not to be disturbed.

What is important in these examples is that none of these countries were large and important enough to matter. The Big Four's
global networks could have survived worst-case exclusion from
local practice in Russia or Italy or India.

It could have been a different and life-threatening story, by contrast, if in 2006, the sanctions[13] imposed on PwC in Japan for its
work on Kanebo had not been so flexible. With the size and
global connectedness of the Japanese economy, PwC dodged a
fatal bullet, being permitted to survive the forced closure of its
local firm by organizing a new local affiliate — which came to
absorb many of its personnel and, vitally, by which it was able to
continue both local work for foreign clients and ex-Japan work
for its clients there.

Which comes back to Saudi Arabia — where, incidentally or
not, Deloitte also audited — until replaced by KPMG — the
Saudi-listed telephone provider Mobily, another investigation target,[14] after profit cuts, a stock price collapse and the suspension
and firing of its chief executive officer.

What remains unknowable is how far abroad the Saudi sanctions might run. In mature regulatory environments, official
enforcement would not cascade into private sanctions across a Big
Four client list. Leadership of a CalPers or PIMCO or Vanguard
would resist imposing a ban on one of the Big Four that would

cause self-inflicted disruption to the companies making up their massive fund portfolios.

Could the same be said of the global holdings of the Saudi royal family?

Demonstrably sensitive to any suggestion of lack of transparency,[15] Prince Alwaleed Bin Talal is the chairman of the Kingdom Holding Company. On his watch, Deloitte's potential consignment to pariah status in his country must be of concern, for example, to Deloitte's firm in the United Kingdom, where it had been the auditor of one of the Kingdom's premier real estate holdings, the massive Canary Wharf development in London.

More to the point, it might safely be predicted that — if the Prince were to have any say in the matter — it would only be if Riyadh freezes over that Deloitte could compete successfully against the incumbents for audit engagements of such prize Saudi holdings as Citigroup (KPMG), EuroDisney (PwC) or News Corp (EY).

The rippling effects of Deloitte's Saudi-originated punishment over MMG could be grave enough. Further, with the acute pressures on auditor choice and replacement arising from mandatory re-tender requirements in the United Kingdom, and the rotations mandated under the legislation in the European Union, the structural impacts beyond a single unpredictable country could only be disturbingly unpredictable on a far wider scale.

AS FOR THE VIEWS OF THE ISSUERS' LOBBY[16]

There is no finding solutions without a proper focus on the problems. Think of the guy in the dark of night, stumbling under the street lamp in search for his keys. The cop on the beat asks, "If you say they were lost over in that dark alley, why are you looking here?"

"Because the light's better," the poor guy responds.

Which pretty much described the January, 2006 report of the US Chamber of Commerce, on the survivability of the large accounting firms, *Auditing: A Profession at Risk*.

With its heart in the right place, the lobbyist for American enterprise said that "action must be taken" so that companies might retain "access to high-quality, reasonably priced auditing services."

Whereupon, the report lost its focus and its way, bumping dimly down the dark streets from one missed opportunity to another. Here were six of them:

First, the Chamber recognized that the audit profession had become effectively uninsurable in the face of litigation costs that threaten immediate destruction of partners' limited capital and their long-term inability to hire and retain personnel.

Yet its observation that legal reform "may be needed" missed the crucial point. Auditor insurability requires the ability to predict, quantify and limit the insured risk — conditions impossible to fulfill under the hazards of unlimited liability.

Second, the Chamber repeated the familiar if unhelpful refrain that auditors should not be held liable for failure to detect or prevent cleverly designed collusive fraud.

That's fine, as far as it goes. But:

- Many corporate frauds are neither particularly clever nor well concealed, but are simply extended shenanigans, perpetrated for generations. Rita Crundwell, now-jailed controller for the City of Dixon, Illinois, made off with $53 million in municipal funds over a 22-*year* period — for which, in October 2013, the regional firm of CliftonLarsonAllen agreed to save its own life by paying out $35 million to settle claims against it. The criminal scheme at Taylor Bean & Whitaker for which, also in October 2013, Deloitte settled its $7.5 billion lawsuit, was described in the indictment of its principals as extending from 2002 to 2009.

- Other "frauds" consist of aggressive use of highly judgmental accounting standards set permissively under the influence of corporate interests themselves.

- In other cases, standards may be questionably flexible to start, and then are pushed past the point of abuse by executives over-reaching the limits of their auditors either to perform or simply to resist.

- Lastly, auditors faced with a crushing liability overhang are forced to forego their courtroom defenses by settling their mega-cases without going to trial.

Third, the Chamber proposed that the PCAOB should promulgate a "safe harbor" standard for fraud detection, to protect the auditors if they could show they had fulfilled the steps required by a regulatory bureaucracy.

Yet it is this very "check the box" approach to requirements for assurance on corporate controls that is the Achilles heel of Sarbanes-Oxley. Companies whose securities trade on US exchanges have since 2002 faced the escalated cost and diminished effectiveness of auditor performance because of the Sarbanes-Oxley requirements.

Fourth, the Chamber served its own broad constituency of small businesses by suggesting that the audit profession's doubtful viability is not helpful to new companies that may be innovative but unfamiliar to the capital markets.

The trouble is, that is not where the real threats lie. It is not the unknowns that have threatened the Big Four with the biggest and most costly claims, but familiar names: Enron, Lehman Brothers, Tesco — and the list goes on.

Fifth, understandably exercised over the Enron-related indictment of Andersen, the Chamber called for legislation to "rein in" the process of indicting whole enterprises.

Here the problem is that unless world trade and commerce unexpectedly achieve an as-yet unknown state of grace, society will expect and call upon its law enforcement officers to indict and prosecute where indicated by the facts. The criminal charges against SAC Capital Advisors in July 2013 and the maneuvering to preserve the licenses and permits of the banks upon their guilty pleas in the spring of 2014 and 2015 are recent examples.

Sixth, the Chamber joined a chorus of concern over the shrinkage down to the Big Four and their audit of nearly all the world's largest companies. But the suggested relocation to smaller firms of nonaudit work is once again off point: Those are not statutory compliance services, where the real legal risks and fatal exposures lie.

To be fair, the Chamber may have been so turned around because it started from a faulty bearing — that Big Audit in its current form actually is central to public confidence in the capital markets. If another of the Big Four should disintegrate amid a litigation catastrophe, it will become obvious that their continued delivery of services will not be something anyone will be able to preserve.

In the small pool of light cast in this darkness, that much was right out in plain sight.

AUDITED FINANCIAL STATEMENTS FOR THE BIG FOUR — SHOULD THE COBBLER'S BAREFOOT CHILDREN HAVE SHOES?

As has been told, a recurring theme through the travails of the Big Four has been their lack of success in persuading either their regulators or their public constituents of the gravity of their fragile position. This should not be surprising, for a profession widely perceived as arcane in its vocabulary, opaque in its own disclosures, important but only to be criticized in times of crisis, and yet handsomely compensated beyond the sympathies of the general population.

When transparency of operations and public access to information are increasingly required for the sake of trust and credibility, the Big Four have declined to take up one opportunity — namely to be as forthcoming with the same kind of detail about their own operations as are their large global clients on whose financial statements they opine.

PCAOB member Steven Harris proposed in a speech at American University on March 20, 2014, "that the large accounting firms make their audited financial statements available to the public."

Harris observed that "many find it ironic that auditing firms in the United States ... resist providing their own financial statements," and saw no reason "that the auditing firms that act as gatekeepers to our securities markets should not be as transparent to investors as the companies they audit."

"Irony spotting" not being a common trait in Washington, Harris did not observe this coincidence — that he was two weeks ahead of the PCAOB's public meetings on April 2–3, 2014, to further address its 2011 proposal for reconsideration of the inadequacy of today's auditor reporting, about which Harris himself had said at the PCAOB's Board Meeting on September 15, 2011:

> "Investors clearly do not believe the current three paragraph, largely boilerplate, binary audit report, is either sufficiently informative or serves their needs."

Suppose that the Harris proposal to impose an audit-reporting requirement on the Big Four were actually taken up and debated seriously.

First of all, it *can* be done. Some country-level firms of the large networks — as for example, in the United Kingdom — already publish IFRS-based financial statements, audited and reported on by colleagues from the smaller firms.

Problems of scale and substance raise questions, but it is noteworthy to the discussion that back in the late 1970s, Arthur Andersen's *global* financial statements were audited and reported on by Haskins & Sells — as the Deloitte firm in the United States was then branded.

Should the Big Four voluntarily offer such disclosures and assurance? Should they be *required* to do so? There would be serious cross-currents and antagonisms in those discussions.

Over the profession's long-standing resistance, there could be considerable public education, both from the information to be disclosed, and from that not furnished.

Consider an extension to their US firms, or to their global structures at large, of the Big Four's audited disclosures in the United Kingdom. For 2016, their revenues there ranged from £2.07 to £3.4 billion, with reported UK firm profits from £374 to £829 million.

Those UK data mainly serve to reinforce the point that the Big Four's business model, running on client receivables and egg-shell-thin capital, is not designed or robust to withstand the ten-figure financial shock that would be inflicted by a truly bad-case litigation or law enforcement outcome.

As to information that similarly designed US disclosure would not make available — there would be two gaping holes:

The first is that, just like the world's other large enterprises — and noting that the Big Four's reported aggregate global revenues for 2016 was near $128 billion — the financial statements of their UK firms are opaque on the extent and quantification of litigation claims and contingency exposures.

The same would be true in the United States — where the *modus vivendi* between the accounting standards-setters and the litigation defense lawyers has long permitted a shroud of confidentiality over the uncertainties of publicly predicted litigation outcomes.

And second, the UK experience makes clear the limited amount of worldwide information to be gleaned only from country-level reporting — which at present offers only the most passing reference, in either words or numbers, to the local firms' membership or participation in the business and funding of their global networks.

The Big Four continue to be on two sides of this structural issue, as they are both obliged and permitted to do under the parochial nature of the profession's organization, regulation and oversight. On one hand, they publish both their revenues and their commitments to seamless service on a global scale. But on the other, they pull back to globally opaque, local-country descriptions for purposes of risk acceptance and cross-border liability.

Arthur Andersen was alone in ever submitting its financial statements to outside audit, and its brief experiment was ended a generation ago in the face of antagonistic resistance from the rest of the Big Eight. Meanwhile, its global network fell in 2002 like a house of cards, under the unwillingness of its ex-US firms to support the US firm in its time of Enron-based travail.

Which calls for one final and irony-tinged observation. Those urging the extension of Big Four reporting transparency might well press Harris and the PCAOB to require the Big Four to follow the initiative of Andersen's global reporting from a generation ago. That *could* be done, under the PCAOB's authority over non-US audit firms participating in the audits of public companies filing in the United States.

But whereas the Big Four's UK firms are audited by firms in the next smaller tiers — who have no significant share of the market for audit services to the world's large global companies — the only auditors having the geographic scope and scale to report on the Big Four's global networks would be those very four networks themselves.

It would be questionable whether, if such a requirement were put in place, the resulting round-robin of mutual Big Four examination and reporting would find public favor. Hostile reactions could be anticipated, among the critics of the accounting profession who are inclined to see malign cartel behavior at every turn.

But candidly acknowledging the ineffectiveness of their relations with legislators and regulators, and to take up a disclosure opportunity having real bargaining value, the Big Four might well find the effort worthwhile.

In any event, the discussion should be worth having — further to the Steve Harris initiative. There would be both hand-wringing and stone-throwing. And it would not be easy to predict who would come out of the tussle.

CONSULTING — A PLAUSIBLE EXIT STRATEGY?

Concern for the viability of Big Audit rests on the unavoidable reality that a single "black swan" litigation could trigger the catastrophically viral collapse of the Big Four — a possibility beyond denial given Andersen's death spiral in 2002.

The only sure alternative is the resolution, on a pre-collapse basis, of the seemingly intractable impediments to a sustainable audit function — including the Big Four's persistent performance quality challenges, litigation liability, financial fragility, uninsurability and independence-based constraints on their scope of services.

There is a new and different new take, however, based on the rapid growth of the Big Four consulting practices — now relabeled for cosmetic reasons as "Advisory." Despite widespread prohibitions on consulting for audit clients, they are all reporting robustly increasing nonassurance revenues.[17] Their 2016 consulting growth rates year-on-year ranged from 8% to 13%, representing steadily increasing percentages of their overall revenue, compared with the largest reported audit revenue growth rate of 6%.

Advisory revenues today at the Big Four — under strategies that include a banquet of acquisitions and alliance building[18] — have reached levels not seen since the large firms' various exits from the consulting business — the bitter divorce between Arthur Andersen and Andersen Consulting that commenced in 1998 and was finalized with the launch of Accenture on January 1, 2001; EY's sale to CapGemini in February 2000; KPMG's 2001 spin-off to create what became BearingPoint, and Pricewaterhouse's sale of its practice to IBM in July 2002.

It presents a tantalizing hypothesis that separation of Big Four consulting might underpin the next logical step in a survival strategy — to firewall and split off altogether from their audit practices.

There would be problems. Not because separation of audit from consulting cannot be done. Plainly it can, as shown by Accenture's growth since birth to an enterprise with 2016 revenue of $32.9 billion, capable of taking on engagements of the very largest scale.

Nor because of the speculative reaction that a Big Four "flight" to consulting would be unlikely, since newly formed "Advisory-only" firms might keep at least minimal audit capacity for the sake of credentials and credibility. That point is readily answered by experience: Accenture not only did not *need* an ongoing relationship with its erstwhile accounting bedmate — it could scarcely wait for the ink to dry on the divorce decree before scrubbing itself of prior history and maximizing the distance between the two.

It is because Big Four division into separate consulting and audit practices would not of itself mark the immediate end of Big Audit.

To separate the Big Four audit practices would not be like a manufacturing company simply firing its workers, exiting a geographic market or shelving a product or shutting down a factory or a division. The Big Audit model may well be fatally flawed and unsustainable, but the large audit practices still generate annual audit revenues in the multiple billions,[19] and globally employ several hundred thousand professionals. These represent jobs and revenue that a consulting-oriented leadership could neither fold up into the surviving practice nor isolate and handcuff under non-compete restrictions.

Instead, what would happen is that freshly jettisoned audit partners would — through some form of spin-off, carve-out or "management buy-out," and perhaps trailing along an ancillary tax division or two — create four (or more) firms — purified as either "audit" or "audit and tax" only.

If so, the outcome would not be the disappearance of Big Audit — at least not yet — but transfer of this poisoned chalice to "slightly-less-big" firms — narrower in practice scope and financially weaker and more exposed to the threats in their litigation portfolios.

Which in turn means that the "audit only" analysis is in the end not wrong, but only incomplete. The eventual day of final reckoning for privately provided Big Audit would not be upon the evolution of the Big Four's aspirations toward the distinct prosperity of consulting, but when one of their offspring should suffer the fate that killed off Andersen.

Sidebar: "What If?" A Contra-Factual

For a comparison to the current troubled state, consider for a moment this contra-factual:

Suppose, back at the end of the booming decade of the 1990s, before the Enron era spun the system into dysfunctionality, that the Big Four had retained their consulting practices — that they resolved their scope-of-services limitations — and that they evolved to realize their potential as the true full-spectrum organizations that were latent within their DNA.

It did not happen, but it could have, this way:

One of two possibilities might have propelled Arthur Andersen to the next level. By one route, its attempted 1989 merger with Pricewaterhouse — which failed under parochial squabbling over either leadership or pension funding, depending on whose version is believed — would have married up the former firm's strengths in innovation, structure and consulting with the unparalleled client list of the latter.

Or, there was an alternative to the combination of greed, distrust and disrespect that underlay the 1998 divorce between Arthur Andersen and Andersen Consulting (reborn as Accenture). Instead, leaders with a different vision might have recognized and realized the synergistic potential of an audit practice that fully utilized and partnered with the strengths of the consultants and their world-class skills in the design, installation and operation of big-company systems for financial recording and reporting. There would have been a model truly fit for purpose in the new century.

With that powerhouse firm on lead, a new model would have been available for ready emulation by the other large accounting networks — as competitors, to be sure, but prepared to join in the creation of a shared vision of the future of redesigned large-company assurance. There would have followed the immediate approval and endorsement by both their global-scale clients and the available sources of outside investment — the latter providing the level of third-party finance needed for investment in the required expansions in technology, methodology and personnel with expanded qualifications, competencies and expertise.

The stage would have been set for a unified and unambiguous private-sector message from the large firms, to the SEC and the other securities and accountancy regulators:

> *"The future has arrived. Fully integrated providers of assurance*
> *and consulting are in place. We decline to be bound any longer*
> *by outmoded constraints on full client service, or by limits on the*
> *deployment of outside capital, based on out-dated notions of*
> *'appearance of independence,' that are obsolete and intolerable."*

By negotiation if possible, or by ultimatum if necessary, a new day would have arrived.

Instead, with the Andersen divorce and the other large firms' dispositions of their consulting practices under the cavils of the regulators about influences perceived as malign, the opportunity to embrace and shape the future was lost.

To avoid misunderstanding — this is not to argue that the nurturing and retention of client relationships is not significantly influential. But the arguably detrimental impact of consulting revenues, in such headline-grabbing cases as Andersen's relationship with Enron, must be weighed against the no-less-influential pressures a client can wield where audit is the only permissible service and therefore *completely* hostage to a client's pleasure.

Empirical studies have never rebutted this proposition: Money may talk, but it does so with equal or greater force when in the form of fees that are audit only.

Unfortunately, evolution can only be based upon available species from which the linear process of survivable mutations can emerge. So today this contra-factual *cannot* occur. Which is severely disappointing, considering what "might have been."

THE FUTURE BELONGS TO "BIG DATA" — THE CHALLENGES WILL BE ENORMOUS

"If I had asked people what they wanted, they would have said faster horses."
— *Attributed to Henry Ford (without authoritative corroboration), on the rollout strategy of the Model T*

Whatever else may happen in the near-future restructuring of the model for financial reporting and the provision of assurance, fundamental changes in the very nature of both are arriving in the era of Big Data and related developments in analytics, cognitive machine learning, drones and robotics and other intelligent mechanical tools.

The introductory primer, *Big Data*, Meyer-Schonberger and Cukier (2013), helpfully defined the mining of comprehensive bodies of data, available for deep analysis and the deployment of new forms of analytics. The authors' shorthand — "N = All" — referred to the gathering of as much data as possible — if feasible, *all* of it. Those doing the analysis would be able to drill far beneath the margins of error that have been undiscoverable by techniques based on the sampling of smaller data sets, with the ability to discover anomalies, patterns and outliers lurking within the masses of normal transactions.

To capture, analyze and report on peta-bytes of public company financial data, on a real-time basis — both for the use of a company's own management and governance but also for public consumption — means that the long-anticipated obsolescence of annual or any other noncontemporaneous reporting will at last have arrived.

Introduction: The Speed and Scope of the Changes

The speed with which Big Data issues have evolved was captured and highlighted by Martin Ford's *Financial Times* business book of 2015, *Rise of the Robots*. There, the ominous message for everyone still believing in job security under the Big Audit model is clear: "They're coming — for your job."

Ford opens with a quick tour of the field increasingly occupied by the machines, surveying the speed and spread of their deployment. According to his source, the International Federation of Robotics, some 230,000 were installed in 2014, with an estimated annual growth rate of 15% projected through 2018.

These items of 2016 news provide additional context:

- Walmart announced that it is testing flying drones to handle its massive warehouse inventories — the goal to do "in a day what now takes employees about a month."

- A Lowe's store in Silicon Valley uses a prototype inventory checker built by Bossa Nova Robotics, using computer vision to recognize bar codes on shelves and a laser to show items out of stock, "automatically perform(ing) a task that humans have done manually for centuries."

- The British government announced its cooperation with Amazon's exploration and actual commencement of drone delivery of packages of up to five pounds — 90% of its sales — while in America the Federal Aviation Administration's new registration rules projected 600,000 commercial drones to be in operation within a year.

- In Rio de Janeiro, the administrators of the 2016 summer Olympics extended the practice, launched for the China games in 2008 and revived in London in 2012, of using a small remote-operated robot truck, rather than human workers, to retrieve the javelins, shot and discuses for return back to the competitors after their heaves — a picturesque practice but with real human and social impact considering the county's double-digit unemployment rate.

- PwC announced its launch in Poland of a commercial drone division — its leaders observing, "the addressable market value of drone powered solutions is over $127 billion" — showing either a complete lack of irony or any self-awareness that their own people-based business was being put at risk.

That last is because of the relevance of these applications to the current Big Audit model. Walmart's drones and Lowe's robots are doing the very counting and data gathering that has traditionally done by squadrons of audit staff — but without quibbling about "quality of life" or gossiping about promotions or dissecting the latest pay raises at the rival firm down the street.

And the ability to analyze data on a comprehensive basis makes obsolete the entire process of audit sampling. The circle returns to the Victorian days of the pioneers of audit, exemplified by Mr. Deloitte and his report in 1850 to the board and shareholders of the Great Western Railway, that in the scope of his work, "every item has been minutely examined."

Across the profession, the transformational loss of the staff jobs to be displaced should be plain — it will hit hiring, team structures, professional training and development at the firms. It will affect career choice-making for students. And the university faculties and professional societies will be pressed, because they depend for their own survival on large numbers of aspiring new entrants to the profession.

The Machines Will Audit Faster, Smarter and Cheaper

A dangerous skepticism can be found around the profession, along the lines that automation has been here forever, and that most will continue to adapt in the future. Not so. Now unleashed, the evolution of technology will not be constrained. The discussion has already shifted from capability to liability and responsibility. It is no longer "if?" — but "how?" and "how soon?"

The fatal accident in May 2016 involving a Tesla Model S in "autopilot" mode, where the car's system was somehow blinded and unable to recognize a white truck turning across its path, will not slow down the arrival of driverless vehicles. The rollout of self-driving taxis in Singapore in the summer of 2016 made the point — not that "this time it's different," but that "the future is already arriving."

Only take note, how far the early stages have already advanced:

- At our daughter's university, the automated system at the school library takes orders and delivers books in ten minutes, making anachronistic the old picture of students and staff rummaging through the dusty stacks.

- Automobiles are parked in fully automated, multistory structures, stored and retrieved without the touch of human hands — benefits include reduced space requirements and air quality improvements due to the elimination of drivers idling in search of spaces.

- The UK government's agreement with Amazon to explore drone delivery moves far to solve the challenges of automating the "last few feet," that contributed to the failure of bubble-era misadventures such as Webvan, where aggressive expansion and lack of appreciation of the grocery industry burned up hundreds of millions before its bankruptcy in 2001.

- Traffic control for the expected squadrons of drones is likely to be administered by the mobile telecoms companies — or at least they so propose with considerable credibility, given their comprehensive network infrastructure and their widespread installed base of control-enabling Sim cards in millions of devices other than telephones themselves.

Examples abound of the types of Big Data usage that illustrate the opportunity for dramatically improved detection and deterrence of financial statement fraud and irregularity — the persistent focus of the profession-induced "Expectations Gap" and the critics' howl, "where were the auditors?" — where sampling processes have throughout history been rife with undetected company fraud and substandard professional performance:

First, a tip-of-the-iceberg example is this beginner's Big Data lesson: a fraud-detection team of internal auditors at a large global company was newly empowered with access to comprehensive data on the activities of the company's entire worldwide employee base. They were enabled, through exception-searching algorithms and analytics, to scrutinize every expense record for the company's 50,000 employees. From this, they were able to identify — and to refer for prosecution — a manager who was routinely submitting expense claims that were both randomly different in amount and just below the policy threshold for mandatory supporting documentation.

In a company of that size, this detection task would have been essentially impossible by traditional "forensic" means. The chances of internal auditors' discovery by old-fashioned sampling methods would have been negligible — and never at all by the outside auditors.

Second, consider the fraud at Satyam Computer Services Limited in India, confessed in early 2009 by its chief executive, Ramalinga Raju, as involving the fabrication of major portions of its revenues.

Real-time access and analysis to Satyam's big data would have made such a fraud almost literally impossible. Ready to hand, as an output of the search algorithms, would have been the revelation that the thirteen thousand alleged "ghost" employees underlying those bogus contracts were unmatched by any of the expenses normally associated with legitimate workers — that is, the costs for desks, telephones and office space, not to mention remittances to local authorities for everything from health insurance premiums to dependent day care to public transit fare cards and employee cafeterias.

Third, decades ago as I was learning the profession's business, the story was widely shared of a Big Eight firm's comprehensive audit of the rolling stock of a Chicago-based railroad. Rail cars being revenue-generating only when in motion, a major part of the engagement involved a fleet of two-seat airplanes — a pilot would locate the trains as they crossed the prairies and fly alongside the tracks, while a flight-suited staffer with a clipboard clamped to his leg leaned out the plane's open window and checked off the serial numbers of the speeding freight cars.

It is not so "Indiana Jones" today. Audit teams can post themselves trackside, and scan the RFID codes on the cars as they roll by. Shortly, a robot will do the code reading, or a drone will fly next to the moving trains. Total human staff for the job, instead of the bygone teams in the field, will consist of an algorithm designer and a machine operator, reporting to the audit manager for analysis and evaluation of this mechanically gathered audit evidence.

Fourth, it was my challenge in an earlier world of traditional audit methods to help defend a Big Eight firm against shareholder class action litigation and a grand jury investigation, unearthing the fraudulent scheme of a publicly held client with a large business in the fitting and finishing of large ships for both civil and military use.

The below-deck interiors of the vessels involved long corridors of identical crew quarters and other spaces. So it was efficient during construction that when a cabin had been fully equipped, fitted and approved, its door would be locked and sealed off, to receive no further attention until final delivery.

The client, feloniously gaming the system by which it could receive advance contract payments based on the state of progress, would simply seal empty cabins — and persuaded the overly trusting auditors not to insist on breaking the seals for eyeball inspection of the actual extent of work completed.

So what of the environment using today's evolved technology? The same protocol of sealing cabins once ostensibly completed could be followed. But a robot or a drone, "walking" the corridors with an RFID reader and a miniature camera slipped under each locked cabin door, could read the codes and "see" the individual bunks, desks, sinks and toilets that legitimate installation would have put in place.

These and other extended Big Data assurance opportunities are nearly too rich, and emerging too fast: when a retail transaction at the cash register generates a stock replacement purchase order and a shipping invoice — when the nationwide spread of epidemics is predicted not by laboratory results at the NIH but by web searches for symptoms and cures — when traffic snarls are reported not by eye-in-the-sky helicopters but by the impeded pace of cell phones carried by car-bound commuters.

Cognitive Technology's Accelerating Learning Rate

If the machines will be able to audit better, smarter and cheaper, the inference is also compelling, that the accelerating learning capability of the algorithms will increasingly displace reliance on human judgment.

To round out the picture of the speed with which high-functioning drones and robots will displace the jobs and careers of the humans in traditional audit, *Rise of the Robots* focuses on the ever-expanding pace with which Big Data analytics, artificial intelligence and cognitive technology can be expected to displace the higher-order roles of human expertise and professional judgment.

The proposition, in summary, is that *any* professional's position is at risk, who sits at a desk and interacts with either words or numbers, or teams up with software that is self-learning and therefore likely to dispense promptly with its human collaborator.

As the author himself puts it:

> *"If you find yourself working with, or under the direction of, a smart software program, it's probably a pretty good bet that — whether you're aware of it or not — you are also training the software to ultimately replace you."*

After a brief reminder of the apparently continued validity of Moore's law — by which, roughly speaking, computational power has doubled every 18–24 months since the advent of mainframe computing and dropped correspondingly in cost — these examples would have been unthinkable only an eyeblink ago:

- Oncological diagnostics are now measurably more accurate as performed by algorithmic analysis rather than by trained human radiologists.

- Artificial newswriting programs now convert the basic data of sports contests into narrative stories on the sports pages — if not with the eloquence of Red Smith or Grantland Rice, every bit the equal of the average pressbox typist.

- High-volume securities trading driven by algorithms now so predominates the markets that major investment in fiber-optics connectivity is done to gain speed advantages measured by the thousandths of a second.

- Alphabet's AlphaGo has now soundly defeated the ancient complex board game's top human competitors from both Korea and China.

And the implications for Big Audit? As with the ability of the drones and the robots to perform mechanical tasks at nonhuman levels of both cost and quality, the strength of cognitive technology will lie in its twofold displacement of traditional auditing techniques and methodologies.

That is, gathering and analysis of *all* of a company's quantitative information will render obsolete the application of sampling-based assurance. Frauds, manipulations and misstatements that have eluded or evaded traditional sampling will become discoverable or preventable when subjected to comprehensive automated capture and analysis of the elements of their scheming.

With search algorithms and comprehensive analytics brought to bear, the very notion of audit by sampling — the bedrock of traditional audit practice — will be rendered obsolete. Whole teams of audit staff, along with their elaborate and costly testing methodologies, will have no more *raison d'être* than buggy whips on an automobile. Incisive programmers scanning for irregularities or evaluating alternative accounting policy implications will search the entirety of a massive data set with the click of a mouse.

There are deep implications for issues involving materiality, audit scope and methods of analysis. Company-level deviations from the tolerable limits of acceptable reporting standards, and shortcomings in audit performance — both discernible from the indicators lurking in and extracted from the pools of newly available Big Data — will be game-changing.

Furthermore, access to the entirety of available data on audit engagement performance will also have implications for both audit practice quality and audit failure prediction.

That is, it has long been an anecdotally supported but unproven hypothesis that incidents of suboptimal audit performance could be predicted from surrounding symptoms. There are said to be signals and "close calls" — that there is never "just one bad apple," or "only one cockroach in the kitchen." But neither regulators nor the profession itself have ever put in place the processes for information gathering and rigorous scrutiny to engage in this form of study.

With Big Data ready to hand, predictive analysis will be able to tease out meaningful indicators from correlations extracted from far broader bodies of information — such as "at risk" audit partners, declining performance in a firm's regional office, or industry sector impacts.

As for the Large Firms' Business Model

Right along with the evolution of the audit process itself, there is the business-model challenge: the *only* participant in this future model, able to possess both the access and the expertise to deliver that assurance, will be the party charged with a mega-system's design, inputs and operation. No "outsider" — traditional auditors included — will be able to endure the cost or justify the duplication of effort and sophistication of such a cognitive Big Data operation.

When the Big Data revolution succeeds in making obsolete the sampling-based audit techniques that have sustained the audit model all these decades, it will at least be uneconomic — and may well be literally impossible — for an audit firm to build and deploy assurance-oriented tools, at the level of data capture and analysis sophistication sufficient to "test" the output of these new-era capabilities.

Which means one of two things: *Either* today's "independent" auditors will fall even further behind in the value delivered by their rapidly obsolescing techniques, *or* they will be obliged, for the sake of their survival, to unshackle themselves from the constraints that today bar them from evolving to be the technology-based auditors of the future.

That is because it is not just the simple data gathering by today's robots that will shortly explode in scope. Profoundly, with such opportunities as the surveying of crops and forests, wind farms or arrays of solar panels, expanded machine capability will cut to the heart of the dialog on independence and scope of practice, and so will challenge the very legitimacy of the Big Audit model.

A drone or a robot gathering crop data, say, will also be able to measure for weeds or pests, irrigation needs or hail damage. A drone viewing a field of wind turbines or an off-shore oil rig will assess efficiency and safety compliance, needs for maintenance, and the timeliness of equipment repairs or replacement.

Those machines and their valuable data will then be wrapped inextricably into the core of a company's operations, performance and strategy. Which in turn means that it will be impermissible under the rules of "independence" for an audit firm's Advisory personnel to provide those functions to audit clients — a serious drag imposed by obsolete constraints on the profession's incentive to invest in and grow such a capital and knowledge-intensive business.

At that time, the only sources of analysis able to provide valuable reporting will be those who "know it all." They may be located within the company itself, or with its outside provider of information collection and management, or as a niche analyst with access to both company and relevant external information.

Who it will not be, for certain, will be those — as in Big Audit today — who are only engaged to apply retrospective or outsiders' techniques and methods. Any gatekeeper or provider of oversight or assurance who accesses *less than all* of a company's financial information will be fundamentally handicapped and incapable of delivering commentary that is either complete, timely or credible.

There are alternative structures for the management and assurance of a large company's big financial data, of course. The historical model of internal corporate ownership of IT, treasury and controllership could continue. Or, the large players in information management could evolve to take up a technology-enabled assurance function as well — whether Accenture or IBM, Oracle or SAP, or indeed Google or Amazon.

As seen through the dark lens of Martin Ford's predictions — jobs and careers in technology-based auditing will be created and thrive and prosper *somewhere* — just not in the business and practice model of the firms of today.

Alternatively, to imagine a world where obsolete prohibitions were eliminated — the Advisory practices of the Big Four could become liberated to do the same, either on their own or in partnership with the existing consultancies that now lack an audit practice, to complement and broaden to full service their existing capabilities.

Meanwhile, the Regulators Are Not On Board

On the regulatory front, the SEC and the PCAOB currently speak about new methods of data analysis. But it must be asked whether those agencies are truly anticipating the rapidly evolving state of

Big Data, or are small-scale and incremental in their vision. For if only the latter, they will not reflect the expected new state nor be transformative in nature, but will be impediments to an evolution that, one way or another, will be irresistible.

This is in part because, whatever form of compliance reporting may still be required by securities regulators — anachronistic as that may be in the new Big Data environment — that assurance will become an essentially trivial exercise in data extraction from the more timely and broadly useful analytics that will already be offered and provided to the information markets — not only using an issuer's own records but to include comparative sector, competitor and geographic comparisons as well.

This realization is not yet apparent in the regulatory mind-set in Washington, where today the attitude toward the Big Data issue threatens to reignite the 1990s brouhaha over the permissible scope of services deliverable by auditors.

One example, as noted above in another context: as an adjunct to his day job as a member of the PCAOB in Washington, Lewis Ferguson had a term as chair of IFIAR, the global collection of national audit regulatory agencies that sprouted around the world in the post-Enron aftermath of Sarbanes/Oxley.

In that capacity, Ferguson was quoted at an IFIAR press conference on April 10, 2014, to the effect that the auditors' search to acquire expertise in the rapidly evolving field of Big Data and its applicability to the practice of auditing "is a source of great concern to all regulators around the world," and "raises serious concerns about differential levels of profitability in these businesses, differential rates of growth, where the economic incentives are and to what extent does audit quality *suffer* as a result" (*emphasis added*).

For Ferguson to suggest that auditors should be either inhibited or constrained from fully realizing the opportunities presented by Big Data was to be on the wrong side of its evolutionary trajectory.

That is because, as with the examples above, the availability of Big Data — and the ability of management, auditors and financial information users alike to grasp and analyze all and every part of the recording and reporting of an enterprise — will shortly rework completely the way in which assurance is performed and delivered.

This would not, of course, be the first time a regulator was behind the transforming consequences of change. Examples in the last decade alone included the unrestrained excesses started in the subprime mortgage market, and the unobserved invasion by the Chinese-based reverse mergers beneath the radar of the American SEC. More recently, regulators were wrong-footed by the legal skimming of the high-frequency traders so entertainingly mapped in Michael Lewis's 2014 book *Flash Boys*.

The point missed by the suggested handcuffing of the auditors' ambition is in the failing to appreciate the implications of inevitable change: the genie of Big Data is already out of the bottle, and will not be returned. If the audit firms do not develop the models and methods for its deployment in the assurance process, and redesign their structures, business models and methodologies accordingly, then new players in the market surely will, with dramatic consequences for the viability of the audit firms and their existing franchise.

To Conclude

As all this transformative uncertainty plays out, it will not be so much that "the machines have won" — because their benefits to company management will be massive and compelling — as that the notion that any value is delivered by an outside "independent" third-party assurance provider will be drained of whatever usefulness survives in today's "pass/fail" report.

At the very least, there is a huge barrier of vision to overcome, as seen in the profession's failure to evolve the basic and obsolete reporting model into assurance that the markets will actually value and be willing to pay for.

And at worst, unless the profession gains credible and active engagement in the public dialog on the compelling case to acquire and deploy the skills and practices needed to bring Big Data to bear in the next generation of Big Audit, they will be setting the stage for a reprise of the disruptions of the 1990s that saw their unfortunate capitulation on permissible scope of ancillary services, nowhere more unfortunately exemplified than in the avoidable debacle of the Andersen/Accenture divorce.

The ability to deploy the sophisticated data analysis tools of the near future will require the auditors to acquire new techniques, tools and personnel to supplant those of the traditional audit. For regulators, rather than see these emerging transformations as invidious developments, they should be concerned lest highly prescriptive standards and restrictions would impose requirements on auditors that would quickly become obsolete or counterproductive.

And if that idea raises the anxiety level among those still committed to the current Big Audit model — it should.

NOTES

1. Updated, the list today comprises Austria, Belgium, China, Cyprus, the Czech Republic, Hong Kong, Ireland, Poland, Portugal and Venezuela — removing Denmark, Hungary, Greece, Luxembourg and Italy — countries with which agreements were reached after that date.

2. Remarks at the SEC's open meeting, February 5, 2014, to approve the PCAOB's budget.

3. *Business Insider*, August 8, 2011, citing unnamed PCAOB members on their visit to China.

4. At this writing the latest exchange in the two countries' competing and antagonistic positions on inspections and document production came with the PCAOB's December 30, 2016, Staff Questions and

Answers, explicitly not constituting agency rules, referencing the Chinese Ministry of Finance position issued in May 2015. The inconsistencies, lack of agreement, and unlikelihood of effective SEC or PCAOB enforcement of the American position were promptly spelled out in Paul Gillis's *China Accounting Blog* for January 2, 2017.

5. The extent of serious issues between the PCAOB and the Chinese and others on inspection, and with the Europeans on mandatory rotation, have been discussed above. Topping up its own show of regional authority and autonomy, the European Commission's June 2016 Decision # 2016/1156, implementing the EU legislation on mandatory rotation and other matters, made a little-noticed gesture of resistance against the aspirations of the PCAOB to give extra-territorial effect to its inspection and oversight program. (For background, joint inspections and access to working papers have been at the core of the PCAOB's endeavor — understandably, given that with a handful of exceptions, oversight agencies in the non-Anglo countries have even less history, experience or success record than the PCAOB itself.) Throwing down a gauntlet of resistance, and revealing a gratuitously up-raised bureaucratic middle finger to the PCAOB, the EC's Decision provided (¶ 11) that only under "*exceptional* circumstances (should) inspections (be) carried out jointly ..., " that transfers of audit papers between systems "should become the *exception*," and that rather than joint inspections, the process should be one of "mutual reliance ... based on the *equivalence* of auditor oversight systems" (¶ 17, *emphasis added*).

6. Indications are that conditions may not have improved in the years since the ten-year anniversary. An academic study in early 2015 in the American Accounting Association's *Accounting Review*, summarized April 29, 2015, in *Accounting Today*, compared the impacts on American public companies reporting internal control weaknesses under the centerpiece requirements of Sarbanes-Oxley section 404, with companies making such disclosures only at the later date of financial statement restatements. The findings indicate that the early-reporting companies were *more* likely, not less, to incur SEC enforcement action, class-action lawsuits, management turnover, and auditor change.

7. M Barnier received a further call to public service in July 2016, from European Commission President Jean-Claude Juncker, to be the EU's chief negotiator with the British over the UK's intended Brexit — a post in which the extent of his commitment and desire for an expanded vision of the regional and international communities was immediately declared through his wish that all meetings and documents be in French.

8. Mr. Connolly, having departed Deloitte in 2011, displayed his visionary aspirations in August 2016, announcing a venture with a private equity investor to build a new firm aiming to challenge the Big Four.

9. For this charming story, I am indebted to Shyam Sunder at the Yale School of Management.

10. *Sputnik News*, January 29, 2008.

11. PwC's relationship with Gazprom lasted until it was replaced by a local firm under the general Russian blow-back against foreign auditors in 2015, part of the politicized stresses arising out of events in the Ukraine.

12. *Forbes*, November 24, 2014.

13. *Kyodo News International, Tokyo*, June 14, 2006.

14. *Bloomberg*, November 24, 2014.

15. *Business Insider*, March 4, 2013.

16. Adapted from my still-relevant column in the *International Herald Tribune*, April 22, 2006.

17. In US$ millions:

- Deloitte, as of May 31, 2016: total global revenue $36.8; consulting and financial advisory $16.4.

- EY, as of June 30, 2016: total global revenue $29.6; consulting and transactional advisory $10.5.

- KPMG, as of September 30, 2016: total global revenue $25.4; consulting $9.74.

- PwC, as of June 30, 2016: total global revenue $35.9; consulting $11.5.

18. Among them, PwC's acquisition of Booz & Co (re-branded as "Strategy&") and its alliance with Digital Asset Holdings; Deloitte's acquisitions of Bersin Associates, the Monitor Group and Casey Quirk; EY's teaming with GE in software and its acquisitions of The Parthenon Group and Thomson Reuters's Tax & Accounting; and KPMG's purchase of Rothstein Kass and its alliance with McLaren Group to give access to the racecar builder's predictive analytics and technology.

19. If "audit and tax only" practices were isolated and spun or carved out of the Big Four, their 2016 global reports would indicate these sizes (US $ billions): Deloitte — $20.4; EY — $19.05; KPMG — $15.68; PwC — $24.4.

V

THE UNCERTAIN FUTURE OF THE BIG FOUR

INTRODUCTION — WHAT COULD BE THE FUTURE?

After what has not been intended as undue doom and gloom, what is the model for the audit of the future?

To enable the continued availability of Big Audit, important issues confront the entire community — issuers and users of financial information, politicians and regulators and the profession itself.

But because, as discussed in Part III, the array of suggested "solutions" are variously irrelevant, unsatisfactory or unachievable, a discussion is required that is broad, open and holistic. Until the issues are candidly recognized and on the table — even if not agreed — the debate goes nowhere. And the risk of catastrophic failure only grows.

The Big Four are not lacking for passionate critics. Harder to come by are possible solutions and paths toward progress. The ideas that follow may not be sufficient, and would no doubt change through the process of debate, modification and adoption. But here they are, in a constructive attempt at a way forward, as an alternative to the collapse of a desirable professional service and the firms that supply it.[1]

All that needs to be known is already at hand, for an agenda and an effective discussion on the reengineering of a sustainable audit function to serve the world's global-scale companies.

That discussion would have these three components:

- Certain basics would be taken as established.

- The over-debated but impractical or unachievable "non-starters" should be taken off the table.

- Focus should be on the handful of central questions, on which views may differ profoundly but which are inescapably important.

In the first category, there may not be consensus on all details, but these propositions are basically beyond debate:

- Other than for purposes of statutory compliance, the standard one-page "pass-fail" audit report no longer serves a function that justifies its cost to issuers or the exposure it imposes on auditors. Evolution to new forms of assurance is essential.

- The concentration of suppliers of large-company audits is down to a critical minimum. A three-firm model is unworkable. A failure of any of the Big Four will disintegrate the entire structure.

- The organizational and capital structures of the Big Four leave each of them exposed to an unsustainable shock, from regulatory or law enforcement proceedings, or a civil litigation outcome in a one to three billion dollar range.

- Regulators and politicians may have the power to kill a Big Four firm, but they lack the vision, authority or means — acting either on their own or collectively — to rescue or sustain one, once a shock tips it into a downward spiral.

In the second category, the catalog of "non-starters" in the current environment includes:

- Liability caps, whether monetary limits or allocated percentages of responsibility.

- Breakup of the Big Four — an act of aggression having neither a rationale in practice nor a basis in law.

- The emergence of new global-scale entrants into the Big Four's large-company market — whether by merger, subsidy or organic growth.

- The injection of outside investment into the current capital structure of the Big Four, or global-scale alteration of existing local-country restraints on their ownership.

- Coordinated mandatory audit firm rotation or replacement at the global level.

- Contingency plans to replace the management of a Big Four network under existential threat.

- Reintroduction of genuine forms of private insurance, by way of "auditor insurance," "catastrophe bonds" or otherwise.

Finally, to table a selection of the hard but unavoidable questions:

- What are the forms of assurance that issuers and users would value and pay for?

- What structural changes are required — competitive, organizational, legislative and regulatory — to enable the evolution of a Big Audit model capable of meeting those needs?

- What form of regulatory oversight, inspection and enforcement would achieve a sustainable balance between investor support and protection and an audit function that is both disciplined and robust?

- In particular, what is the necessary form and amount of government involvement and support — whether an investor protection fund, insurance of last resort or otherwise?

- Under a newly structured audit delivery model, and with a comprehensively refreshed legislative mandate, what are the proper limits and guidelines on the scope of services deliverable to audit clients, and what revisiting of concepts of auditor independence and conduct are indicated?

The envisioning and convening of a forum of senior-level players devoted to such an agenda has yet to occur. Until it does, and the process moves on to real substance, the stability is at risk of both the current Big Audit model and the Big Four that provide its delivery.

Medical Checkups and Annual Audits — If Your Doctor Reported Like Your Auditor

It is well to start with the very basic question of the appropriate scope and content of the traditional audit report itself. Here is a telling comparison.

Consider the comparability of a financial statement audit and a personal physician's examination.

When the question of personal health is raised around a table of the reasonably responsible, the "organ recitals" of those surveyed include general familiarity with their own particular concerns — whether blood pressure, good and bad cholesterol levels, resting pulse, bone density or hormone levels.

To achieve that awareness, on a periodic and routine basis, patients are poked and prodded and invaded in various intrusive and unpleasant ways. They give up samples of fluids and tissue for laboratory scrutiny, and they are screened and hitched and wired to exotic and expensive diagnostic machinery.

Diligent patients are also submitted to questioning by their doctors about their major behavioral risks — does their personal "control structure" includes taking their medications, watching their cocktail intake, wearing seatbelts and avoiding handguns.

And then they receive several pages of detailed results, calibrated to standard norms of tolerance and a briefing on what their trends are and what they might need in aide of maintaining or improving their well-being.

Suppose instead, along with an invoice whose magnitude is itself a threat to good health, a physician delivered this report:

> *"We've done a number of tests, the scope and results of which we have but you don't, and we have chosen not to do a number of other, unspecified procedures.*

> *"We're not sure, but we think you're unlikely to die of natural causes any time soon.*

> *"Thanks — we'll see you next year. Be sure to settle your bill on the way out. And have a nice day."*

Unacceptable — even with the systemic impediments that make American health care delivery a lagging embarrassment among the world's developed countries.

Does an audit report convey anything more about the health of a corporate body? A company's management may be well informed, or sclerotic. Its products and strategies may be world-class, or senescent. It may be the equivalent of a gold-medal athlete, but with a malign and life-threatening growth lurking or metastasized.

Does the company need the corporate equivalent of a slimming regime of diet and exercise? Are prescriptions indicated to bring the basic operational chemistry within tolerable limits? Something surgically targeted like joint replacement or a major arterial by-pass? Radical intervention or experimental drugs?

The only available opinion from today's Big Audit is that, within the tolerance of undisclosed measures of materiality, the company's financial health is generally fair. No detailed diagnosis is on offer, even at great cost — only a single bland page, in the same language handed out once a year to every other patient who passes through the annual audit clinic.

An auditor's report tells less about a public company's health than a doctor's report tells about an individual — in scope, detail and precision. And if investors and other financial information users are not happy, they are doing nothing effective with their dissatisfactions.

It may be, as Mary Poppins put it, that "a spoonful of sugar makes the medicine go down." But in the audit environment, patients are getting only sweets and placebos — and still paying for the dubious privilege.

What Should Be in the Auditors' Report — Would Users Know When They Saw It?

> "I shall not today attempt further to define the kinds of material I understand to be embraced within that short-hand description; and perhaps I could never succeed in intelligibly doing so. But I know it when I see it ...."
> — *United States Supreme Court Justice Potter Stewart,*
> *on pornography, Jacobellis v. Ohio, 1964*

A host of different interests are calling for a rethink of the standard auditor's report. What form of assurance is really desired, what do users really value and what will they pay for?

Available pronouncements have been so lofty as to be unhelpful — such slogans as in PCAOB chairman Doty's May 5, 2011 speech, that "the audit embodies core societal value and relevance," or the same month's hyperbole from the European Parliament's Committee on Legal Affairs, that the statutory audit is "an absolutely fundamental component of the democratic economic and political system."

Two other and more helpful generalizations may be made:

The first, addressing the tumult in the years of the financial crisis of the last decade, is that users are emphatically dissatisfied with the "clean" assurance that was delivered within weeks or months of an issuer's demise — the unqualified opinions on such casualties-in-waiting as Bear Stearns, Lehman Brothers, Merrill Lynch, Citigroup, General Motors and AIG.

The other unreality — the reemerging credibility gap between the traditional one-page report and the market behavior of investors — reprises the roller coaster of the late 1990s in the current wave of "new media" and other darlings — where stock prices, enterprise valuations and near-hysterical crowd behavior give every indication of a new bubble well inflated.

In the exuberant reception of the new media IPOs, rational attention to the boundaries of quality accounting and reporting was overtaken by investor frenzy. The poster child might have been LinkedIn, with its IPO on May 19, 2011, at an upwardly adjusted $45 and its first-day explosion to $122.[2]

At that, LinkedIn's indicated post-offering enterprise value paled next to the $15 billion for Groupon and the staggering $50 billion for Facebook — figures bearing no terrestrial relationship to the companies' available financial data.

Or take Alibaba — in September 2014, the world's largest initial public offering — priced at $68 and rising its first day above $92.[3]

By way of these two central themes — the uncertain commodity value of a "clean" audit report, and the lack of linkage between financial reporting and share pricing — it is knowable both what financial statement users do not want at all, and what they will completely ignore.

The Value of Today's Audit Report — Military History's Metaphor for "Expensive, Obsolete and Irrelevant"

On a recent holiday, I had the moving experience of touring one of the surviving fortresses of the Maginot Line — the defensive installations named for France's Minister of Defense, built in the 1930s and left largely unscathed when the invading Germans simply and speedily flew their planes and drove their tanks over and around.

Dug deep into the Alsatian hills, these brutal piles of 1920s military technology — built for three billion francs and among the largest public projects in France since the construction of the Gothic cathedrals — are derided by history as a strategic failure, because they were rendered irrelevant by the German circumvention.

Yet consider the success — in terms, the Maginot Line did its job. It was evaded, rather than destroyed by direct attack; it was surrendered largely whole, rather than bombarded; and it was only thereafter abandoned by postwar French governments to the effects of tourism, rust and decay.

Much the same is true for the modern-era audit report:

- Conceived in an earlier and simpler time, oriented to the avoidance of problems no longer meaningful, and now ignored by aggressors with superior tools in their armory.

- Consuming vast sums of defensive budgets, engaging battalions of trained and expensive manpower in an endeavor of questionable value.

- Achieving no obvious deterrence against threats on a scale of systemic corporate collapse.

Life for the French garrisons would have been misery: cramped underground in caves of steel and concrete; enclosed by machinery, ducts and wiring; ventilators struggling with the confluent mixture of petrol, dangerous explosives and close human quarters.

Compare with the modern audit engagement team — inflicting vast costs on their clients for a marginal purpose, toiling away to tick the boxes required by Sarbanes-Oxley and its equivalents, facing a hostile world through the narrow visor of confining reporting requirements and a crude and outmoded arsenal of opinion language, and exposed to being outflanked or overrun without warning by antagonists of superior mobility and strategic imagination.

Just as the Maginot Line proved its worth as an obsolete but ironic success against an invasion that never came, the current audit report stands as a bulwark effective only against the kind of assaults about which no one cares.

Instead, just as the hapless French troops were obliged to surrender without a struggle when overtaken from the rear, the modern system of assurance has been revealed as dug in and powerless against such invasive forces as the exotic financial derivatives of the credit crisis or the guerrilla tactics of a Bernie Madoff or an Allen Stanford.

And to what end? The metaphor can be pressed one step further. By surrendering the Maginot Line's indefensible position, the French cut losses that would otherwise have been catastrophic, and survived to be joined by their allies in a strategic regrouping.

As with supplanting the dimly misguided André Maginot, might the regulators yet find in their ranks the likes of a Churchill or Roosevelt or DeGaulle.

And What a Truly Useful Report Might Say

"When you play the 12-string guitar, you spend half your life tuning the instrument, and the other half playing it out of tune."

— *Pete Seeger*

Researchers in group psychology have long known that human attitudes are asymmetrical toward rewards and detriments: people seek risk on the upside, but are risk-averse on the downside.

Which means that the pain of a losing investment will outweigh the pleasure of a similar gain.

Therein lies the fallacy behind the traditional "pass-fail" audit report. Investors will ignore all cautionary limitations within a clean report on such bubble companies as LinkedIn or Alibaba — or the nature of the accounting proffered ahead of the launches of Facebook or Groupon. But on the other hand, they will never admit to being satisfied, absent an advance "fail" signal, for a company poised for collapse — Lehman Brothers, Bear Stearns, Countrywide, AIG, Fannie and so on. That is not because the real desire is for a coherent and comprehensible articulation of a business model destined to failure, but to avoid the failure itself, *at all.*

This "second-order" disconnect means that auditors are truly at one long step removed from the core issue in today's world of short-term score-keeping: financial reporting is seen by investors, essentially if emotionally, as a proxy for the ultimate future success of the management team leading the reporting enterprise. So it misses the point to keep belaboring the messenger.

That is, it must be for the issuing companies, not their auditors, to fully satisfy the disclosure desires of regulators and investors — regarding, for example, the achievability of results dependent on management's judgments, the critical estimates, and the difficult choices among permissible or alternative accounting policies. All of these contain and reflect the company's business, operational and strategic risks, on which actual results depend.

Accountants then would have two socially useful but limited roles:

- The reporting role: to provide the necessary technical and professional competence to assist issuers in navigating through their many politicized and judgmental reporting choices — a process, by the way and as discussed in Part I, which reminds and brings back to the fore the many irrationalities involved in the unending problems of "convergence" among standards and the essentially irreconcilable inconsistencies between and among IFRS and the various versions of GAAP.

- The assurance role: to support — to the extent possible — the clarity and transparency of the representations made to the community of users in the financial statements themselves.

That is it — only so much, and no more.

What may this mean for legitimately useful audit report language? Messages are required like, "We don't know .... we cannot tell from the evidence .... we cannot test or provide a meaningful comment ...." The profession's leaders have been leery of any such rationalization of their role — a fear with three drivers: the economic self-interests in the current model, the looming ever-presence of the shareholder plaintiffs' lawyers and the denial and unwillingness to confront the fragility of the Big Audit model.

Staying the present course, however, risks their being revealed, like the Wizard of Oz, as diminished figures behind the curtain, puffing smoke and noise of no value or significance.

With the spreading concern about the real value of the statutory auditor's statement — what has been remarkable is the complete absence of debate or even contemplation of "the day after." What would happen if, or when, the audit report as it has been known since early in the last century is no longer available?

Nothing. Here is why:

Imagine a late-winter morning after the deadline for the filing of annual accounts for the preceding year. One of the surviving Big Four has just been driven out of the business of issuing auditors' reports, in another of the highly publicized scandals to taint the standing and reputation of the entire profession. Partners are fleeing the practice, and national firms are splintering away from a collapsing global network.

As a result, a large and growing percentage of the world's global companies will be unable to file audited financial statements with their securities regulators, for want of an available provider at any price.

But suppose a large number — say, 50% — of the companies in the FTSE 350, the CAC 40, the DAX 30 and the S&P 500 — offer to their regulators and stock exchanges a report in this form:

> To: *The Members of the Audit Committee of Large Global Company Inc. (the Company)*
>
> *The accompanying statement of financial position, results of operations and changes in financial condition of the Company, as of and for the period ended December 31, 201X (the financial statements) have been prepared by the Company, with our assistance.*

So far so good.

> *In the opinion of the Company and its senior management, the financial statements are free of material error and are fairly stated in accordance with preferred accounting principles. These principles, based upon International Financial Reporting Standards, may or may not be deemed "generally accepted" in the Company's headquarters country or any of the countries in which it has significant operations.*
>
> *We have performed those audit procedures respecting the financial statements that we reasonably believe necessary, and in accordance with the International Statements on Auditing. On the basis of those procedures, we are of the same opinion.*

Up to this point there are tweaks in emphasis, mainly for the scholars. But now buckle up.

> *For purposes of our procedures and opinion, items and transactions less than $XXX million — approximately Y% of the Company's pre-tax profit and Z% of its equity — individually and in the aggregate, have been deemed not material.*

*We are not the Company's statutory auditor. We are also
not independent under the rules of the Securities and
Exchange Commission or any other securities regulator
claiming jurisdiction over the Company and its securities.*

*We have designed and built and currently operate the
Company's systems for the recording and reporting of its
transactions, for which we have been paid $XXX million
in the period covered by the financial statements, pursuant
to an engagement approved by the audit committee of the
Company's board of directors.*

Signed: Surviving Accounting Firm

And to make plain that this really is a new day, the report carries the following footnotes:

1. *This report and opinion are available to interested persons
   through the Company website. In accordance with the terms of
   use there, persons obtaining access to this report and opinion
   agree that we have no liability with respect thereto except in
   the event of a final judicial determination of our knowing and
   willful fraud in the conduct of our audit.*

2. *In addition to this report and opinion, we also perform certain
   procedures from time to time with respect to the Company's
   financial statements and operations, and periodically report to
   the Company's management and its board of directors and the
   audit committee of the board on the results of those procedures. Persons interested may, subject to certain limitations of
   liability and other conditions, have access to these reports, on
   the Company website.*

This report essentially says: "We have done the best we could,
given the time and money allotted us. We are also a clearly interested party, doing work that adds value to our report, and which
you should clearly know up front. We can help you to know

more. But both our undertakings and our exposure to you are strictly limited."

What would happen? Politicians and regulators would have an apoplectic moment. And the world's stock exchanges would open as usual.

Even in these hypothetical uncharted waters, real-life markets would ripple gently and then would speed along. Because if markets move on information and founder on obscurity, this report would have the dual virtues of providing the first and relieving the second.

Delivering a Tailored Report[4]

And if a report as just outlined became standard, what else might be available?

If the accounting firms did rework their "compliance reporting" as outlined, or if they withdrew voluntarily from the issuance of compliance-oriented assurance reports? Or following the systemic collapse of the Big Four franchise, which significant national or niche practices might be able to survive — and what then?

The option of a new form of nonstatutory assurance would emerge.

The global capital markets would decide the scope and value of differentiated reports, having characteristics fundamentally different from today's report. New reporting would be decoupled from statutory standards. The issuing firm would disavow the requirements of the securities regulators.

Those reports would also be decoupled from the obsolete impositions of "independence." The shift would be emotionally traumatic for those wedded to the mantra of the "independent auditor" — a mind-set that likely explains a good deal of the denial and resistance to change within the profession itself. It would however cause no loss to the firms if they no longer had any protection, stature or credibility under the independence requirements, from which they derive no real benefit today.

There are a multitude of special reports that a savvy post-Enron chief financial officer might commission. Three examples ripe for attention, even going back before the tumult of the 2007–2008 financial crisis, could have been addressed — Shell's petroleum reserving, the internal trading controls regime at Société Générale and the black hole of inter-company money transfers at Parmalat.

Down to date, current examples would include the financial portfolio models of the large investment banks and other institutions — consider Fannie Mae and AIG and the "London Whale" of JP Morgan Chase — for their holdings of sovereign debt and such complex financial instruments as derivatives and finite insurance.

Or the efficacy of operational and strategic controls, after the misadventures of Bernie Madoff or MF Global. Or the stability of the high-frequency trading software of the firms exposed to hazards of the type fatal to Knight Capital's survival as an autonomous entity. Or the manipulations of LIBOR and FOREX indices exposed as widespread across the trading desks of the world's largest banks.

Or, consider the impact on public credibility had there been legitimate leadership at *FIFA*, who — unlike the arrogant and insulated Sepp Blatter — could have commissioned root-and-branch auditor scrutiny of the potential for local-country bribes and payoffs, rather than suffer a crash under the ultimate weight of an ex-prosecutor's investigation and the resulting charges of pervasive criminality.

Or the smorgasbord of accounting issues at Hertz Corp., that caused it on June 6, 2014, to withdraw the last three years' statements and cost it an 11% whack to its share price — items ranging from the capitalization and depreciation timing for "certain non-fleet expenditures," to adjustments for allowances for doubtful accounts in Brazil, to allowances for uncollectible amounts from renters for damaged vehicles and other obligations under facility leases.[5]

Or, on a scale that threatens political instability on a national scale along with hemispheric financial disruption — PwC's declining to report on the financial statements of Brazilian giant Petrobras, as of its third quarter of 2014 — after which the company's ultimate release of 2014 figures, on April 2, 2015, included a two billion dollar provision as the best available estimate of the cost of corruption running through the enterprise.

Investment banks and investors in search of best-in-class assurance would line up for such information. They would agree to terms of access that would eliminate ruinous auditor liability. And they would not give a tinker's damn for auditor independence. Their focus, and their expectation, would be on top-level qualifications and good-faith performance.

But not today. The combination of ossified compliance requirements, obsolete practice restrictions and runaway liability means that auditors today could not sell such products even if they wanted to.

Those who pine for the days when an auditor earned broad professional respect by detailed examinations of the distinct items in corporate accounts are entitled to mourn. What they cannot avoid, however, even through the best-intentioned sentimental wishes, is the evolutionary course that has taken Big Audit to the brink.

Valuable forms of financial statement assurance remain to be created and brought to market. What form the profession will take that will do so remains a vital question. The only certainty is that the structure will be different from the one that exists today.

Roguery at UBS Provides a Teaching Moment

When he launched the PCAOB's concept release on the auditors' report, Chairman Doty's June 21, 2011, statement acknowledged, "generalized investor dissatisfaction with the pass-fail model, and generalized frustration with auditors who had issued unqualified opinions on the financial statements of banks that later failed."

On the dialog about that dissatisfaction, Kweku Adoboli, the rogue trader at the London desk of UBS, made a contribution in the fall of 2011.

Many others could not say the same. They included the senior management threesome at UBS — Oswald Grüber, Carsten Kengeter and Maureen Miskovic — the bank's chief executive, head of investment banking and senior risk officer — whose balance sheet the 31-year-old trader blew up to the tune of $2.3 billion, through the unimaginative if devastating use of fictitious customer trades to mask his massive wrong-way bets on the S&P 500 and other major indices.

Adoboli wound up in the law's extended custody in London — nine months pretrial and two and a half years of the seven-year sentence that followed his November 2012 conviction — while UBS teams in Zurich pursued the extended process of damage assessment and control of this latest outbreak at the troubled bank.

Arrested on the third anniversary of the collapse of Lehman Brothers, Adoboli not only exemplified the inevitable eruption of large-scale unmanaged risks in complex systems. He also replaced Société Générale's Jérôme Kerviel as the answer to the question, "Where's the latest rogue?"

Adoboli freshly demonstrated, at UBS, that compliance-oriented risk systems —limited in concept, execution and assurance to the narrow and unsatisfactory conclusion that "most things are working, most of the time" — are both wasteful and ineffective to detect or deter a threat on a "black swan" scale.

It is as true for a rogue trader as for a suicide terrorist: doing pat-downs or box-ticks of an entire population, whether grandmothers on airplanes or bank clerks writing customer orders, will not stop the dangerous deviant capable of causing a blowup — however much those intrusive and costly procedures may serve the politically correct goal of lulling both leaders and constituents into a false if harassed sense of security.

In context of Adoboli's shenanigans, dating back to 2008 when UBS itself was bailed out of the consequences of its ill-fated venture into subprime mortgage-backed derivatives, on through its difficulties with the Justice Department over the business of sheltering US taxpayers, it is painful to read the bank's self-congratulation on the subject of its risk management.

Take, for example, these excerpts from the UBS 2010 annual report:

> "*Operational risk is the risk resulting from* inadequate *or* failed *internal processes, human error and systems failure, or from external causes (deliberate, accidental or natural). Events may be manifested as direct financial losses or indirectly in the form of revenue forgone as a result of business suspension. They may also result in damage to our reputation and to our franchise causing longer-term financial consequences.*

> "*Managing risk is a* core element *of our business activities, and operational risk is an inevitable consequence of being in business. Our aim is not to eliminate every source of operational risk, but to provide a framework that supports the identification and assessment of* all *material operational risks and their potential concentrations in order to achieve an appropriate balance between risk and return.*

> "*... Management, in all functions, is responsible for establishing an appropriate operational risk management environment, including the establishment and maintenance of* robust *internal controls and a* strong *risk culture*"
> (emphasis added).

With that, a strategic question could have concerned the bank's reporting that it paid 2010 fees to EY, its outside audit firm, of 67.4 million Swiss francs, of which ChF 58.5 million were classified as audit, to obtain the latest annual version of a standard auditor's report:

> *"With hindsight, how badly would you have wished to re-direct some portion of that audit fee to conduct precise, deep and effectively directed scrutiny of the controls at the sections of your bank having potential to inflict multi-billion dollar harm?"*

There lay both the puzzle, about the unavailability of such valuable assurance to replace today's outmoded product, and the unrealized opportunity.

The Attributes of a Differentiated Assurance Report

Turning back from the many forms of assurance that in a new environment could deliver value to issuers and users alike, the content of a new form of general-purpose assurance report, and the terms governing its availability for the use of investors and other third parties, would include the following:

- Scope of work and limits would be clearly defined.

- Materiality thresholds and limits would be explicit.

- Accounting and auditing standards would be clearly identified, including the use and availability of issuer and auditor judgments.

- Reliance on management predictions or expectations as primary or sole sources of audit evidence would be clearly stated.

- Disavowal of statutory compliance and independence would be explicit.

- Contractual rather than statutory relationships would underpin strictly controlled scope of duty, liability and limitations of damages. Third-party users would accept responsibility for their own due diligence and the limits of their reliance.

Untied from the varying compliance obligations imposed by local securities laws and regulations, a new assurance report would not need to cover an entire consolidated global business. Just as well, if a result of Big Four disintegration were that no global firms survived, with the capability of delivering such a product. But new audit firm structures and new niche entrants would be able to emerge and develop, putting their focus on industry, geography and individual components of the operations of the large international enterprises.

Among the most significant changes would be the roles and responsibilities of the chief financial officers and the audit committees of global companies. These agents of the enterprises would be both enabled and obliged, on behalf of their companies, to assemble an appropriate bundling of assurance reports to satisfy the needs of the capital markets.

As a message of optimism for the profession as it now stands, these CFOs and directors would require and draw upon the resources of both the national accounting firms that would survive a Big Four disintegration, and the new niche practices, by industry and region, that would be able to emerge and thrive in a reengineered regulatory and legal environment.

Market needs would drive the practical obligation for users to seek out this information. Companies offering a differentiated assurance picture would enjoy a competitive advantage in the capital markets.

The landscape for the raising and movement of capital and the trading in securities would be significantly redefined. A turbulent period of adjustment, and the emergence of several new classes of players and a reworked set of relationships, would be defining events in the dynamism of the marketplace.

Recapping the Prescription — A Dose of Real Medicine

"Reality must take precedence over public relations, for
nature cannot be fooled."
*—Physicist Richard Feynman's appendix to the Rogers Commission
Report on the space shuttle Challenger disaster, January 28, 1986*

A reader once chided me. Although he acknowledged the sterility
of the dialog, the doubtful status of the standard auditors' report
and the deep threat to the survival of the Big Four, I was — he
said — offering only "bromides" rather than substantive ideas.

After the Enron debacle, Sarbanes-Oxley and the many-faceted
events of the financial crisis, full-length treatment is, *faute de
mieux*, reason enough to respond.

As a transition from the present state to a sustainable future,
then, here is a recap of the basic background assumptions:

*The threat hanging over the Big Four's complete domi-
nance of the large-company audit market — the "supply
side" — is simply not addressed by any of the so-called
"solutions" addressed to market concentration.*

*There is no credible case for government-controlled deliv-
ery of audits that is worth the effort, disruption and
expense — whether by direct execution, engagement
assignments or otherwise. The output of the artificial
"profession" that would exist under such regimes would
be inferior to today's unsatisfactory conditions, much less
to the evolved requirements of the future.*

*A forthright reading of the projects to re-consider the stan-
dard auditors' report, by the PCAOB and the IAASB
among others, confirms the emerging consensus that the
current "pass/fail" report is obsolete, serves no purpose
other than securities laws compliance, and should be
supplanted by assurance of real value.*

Third-party equity capital must be allowed and encour-aged, to enable the significant investments in technology, research and expertise required to enable the design and delivery of a large-company assurance function useful and valuable in the 21st century.

It is time to acknowledge that the entire fragile structure of auditor independence is anachronistic, ill-suited to today's conditions, and deleterious to both performance quality and the potential for useful change.

Re-design is required of the legal regimes by which to assess and impose auditor liability, because the survivabil-ity of a large international network cannot be left to the unpredictability of the civil courts.

A framework does exist for regulators to license or charter sus-tainable audit-only firms. But — *if and only if* — a reconfigured legal and regulatory environment both permits, invites and encourages:

- Full-service relationships between auditors and providers of other ancillary but client-valued services.

- The appropriate involvement of meaningful regulatory over-sight, performance quality enforcement and investor rights recognition.

- The emergence of geographic and industry-based new competitors.

- And, perhaps, even the return of today's understandably reluc-tant insurance sector.

Under such a fundamentally reengineered regime, truly new and valuable forms of reporting could be designed and delivered.

These would be responsive to the needs of financial manage-ment and audit committees, welcomed by both executive teams and directors alike and subscribed to by users under sustainable liability terms. They could be, at the same time, respectful of the value perceived by shareholders and others of the influential presence of "outside experts."

Simultaneous attention to all aspects of this framework is essential, however, because until then — as the current impasse shows — neither issuers nor auditors have any incentive to take on the increases in both cost and liability imposed under today's exposed conditions.

AUDIT QUALITY AND FAILURE STUDY — A MODEST PROPOSAL

"You can't hope to improve, if you can't tell whether you're good or not."

— Maxim of experts in failure study

A brief pause here, before the final section of this fulsome story will close with an outline of what the possible future structure of Big Audit might be, to consider one of its necessary building blocks — a means by which to explain, and perhaps to move toward solving, the accounting profession's long-standing inability to respond to the persistent thematic question, in every case of significant financial breakdown, corporate malfeasance or share price collapse: "Where were the auditors?"

This reason is suggested, why that question remains unanswered:

Unlike other business and professional sectors where the scrutiny of performance quality involves detailed case-by-case examination and self-criticism, the auditors have no common forum where experiences can be shared, penetrating questions asked, data collected for pattern analysis and lessons learned and put into practice.

At the level of user dissatisfaction and the firms' own structural and financial fragility, in short, they have no shared platform for "failure study" — no systematic support for their legitimate but unaccomplished aspirations to "get better."

Considering the importance attributed to independent audits, for the benefit of investors and to support the successful operation of the capital markets, the community of users might have expected the profession to have figured out and solved the "Expectations Gap" by now. After all, the franchise of privately delivered assurance on the financial statements of public companies was invented back in the Victorian era, and in American the auditors have had over eighty years of experience under the country's major securities laws.

Yet dramatic incidents continue to erupt. The financial debacle of 2007–2008 — with its failure or bailout of a parade of iconic companies, all bearing clean audit opinions — came half a decade after the ostensible improvements touted for the Sarbanes-Oxley law. Since then, fresh occurrences have continued to erupt, in the US and around the globe.[6]

Public criticism, expectations and calls for accountability are broad. Challenges to auditor performance extend from shortcomings in GAAS execution to issuer abuse of the principles of accounting and reporting, including the auditors' distance from management misconduct having effect on financial reporting and share prices.

In all these areas, public expectations are that auditors perform with "zero defects." That is, investors being neither informed nor concerned with the degree of actual auditor conformity with professional standards, their interest is that investment values not be impacted by corporate malfeasance. So viewed by investors, the auditors are indeed expected to be the watchdogs guarding investor value.

So the absence of a forum by which to scrutinize the profession's humanly inevitable instances of suboptimal performance reveals a gap that is equally as broad as its exposures. The profession's traditional defensive assertions — "not in our scope" or "isolated exception" — are neither responsive nor publicly satisfactory.

Examples in Other Sectors

Failure study is an article of faith and long applied elsewhere — even in areas where instances of breakdown are far less frequent and less consequential in broad public impact than among the auditors and their public company clients.

Hospital surgeries and emergency rooms study their cases — often literally *postmortem* — to improve procedures and patient outcomes. Engineers dissect the causes of collapsed dams and bridges and fallen buildings. Assembly lines are halted until defects are identified and cured.

The National Transportation Safety Board, charged by legislation to investigate civil aviation and other transportation accidents, puts forensic teams on the site of crashes as soon as possible. There, even "close calls" and other deviations are examined and reported, providing learning that is unavailable in less dedicated sectors where "minor" matters are viewed merely as dodged bullets and passed over as incidental.

Notorious public tragedies are also learning laboratories. In 1912, *RMS Titanic* was in literal compliance with the rules on the number and deployment of lifeboats, and was extolled as representing the best of marine engineering — until its iceberg encounter created the opportunity for study and revision of both.

The twin towers of New York City's World Trade Center were considered so safe that 50,000 people worked there daily in complete confidence — until with the results of engineering studies after 9/11, the diagnosis and appreciation of their fateful design weaknesses now assure that the deficiencies in their construction will never be replicated.

A Vacuum of Opportunity

The reasons why the accounting profession lacks structures and protocols for failure study provide explanations, if not satisfactory justifications:[7]

- There is an absence of incentives. The commodity language of the auditor's report is mandated by law and regulation. At the same time, a reader has no way to extract any quality differentiation — one way or another. Users have no way to discern a "good quality" audit from a poor one, while the profession has lacked sufficient motivation to search for a fix, for a system not perceived as broken.

- Legal advisers profess with passion their deadly fear of the adverse litigation hazards of generating discoverable *post hoc* analysis. The impenetrable armor of attorney-client privilege is clapped around work done in litigation defense, shielding attempts at learning and improvement even from internal sharing, much less from transparent exchanges across the profession or with users and standard-setters.

- And with the customary human desire to admire the upside and claim "success" wherever possible, the profession has absorbed the intrusive inspections of its regulators — the PCAOB and its counterparts around the world — along with the occasional official wrist-slaps and the survivable settlements of its lesser litigations, and taken pride in steadily expanded revenues and accelerated diversification into new areas of practice.

In response to the profession's enthusiastic proclamations of attention to indicators of improved quality — that is all very well, at the level of process and routine execution, *most* of the time. But the inability to achieve the publicly expected "zero defects" means that the firms have not solved their recurring exposure to the mega-cases that would blow up their capital-thin balance sheets — as recently shown by the painful settlements by Deloitte and PwC of their litigations relating to Taylor Bean & Whitaker, Colonial Bank and MF Global.

Structure and Operations

Taking as a target population the list of public companies reporting under the aegis of the SEC, what would a useful forum for "audit failure study" look like and what would be required?

It should not be difficult to articulate the broad terms of reference for such a body — which, to keep the emotive nature of the nomenclature to a minimum, could be named the National Audit Performance Board.

The Board could, by design and legislative authorization, be housed within one of the existing federal agencies — the SEC or the PCAOB being, with adjusted mission definition, likely candidates. Or, authority could be devolved to a private body — either newly formed or evolving from one already in place — whose scope and performance would function under official delegation, monitoring and oversight.

The remit of the Board would need to be broadly stated — to investigate and report on incidents of allegedly inappropriate accounting and reporting, audit performance insufficiency or personal malfeasance — at either the audit firms or their issuer clients — for lessons and areas for improvement.

Selection criteria by which incidents would be identified would include those attracting shareholder or other litigation, proceedings by agencies of law enforcement or oversight, material restatements of financial results, large-company bankruptcies, bailouts or rescue interventions.

Other matters possibly within the Board's authority could include third-party complaints, as well as voluntary submissions of cases of complex accounting or other judgments in the course of engagement performance — either to obtain advisory advance guidance in individual cases or to flag an emerging issue for broader inquiry and dialog.[8]

Notification would be made and pursued promptly on the arising of an issue, for the sake of realistically timed investigation and advances in learning — unlike the delayed and unsatisfactory timetables of either today's PCAOB inspection program or its antecedents in the old SEC Practice Section of the AICPA.

Staffing of the Board would include senior-level experts across the relevant disciplines, drawn by volunteered secondment or direct hiring from the profession and also from industry executive and finance personnel — along with the support of the research academics and the professional and legal standard-setters.

Competencies would include auditing and accounting standards, engagement and methodology design and execution, risk analysis and management, forensics, data analytics and behavioral evaluation. Secondments of junior staff from the firms, as with the fellowship opportunities at the SEC, would be seen as valuable sources of experience and serious career enhancements for those signing on.

Outputs of the Board would cover a spectrum of reporting and commentary:

- Post-event reports on individual cases including analysis of performance quality and behavior, application and evaluation of standards and judgments, and event causation.

- Broader studies based on identification of trends and patterns for onward reference to standard-setters and other bodies.

- Articulation of optimal practices — actually "raising the bar" above the minimal satisfaction of generally accepted standards — drawing on the Board's accumulated experience and, optimistically, its capacity to identify cases of affirmatively superior performance.

Operationally, while the willing participation of the audit firms and corporate issuers would be essential, to capture and build a body of data complete and robust enough to be informative and credible, a federal-level legislative mandate would be required — among other reasons, both to have the necessary regulatory buy-in and also so that the entire exercise would be protected from hostile use and effect in civil litigation.

Concerns for exposure would be reasonably manageable thereby — as by analogy, the results of NTSB investigations and determinations of probable cause cannot be used as evidence in courts of law, nor typically can ameliorative company acts in such areas as consumer product safety.[9]

It being easy to see that compulsory participation in a failure study forum, based on government coercion and resistance, could be frustrated by the profession and the business sector and doomed to fail from the outset, it is also clear that to achieve a productive state of virtuous cooperation, as an evolution from today's environment of hostility and antagonism, would be no small task.

As a matter of cultural change, the firms, the profession's leaders and the communities of information issuers and users would need to be willing participants — endorsing the value of the forum as a matter of mutual trust and appreciation for its value.

Benefits and Support

Those standing to benefit from a robust and transparent program of audit performance evaluation would include all players in the Big Audit community:

- The profession's claims on behalf of their programs for improvement would acquire a measurable base of empirical evidence.

- Standard-setters would build a base of experience on which to evaluate and evolve their guidance.

- Corporate issuers would achieve increased credibility for their commitments to quality governance and reporting.

- Government agencies of oversight and law enforcement could legitimize their claims for leadership in cooperative efforts to elevate audit performance quality.

- Investors and other users would see increases in convergence and comparability of information, along with the particulars of divergence of issuers' positions in areas of complexity.

The broad outlines of this concept are readily available. What is now wanted is uptake across the financial information community.

FEDERAL "CHARTERS" FOR ACCOUNTING FIRMS AND THEIR PERSONNEL — A BLANK-PAGE APPROACH

Now a decade and a half beyond Andersen's disintegration, in a discussion grown steadily louder but not more productive — how would a truly valuable audit report of the type just outlined be delivered? What would be the business model for the new and sustainable Big Audit?

A framework for a blank-page approach is at hand — although it would require a clean, robust and full-blown debate and a fresh legislative mandate. What is lacking, but essential in the organizational and legislative discussion, is the necessary breadth of support and ready participation that might actually replace today's antagonistic finger-pointing.

Elements of that framework would include these:

Newly organized and restructured firms would be authorized and regulated to deliver audits for all public companies. The nomenclature for this freshly conceived form of public company audit license is less important than the concept itself. For purposes here, let it be called a national-level "charter" — drawing on the vocabulary still used in the United Kingdom, the profession's home of origin in the 19th century.

Applied in the United States — the key jurisdiction necessary for any worldwide solution — this new system for Big Audit licenses would be administered at the federal level, by analogy to the government oversight of American stock exchanges, credit rating agencies and broker-dealers.

Newly organized firms holding these charters could be in their current form, generally as limited liability partnerships. They could also be organized in corporate form, in any of the permutations long familiar to creative business designers and strategists.

They could be organized by and evolve out of the existing accounting networks, or be acquired or built afresh by other new market entrants. Their resources — personnel, methodologies and technology — could be internally supplied, or could be outsourced from the existing Big Four or from emergent niche competitors and suppliers.

Charter-holding audit firms could be stand-alone enterprises. Or, if strategic, they could function as subsidiaries or affiliates of other enterprises — offering the design flexibility of both ownership and capital structures that would enable and support their varying strategies and service models.

Because these SEC licensees would be "audit-only" enterprises, the multiple overlapping restrictions on their scope of services would be finessed. The endless debate over independence and permissible ancillary services could at last be ended.

At the same time, the chartered firms' affiliated companies would be empowered to deliver all legitimate services within their scope and aspirations — all forms of consulting and advice including systems design, installation and management; merger and acquisitions advice; investment banking; tax and legal services; technology, data processing and analytics; drones, robotics and artificial intelligence.

These associated nonaudit entities — whether parent or affiliate companies — would not, in terms, be "accounting firms" at all. By this means, they would be declared free from independence and compliance requirements. This approach would explicitly address, and acknowledge out loud and for the first time, the elimination of the obsolete and dysfunctional concepts of auditor "independence" — a necessary step in any event in the evolution of a modern and responsive assurance function.

As for the remaining strictures of "independence" in this new world, client approval and disclosure of the portfolio of services so provided would be required — desirably at the audit committee level, to satisfy the aspirations to quality of governance. The limitations on auditor investments in clients, presently located in the SEC's regulation S-X,[10] would be preserved, and above minimal thresholds to be set, chartered firms would not audit their own investors, affiliates or parents.

Minimum capital requirements could be set, geared to those new firms' turnover or the capitalization of their client list. Necessary modifications of existing legal regimes would include revision of the incentives of the tax codes that presently maximize the speedy distribution of current profits to their partners.

Governance structures could include measures not presently achievable under the constraints of state regulation and the laws of partnership and bankruptcy: independent outside directors, accountable audit committees and financial transparency. This last would include the achievable requirement — already explored here — that the chartered firms and their ownership structures would publish their own audited financial statements, a step even today within the capacity of the Big Four networks.

With this array of stabilizing governance changes in place, new audit firm structures could at last be attractive to outside capital, which these offerors of new services would require in order to fund their needs for research, personnel and technology.

Newly structured audit firms would be flexibly able to evolve their deliverables to clients beyond the one-page statutory report that now looks so obsolete. Targeted assurance reports could be designed for their value to users in the capital markets.

In aide of enhanced competition and expanded auditor choice, segments of the public company audit market could be specifically identified to encourage new entrants. Separate charters could be issued for the auditors in high-risk or technically specialized sectors, such as IPOs, troubled companies or financial services. Audits of targeted companies could be separately underwritten and priced, as now done with high-risk insureds.

In competition with each other and all other entrants in this competitively expanded environment, this new form of chartered auditors would come within the ambit of the rapid and landscape-changing evolution in the world of technology.

The prospect of life-threatening litigation liability remains the elephant in the room, and requires a solution. So — take at their word the investor advocates who would prefer improved information and communications from auditors, over the caprice and low return of the litigation lottery.

For historical reference, revival and extension would be timely of the proposal floated in the 1950s by Leonard Spacek, who had succeeded to the leadership of Arthur Andersen on the death of its founder in 1947. Asserting that the complexity of modern accounting and reporting surpassed the capacity of the traditional court system, Spacek called for the creation of a federal-level "accounting court."

A broader mandate is called for. A specialized "accounting and audit tribunal," made up of experienced experts, would have jurisdiction to hear all claims relating to auditor performance regarding the financial statements of an SEC-regulated company — whether instigated by agencies of oversight and law enforcement or as brought by investors or others claiming actionable injury.

Drawing on the authority of the federal securities laws to preempt the role of the existing federal and state court systems, this tribunal would adjudicate issues of auditor fault and responsibility, allocate and apportion liability and contribution as between the auditor and issuer management or others, and fix damages to be assessed. It would levy fines and impose sanctions against those found liable for wrongdoing, both firms and individuals.

Compensation for legitimately damaged investors and other claimants would be determined through this tribunal process, rather than under the unpredictability of juries and the inefficiencies of settlements.

To recognize the importance and legitimacy of "too big to fail," the magnitude of a fine or damages assessed against a chartered firm's ownership would have a survivability ceiling, which could be calculated as a multiple of fees, a percentage of revenue or a maximum charge to the capital of partners and other owners.

Funding would be through a system of fee schedules rather than the hazards of the firms' limited partner capital. Contributions to a compensation fund would be geared to the revenue or capitalization of registrants (noting that the benchmark of audit firm revenue could be subject to measurement issues in the newly permissible ownership structures). The fund would be administered by regulators as a form of "last-resort" compensation, in lieu of the now-vanished and insufficient structure of private-market auditor insurance from which that industry has effectively withdrawn.

However, with this expert tribunal supplanting the unpredictability of the courtroom, and with firewalls of corporate organization and bankruptcy infrastructure in place to limit liability, the conditions for insurability could be brought once more into alignment with manageable litigation and enforcement risk. In that context, the compensation-fund obligations of the regulatory agency could be assessed for risk, arrayed by underwriters into tranches of varying exposure, and marketed to the insurance sector and other sources of risk capital as a form of private-market reinsurance or a variant of the "cat bonds" now lacking appeal in that market.

This proposed outline contemplates a variety of complex and demanding tasks and responsibilities on the part of an evolved government agency of oversight and enforcement, to whom the newly chartered accountants would be accountable. These could be housed in an entirely new agency, or could be expansive of the existing and continuing roles of the American SEC and PCAOB, under whose authority it would still be the enforceable legal duty of corporate issuers to report financial information that is fairly stated and free of material error.

In summary of the foregoing, the collective remit of the agency would include:

- Chartering of both firms and individuals.
  - o For quality and enforcement purposes, audit engagement personnel would be individually chartered along with their firms, in coordination between federal authorities and existing state regulations over education, examination and training.

- Quality inspection and review of chartered firms and individuals.

- Enforcement of findings of unsatisfactory performance.

- Accounting, reporting and auditing standard setting.
  - o Which could in turn involve a devolution to the private sector, as a revival of the system pre-Sarbanes-Oxley by which auditing standards could evolve — returning "generally accepted" to a meaning that would be nontechnical, flexible and adaptable to change.

- Operation of the claims tribunal.

- Administration of the compensation fund, including the design and offering of auditor cat bonds.

- Administration and oversight of an appropriately funded, expertly staffed and privileged "audit failure study" forum.
  - As discussed just above, this last would remedy the yawning gap in the profession's ability to learn from its experiences. That is, the suggested NAPB would be organized to identify, investigate and report on incidents offering lessons and areas for improvement, at both audit firms and their clients.

The activities sketched here are, it is suggested, within the realm of credible legitimacy and justification. Keeping the existing agencies in place, with greatly expanding and evolved duties, might be thought a cynical or pragmatically political response to an argument that it would be preferable that they be better abolished in their entirety and replaced. But political accommodation would no doubt be required, to satisfy the most passionately significant imperative of bureaucrats *in situ* — namely the protection and preservation of the very existence of their agencies and the robust state of their budgets and their continued employment.

In other words — the SEC and the PCAOB should support this program — because their functions would retain value and their good employees would still have a place to report for work.

The bare bones of this proposal should include something to excite or insult nearly everyone — a signal that it is broad enough to be worthy of pursuit.

NOTES

1. Acknowledgment and thanks to Bob Mednick, a long and widely recognized expert in the profession's field of ethics and standards — also my neighbor, friend and long-time fellow partner at Andersen. Bob challenged my early writing about the issues. "It's all very well to complain," he put it, "but you have to bring solutions."

2. LinkedIn's stock went through a gradual post-offering descent back in the general direction of reality, bottoming around $74.

All after-market purchasers were left under varying depths of water —
until it went again on an upward tear, through its capital raising of $1.2
billion in September 2013 at $223 a share and topping above $250. The
wild ride continued as it dipped to $140 the following spring, bounced
back around $200 through mid-2015, halved to $100 in March 2016
and jumped back in June to $190 with its announced purchase by
Microsoft for $26 billion.

3. Alibaba rose to $115 in November, then slumping in January 2015
below that first-day price, breaking in August below its IPO price and
languishing until its recovery beginning in February 2016.

4. Adapted from the original in the *International Herald Tribune*, April
8, 2006.

5. A full two years on, the problems at Hertz continued to cascade. On
May 14, 2015, the company announced that while it would not be able
on a timely basis to file its 2014 annual report or its previously withdrawn reports for the two prior years, it had identified an additional $30
million in errors, bringing to $183 million the total negative three-year
impact on its pre-tax income. November 8, 2016, saw a 23% stock price
drop with the company's announcement of a comprehensive failure to
meet targets across such core issues as costs, lowered used-car values
and customer-driven revenue declines.

6. Examples in the US alone have run from the likes of Bernie Madoff
and MF Global, more recently to Hertz and Valeant and Wells Fargo
and the Academy Awards, with equally impactful examples elsewhere —
Tesco and Autonomy, Toshiba and Olympus and Petrobras, FIFA and
Volkswagen — and others certain to come.

7. There is history to the ideas here, as I have been pleased to be
reminded, in particular by accounting professor and author Sri
Ramamoorti of Kennesaw State University. In March 1993, the nearly
forgotten Public Oversight Board, whose remit covered the SEC Practice
Section of the AICPA, issued its entirely forgotten report, "In the Public
Interest — Issues Confronting the Accounting Profession." As reported
in the December 1993 *CPA Journal*:

> *"The Board observed the auditing profession does not have a
> system to dissect its failures, ferret out the causes, identify the
> symptoms related to those causes, and develop methods to pre-
> vent their recurrence."*

Predictably, the proposal was met with indifference and inaction — overcome by the antagonistic reactions to the Board's more immediately provocative proposals on such difficult subjects as auditor liability, internal controls reporting, fraud detection, and the role of audit committees.

Viewed through the long lens of hindsight, the Board's proposals in general retain considerable relevance to issues of unresolved urgency today — of which the absence of a failure study forum is only one.

8. Also within both the remit and the aspirations of the Board — especially once it had attained maturity and a base of experience, and drawing on the scope of the NTSB's inquiries — would be the "close calls" — cases where a serious problem did not materialize, but *could* have — the "near misses" avoided or averted perhaps by good performance or perhaps by luck, or perhaps only rationalized away, to lie quiet and festering until the conditions for breakdown might emerge.

9. As a reality check, the accounting profession's long and futile attempts to reduce its legal exposures suggest that to obtain a trade-off by which submission to the Board's inquiry process would include actual reworking of liability thresholds — through the creation of "safe harbors" or other means — would be a step politically too far.

10. § 210.2-01(3)(c)(1)(i).

CONCLUSION

The alert delivered half a century ago by the Noble prize-winning poet/songwriter Bob Dylan, that the times would be changing, included the warning that the disruption would involve shaking the windows and rattling the walls.

No less for Big Audit. Achievement of the possible positive outcomes sketched here can readily be seen as difficult at best, given the deeply ingrained environmental antagonisms and dysfunctionalities.

There may be some grounds for hope and optimism:

- The UK's re-tender rules *may* dampen the consequences of the EU's misguided rush to impose mandatory rotation.

- The clumsy US requirement for disclosure of the lead audit partner *may* do little substantive good, but the cosmetic effect would at least have little downside.

- Tentative steps to improvement in audit report disclosure — quantification of materiality measures and identification of key or critical matters for attention by both auditors and those in company management and governance — *may* refocus the appropriate measure of responsibility between issuers and their auditors.

- The expansion of Big Four consulting and advisory practices *may* threaten a reprise of the Andersen/Accenture divorce, and the consequent emergence of diminished and weakened "audit only" practices. Instead, if long memories and proper vision prevail, a real revision of permissible scope of services and independence requirements could support the evolution to tailored and multi-disciplinary forms of truly valuable assurance.

As a concluding message to all those having an interest: whistling past the graveyard is not a strategy. Nor are the partial steps surveyed here — either individually or collectively — structurally significant enough to be more than bandages on a patient requiring life-saving surgery.

But with the Big Four's history of valued service to society, their story deserves a happier course and a healthy future.

APPENDICES

APPENDIX A

Opinion of W. W. Deloitte, Accountant, on the General Statement of Receipts and Payments to the 31st December 1849, of the Great Western Railway, dated 8th February 1850:

Great Western Railway.

GENERAL STATEMENT OF RECEIPTS AND PAYMENTS TO THE 31st DECEMBER, 1849.

Audited and approved, 8th February, 1850.   W. W. DELOITTE, Accountant.

APPENDIX B

EY's report dated October 26, 2016 on Apple's financial statements for the year ended September 24, 2016 (page 70 of the Form 10-K of Apple Inc.):

REPORT OF ERNST & YOUNG LLP, INDEPENDENT REGISTERED PUBLIC ACCOUNTING FIRM

The Board of Directors and Shareholders of Apple Inc.

We have audited the accompanying consolidated balance sheets of Apple Inc. as of September 24, 2016 and September 26, 2015, and the related consolidated statements of operations, comprehensive income, shareholders' equity and cash flows for each of the three years in the period ended September 24, 2016. These financial statements are the responsibility of the Company's management. Our responsibility is to express an opinion on these financial statements based on our audits.

We conducted our audits in accordance with the standards of the Public Company Accounting Oversight Board (United States). Those standards require that we plan and perform the audit to obtain reasonable assurance about whether the financial statements are free of material misstatement. An audit includes examining, on a test basis, evidence supporting the amounts and disclosures in the financial statements. An audit also includes assessing the accounting principles used and significant estimates made by management, as well as evaluating the overall financial statement presentation. We believe that our audits provide a reasonable basis for our opinion.

In our opinion, the financial statements referred to above present fairly, in all material respects, the consolidated financial position of Apple Inc. at September 24, 2016 and September 26, 2015, and the consolidated results of its operations and its cash flows for each of the three years in the period ended September 24, 2016, in conformity with U.S. generally accepted accounting principles.

We also have audited, in accordance with the standards of the Public Company Accounting Oversight Board (United States), Apple Inc.'s internal control over financial reporting as of September 24, 2016, based on criteria established in *Internal Control — Integrated Framework* issued by the Committee of Sponsoring Organizations of the Treadway Commission (2013 framework) and our report dated October 26, 2016 expressed an unqualified opinion thereon.

/s/ Ernst & Young LLP
San Jose, California
October 26, 2016

TIMELINE: AN ABBREVIATED HISTORY — THE ORIGINS OF THE BIG EIGHT, AND HOW THEY SHRANK TO FOUR

Circa 3400 BC — Systems for inscribing accounting records on clay tablets are developed in Sumeria.

1458 — Benedetto Cotrugli composes his *Libro de Larte dela Mercatura* in Naples.

1494 — Franciscan friar Luca Pacioli publishes his *Summa de arithmetica, geometria, proportioni et proportionalità*.

1844 — The Joint Stock Companies Act in England requires railway companies to appoint bookkeepers to keep and maintain their accounts, and to appoint "auditors" from among the shareholders.

1845 — William Welch Deloitte founds the firm that bears his name.

1849 — Samuel Price and Edwin Waterhouse form their London partnership. Frederick Whinney joins the London firm of Harding & Pullein, formed that year, renamed Whinney Smith & Whinney in 1894.

1850 — Mr. Deloitte joins the shareholder/auditors of the Great Western Railway in signing the report, "Audited and approved," on the company's half-yearly accounts for the period ended December 31, 1849.

1854 — William Cooper founds his London firm, to be joined by his brothers as Cooper Brothers & Co., 1861.

1867 — William Peat establishes his practice in London.

1886 — Charles Haskins begins his New York practice, partnering with Elijah Sells in 1895.

1887 — James Marwick opens in Glasgow, opens in New York in 1896 and partners with Roger Mitchell in 1897, merges with Peat in 1911.

1894 — Arthur Young opens an office in Chicago, joined by his brother Stanley to form Arthur Young & Company in 1906.

1898 — William Lybrand, Adam and Edward Ross and Robert Montgomery found their firm in Philadelphia.

1900 — George Touche and John Niven form their partnership in London.

1903 — Alwin and Theodore Ernst form their firm in Cleveland.

1913 — Arthur Andersen and Clarence Delaney form their partnership in Chicago, which becomes Arthur Andersen & Co. in 1918, re-branded as Andersen in 2001.

1924 — Ernst & Ernst allies with Whinney, Smith & Whinney.

1933–1934 — The Securities Act and the Securities Exchange Act are passed in the United States.

1952 — Deloitte, Plender, Griffiths & Co. in the United Kingdom merges with Haskins & Sells, globally adopting the name Deloitte Haskins & Sells in 1978.

1975 — Tohmatsu Aoki & Co, based in Japan, becomes part of the Touche Ross network.

1979 — Ernst & Ernst merges with Whinney.

1986 — Peat Marwick merges with Klynveld Main Goerdeler, forming KPMG.

1989 — The shrinkage of the Big Eight begins. Deloitte Haskins & Sells merges with Touch Ross in the United States and elsewhere. Ernst & Whinney merges with Arthur Young, re-branded as EY on July 1, 2013.

1998 — Price Waterhouse merges with Coopers & Lybrand, as PricewaterhouseCoopers, re-branded PwC in 2010.

2002 — Andersen is indicted in Houston on March 14; after trial, the jury's guilty verdict is returned on June 15; Andersen surrenders its professional licenses and ceases to practice as of August 31.

GLOSSARY — ABBREVIATIONS, ACRONYMS AND CAST OF CENTRAL CHARACTERS

AICPA

The American Institute of Certified Public Accountants, which represents the profession in the United States, traces its history to 1887. Its activities include advocacy, certification and licensing, communications, recruitment and education, and standards and performance. Until 2002, when the PCAOB was created by Sarbanes-Oxley and given authority to set generally accepted auditing standards and to inspect and oversee auditors of public companies in the United States, these functions were carried out under the auspices of the AICPA.

CAQ

The Center for Audit Quality is a policy advocacy organization, affiliated with the AICPA, whose members are US accounting firms registered with the PCAOB. It formulates and advances positions on policy issues facing the public company auditing profession and the capital markets.

EU

In 2002, the European Union adopted IFRS as the required financial reporting standards for the consolidated financial statements
of all European companies whose debt or equity securities trade in
a regulated market in Europe, effective in 2005. The adoption of
IFRS was done by enactment of Regulation (EC) No. 1606/2002
of the European Parliament and of the Council of 19 July 2002
on the application of international accounting standards.

The portfolio of the EU Commissioner for Internal Market and
Services, a member of the European Commission, concerns the
development of the European single market and its movement of
people, goods, services and capital.

The tenures of Commissioners Charlie McGreevy (2004–2010)
and Michele Barnier (2010–2014) led eventually to the passage
by the European Parliament in April 2014 of legislation having
potentially far-reaching effect on auditor tenure, non-audit services by auditors, and the form and content of auditor reports.

FASB

The stated mission of the Financial Accounting Standards Board is
to establish financial accounting and reporting standards for publicly held companies in the United States (US GAAP). Although
having statutory authority to do so under the Securities Exchange
Act of 1934, the SEC has throughout its history relied on the private sector for this function — designating the FASB to establish
standards of private sector financial accounting that govern the
preparation of financial reports by nongovernmental entities. The
FASB's standards are thus officially recognized as authoritative by
the SEC and the AICPA.

Chairmen of the FASB over the relevant years:

Robert Herz (2002–2010)

Leslie Seidman (2010–2013)

Russell Golden (2013–)

FRC

The Financial Reporting Council sets the standards framework within which auditors, actuaries and accountants operate in the United Kingdom, and sponsors the UK Corporate Governance Code for companies. It sets, monitors and enforces standards for corporate reporting, audit and actuarial practice.

FSA/FCA/PRA

In 2012, the responsibilities of the Financial Services Authority, as the national financial services regulator in the United Kingdom, were divided between the Financial Conduct Authority and the Prudential Regulation Authority. The FCA now has responsibility for regulating financial firms, market infrastructure and listings for securities issuers. The PRA, as a subsidiary of the Bank of England, is responsible for the supervision and regulation of banks, building societies, credit unions, insurers and investment firms.

IAASB

The International Auditing and Assurance Standards Board develops auditing and assurance standards and guidance, including the international standards on auditing (ISAs), which are used or are in the process of adoption in more than 90 countries. The structures and processes supporting the operations of the IAASB are facilitated by the International Federation of Accountants (IFAC), a global organization whose 175 members and associates are professional accountancy organizations in some 130 countries and jurisdictions — examples would include the AICPA in the United States and the ICAEW in the United Kingdom.

IASB

The International Accounting Standards Board is responsible for the development and publication of the International Financial Reporting Standards (IFRS) and related interpretations. Its 14 members have a mix of experience in preparing, auditing, or using financial reports and in accounting education.

Chairmen of the IASB over the relevant years:

David Tweedie (2001–2011)

Hans Hoogervorst (2011–)

ICAEW

The Institute of Chartered Accountants in England and Wales was given a royal charter by Queen Victoria in 1880. It seeks to achieve its vision on behalf of the accountancy and finance profession, through advancing the theory and practice of accountancy, finance, business, and commerce; recruiting, educating, and training the profession's members; preserving professional independence; and maintaining high standards of practice and conduct.

IFIAR

The International Forum of Independent Audit Regulators was established in 2006 by audit regulators from 17 jurisdictions, and has grown to have members from 51 jurisdictions with the establishment of new audit regulators around the world. Its focus includes sharing knowledge and experience concerning audit regulatory activity with a focus on inspections of auditors and audit firms, and promoting collaboration and consistency in regulatory activity.

IFRS

The International Financial Reporting Standards comprise a set of accounting standards, developed and maintained by the IASB, intended for application on a globally consistent basis. IFRS are mandated for use by more than 100 countries, including the European Union and by more than two-thirds of the G20.

IFRS are developed and issued by the IASB, the standard-setting body of the London-based IFRS Foundation, through an international consultation process, involving interested individuals and organizations.

PCAOB

The Sarbanes-Oxley Act of 2002 created the Public Company Accounting Oversight Board, as a nonprofit corporation to oversee the audits of public companies, requiring for the first time that auditors of public companies in the United States be subject to governmental agency inspection and oversight. As part of its mandate, Sarbanes-Oxley gave the PCAOB final authority over generally accepted auditing standards (GAAS), regulation and professional practices for auditors and audits of public companies — functions previously and traditionally exercised under the auspices of the AICPA.

The SEC has oversight authority over the PCAOB, including the approval of the Board's rules, standards and budget. The members of the PCAOB Board are appointed to staggered five-year terms by the SEC, after consultation with the Chairman of the Board of Governors of the Federal Reserve System and the Secretary of the Treasury.

Chairmen of the PCAOB:

William McDonough (2003–2005)

Mark Olson (2005-2009)

Daniel Goelzer (acting, 2009–2011)

James Doty (2011–)

Sarbanes-Oxley

The Sarbanes-Oxley Act of 2002 (Pub.L.107-204, 116 Stat. 745, enacted July 30, 2002) was also known as the "Public Company Accounting Reform and Investor Protection Act" (in the US Senate) and the "Corporate and Auditing Accountability and Responsibility Act" (in the House). It is known after its principal legislative sponsors, Senator Paul Sarbanes (D-Md.) and Representative Michael Oxley (R-Ohio), sometimes also Sarbox or SOX.

The law created the PCAOB, charging that agency with over-seeing, regulating, inspecting and disciplining auditors of public companies, and also addressed auditor independence, corporate governance, internal control assessment and reporting and financial disclosure.

SEC

The Securities and Exchange Commission is the primary overseer and regulator of the securities markets in the United States. The two principal pieces of legislation framing the American regulatory scheme are the Securities Act of 1933 and the Securities Exchange Act of 1934.

The 1933 Act established the requirement of registration of securities offered for public sale, intending that investors receive financial and other significant information. The 1934 Act created the Securities and Exchange Commission, giving it broad authority over the securities industry, brokerage firms, transfer agents, and clearing agencies as well as the nation's securities exchanges. The 1934 Act also identifies and prohibits certain types of conduct in the markets and provides the Commission with disciplinary powers over regulated entities and persons associated with them, and empowers the SEC to require periodic reporting of information by companies with publicly traded securities.

The SEC is authorized to set national accounting standards — US GAAP — a function it has traditionally delegated to the private sector in the role of the FASB. Under Sarbanes-Oxley, it exercises supervision over the PCAOB and its functions in respect of auditors and audits.

Chairs of the SEC over the relevant years:

Harvey Pitt (2001–2003)

William Donaldson (2003–2005)

Christopher Cox (2005–2009)

Mary Schapiro (2009–2012)

Mary Jo White (2013–2017)

NOTE ON SOURCES

News, information, scholarship and research all now being located online, materials quoted or referenced here are — with very few exceptions — from publicly available and readily accessible sources.

For simplicity:

- Information on the Big Four and the other accounting firms is found on their global and country-level web sites. Information on their clients, the large global companies, is likewise for the most part on the respective web sites.

- Materials originating with the regulatory and oversight agencies and the professional standard-setters are found on their web sites, referenced here where helpful to the way they organize — releases and proposals, enforcement orders, speeches and meeting presentations, etc.

- News reports are identified by dates, and are mainly found on the web sites of the general or business media sources — the *Financial Times*, the *New York Times*, *Reuters*, *Bloomberg* — identifying by name the more specialized local or industry sources such as the newsletters, journals and blogs covering the accounting profession.

- Materials from academic journals and consultancy papers are shown by issuer, title and date.

I have tried to avoid citations involving paywalls or subscription requirements, which may however be affected by the passage of time or changed policies of the publications involved.

THANKS AND ACKNOWLEDGMENTS

The list of people who have provided their experience, wisdom and endorsement is, I regret, much too long for the available space. My appreciation and gratitude go especially to the following:

First, my clients, partners and friends in the accounting profession — whose travails provided me both an education and a career. Among those far too numerous to name, two calling for special mention are Duane Kullberg and Bob Kelley.

The fraternity of in-house lawyers at the large firms, among whom our most colorful shared exploits must remain forever unrecorded — with special thanks to Rick Murray.

The inspired supporters of my column at the *International Herald Tribune* — an adventure that returned me to journalism, the field I had nearly pursued after college but for an unexpected "black swan" offer from a law school admissions office.

Francine McKenna, for her help and support in my migration across media platforms; and all the readers of my blog, *Re: Balance*, whose interest, loyalty and sharp-edged critiques have kept me going.

The deans, administrators and all my terrific students in Risk Management at DePaul's Kellstadt School and the law schools of the Universities of Chicago, Illinois, and Cergy-Pontoise.

The many friends and colleagues who have listened patiently, read and criticized early drafts, and steered me in productive directions and away from pitfalls and errors — the ultimate responsibility for which rests with me and not with them.

My wise and helpful agent Carol Mann.

Emerald series editor Gary J. Previts, and the entire team at Emerald for their vision in seeing this project to realization.

And above all, Kat and Julie for their sustaining love and support.

ABOUT THE AUTHOR

Jim Peterson is an American lawyer, concentrating on complex multinational disputes, litigation and financial information.

He has represented the international accounting firms and large global companies in disputes, negotiations, government agency proceedings and standard-setting.

After ten years in the litigation department of a Wall Street law firm, in 1982 he joined the internal legal group of the Arthur Andersen firm. He became a partner of Andersen Worldwide in 1985, based in Chicago and later in Paris. He retired from the firm in 2001 and established his solo law practice.

"Balance Sheet," his financial and accountancy column, ran biweekly in the *International Herald Tribune* from 2002 until 2008, when he migrated his writing to his blog, "Re:Balance."

Since 2009 he has taught a graduate-level course in Risk Management at business and law schools in Chicago — the University of Chicago Law School, DePaul University, and the College of Law of the University of Illinois — and in Paris at the law school of the University of Cergy-Pontoise.

He is a graduate of Phillips Exeter Academy, Yale College and the Yale Law School.

He divides his practice, teaching and residential time between Paris and Chicago.

INDEX

AAI (American Antitrust Institute), 51, 52, 55

Accenture, 242, 244, 256

Accounting networks, 24, 26, 51, 135, 244, 293

Accounting partnerships, 47, 62, 122, 137, 164, 225

Accounting principles, 22, 46, 49, 68, 75, 140, 141, 274, 304

Accounting profession, 15, 17, 33, 34, 37, 53, 56, 96, 101, 125, 217, 221, 241, 285, 288

Accountancy Europe, 204n18

Ackman, Bill, 95–96

Adelphia, 21, 173

Adoboli, Kweku, 103, 279, 280

Advisory Committee on the Auditing Profession, 149–152, 203n8

Aguilar, Luis, 208–209

Ahold, 21, 103

AICPA (American Institute of Certified Public Accountants), 6, 290, 299n7, 309

Aiding and abetting, 169

AIG, 10, 21, 103, 130, 131, 269, 272, 277

Algorithmic trading (algorithms), 250, 252, 253

Alibaba, 269, 272, 299n3

AlphaGo (Google), 253

Alwaleed (Prince Alwaleed Bin Talal), 234

Amazon, 44n16, 247, 249, 256

Analysts, 22, 23, 82

Analytics, 9, 246, 250, 253, 257, 293

Andersen, Arthur. *See* Arthur Andersen

Andersen, Arthur Edward, 196

Andersen Consulting, 242, 244

Andersen Worldwide Société Coopérative, 135

Appearance of independence, 9, 15, 25, 36, 90, 92, 94, 96, 244

Apple Inc., 42n10, 303, 304

Arthur Andersen, 1, 3, 41n1, 41n2, 65, 85, 106n1, 135, 239, 240, 242, 244, 295

Assurance, 8, 9, 13, 15, 17, 19, 21–22, 24–25, 28–30, 33–35, 37–38, 45–46, 56–57, 64, 78, 79, 85, 91, 92, 94, 97, 102, 116, 122–123, 126, 128, 130–133, 136, 142–143, 156, 161, 177, 180, 212–214, 218, 221, 228, 231, 236, 239, 245, 254, 256–259, 264–265, 268, 271, 273, 278–279, 281–283, 286, 302, 304

Assurance model, 35, 156

Assurance services, 8, 116

Atkinson, Richard, 30

ATT, 122

Audit committee, 9, 88, 111, 123, 155, 159, 175, 274, 275, 294

Audit competence, 144, 188, 225

Audit deficiencies, 217–220